Wordsworth's Literary Criticism

The Routledge Critics Series

GENERAL EDITOR: B. C. SOUTHAM, M.A., B.LITT. (OXON.)
*Formerly Department of English, Westfield College,
University of London*

Titles in the series

Wordsworth's
Literary Criticism

Edited by

W. J. B. Owen

Professor of English
McMaster University

Routledge & Kegan Paul

London and Boston

First published in 1974
by Routledge & Kegan Paul Ltd
Broadway House, 68–74 Carter Lane,
London EC4V 5EL and
9 Park Street,
Boston, Mass. 02108, USA
Set in 'Monotype' Ehrhardt
and printed in Great Britain by
W & J Mackay Limited, Chatham

ISBN 0 7100 7849 8

Library of Congress Catalog Card No. 74-75858

General Editor's Preface

The purpose of the Routledge Critics Series is to provide carefully chosen selections from the work of the most important British and American literary critics, the extracts headed by a considerable Introduction to the critic and his work, to the age in which he was writing, and to the influence and tradition to which his criticism has given rise.

Selections of a somewhat similar kind have always existed for the great critics, such as Johnson, Wordsworth, Arnold, Henry James, and the argument for their appearance in this series is that of re-appraisal and re-selection: each age has its own particular needs and desiderata and looks in its especial own way at the writing of the past —at criticism as much as literature. And in the last twenty years or so there has also been a much more systematic and intelligent re-reading of other critics, particularly the lesser-known essayists and reviewers of the Victorian period, some of whose writing is now seen to be criticism of the highest order, not merely of historical interest, but valuable to us now in our present reading of nineteenth-century literature, and so informing us in our living experience of literature as well as throwing light upon the state of literature and criticism at particular moments in the past.

B.C.S.

Contents

Preface

The title of this book differs in form from those of its companion
volumes because, when I was invited to prepare it, I had already
allotted the title *Wordsworth as Critic* to a detailed exposition of
Wordsworth's literary criticism published in 1969 (University of
Toronto Press; London: Oxford University Press). With some
exceptions, my introductory sections in the present volume represent
a severely condensed rewriting of that book; for it does not seem
possible to expound the same texts in a totally new way without
confessing that one's earlier ideas were either markedly erroneous
or grossly incomplete. The main exceptions are my observations on
the nature and origins of Wordsworth's criticism (Introduction,
section I), and on the literary tradition of the Preface to *The Borderers*
and the Note to 'The Thorn' (Introduction, sections II and III).
Consideration of the nature of these two documents has permitted
me to trace to an earlier stage than in 1969 the step-by-step progress
by which Wordsworth's critical ideas move forward.

My introduction confines itself to formal discussion of the formal
literary criticism printed here; I have not discussed, except incidentally, the five important letters which I have included. Their
relevance to the formal essays will be obvious: the letter to Fox to
Lyrical Ballads and its Preface; the letter to Wilson to *Lyrical
Ballads* and its Preface and, at a remoter distance, to the ideas on
originality which appear in the Essay, Supplementary; the letters to
Lady Beaumont, to Coleridge, and to Catherine Clarkson to the
Preface and Essay, Supplementary of 1815.

My texts, with some concessions to the style of this series, are
drawn from Wordsworth's own printed editions, where appropriate,
and where they depend on manuscripts, from the Oxford editions of
Wordsworth's *Prose Works* and of his correspondence. I am indebted
to the Delegates of the Clarendon Press for permission to use these
texts. The source of each text is indicated in the headnote; where no

other considerations are relevant, my text is the last of which Wordsworth authorized the printing, or represents what seems to be his final intention in the case of works surviving only in manuscript. My annotations to the texts are confined usually to the identification of quotations and explanations of obvious allusions, with occasional comment on the sense of the text. For fuller discussion of verbal difficulties, detection of concealed allusions, and indications of Wordsworth's sources and analogues, the reader is referred to the commentaries in the Oxford *Prose Works*.

Although she has made no direct contribution to the present book, my frequent references to that edition will be some measure of my general debt to a long and profitable collaboration with Professor Jane Worthington Smyser.

W. J. B. O.

Abbreviations

Biog. Lit.	S. T. Coleridge, *Biographia Literaria*, ed. J. Shawcross, 2 vols, Oxford, 1907.
CL	*Collected Letters of Samuel Taylor Coleridge*, ed. E. L. Griggs, 6 vols, Oxford, 1956–71.
Dennis	*Critical Works of John Dennis*, ed. E. N. Hooker, 2 vols, Baltimore, 1939–43.
Exc.	*The Excursion*, in *PW*.
EY	*Letters of William and Dorothy Wordsworth: The Early Years*, ed. E. de Selincourt. Second edition, revised by Chester L. Shaver, Oxford, 1967.
HCR	*Henry Crabb Robinson on Books and their Writers*, ed. E. J. Morley, London, 1938.
Journals	*Journals of Dorothy Wordsworth*, ed. E. de Selincourt, London, 1941.
Lives	Samuel Johnson, *Lives of the English Poets*, ed. G. Birkbeck Hill, 3 vols, Oxford, 1905.
MY	*Letters of William and Dorothy Wordsworth: The Middle Years*, ed. E. de Selincourt. Second edition, revised by Mary Moorman and A. G. Hill, 2 vols, Oxford, 1969–70.
Prel.	William Wordsworth, *The Prelude*, ed. E. de Selincourt. Second edition, revised by Helen Darbishire, Oxford, 1959.
Prose	*Prose Works of William Wordsworth*, eds W. J. B. Owen and Jane Worthington Smyser, 3 vols, Oxford, 1974.
PW	*Poetical Works of William Wordsworth*, eds E. de Selincourt and Helen Darbishire, 5 vols, Oxford, 1940–9.

Introduction

I General

Wordsworth's literary criticism springs from his creative writing: it is almost invariably an exposition or a defence of his own poetry. Thus the Preface to *The Borderers* (No. 1) and the Note to 'The Thorn' (No. 4) expound dramatic characters which (the poet conceives) the reader may find hard to accept as credible. The Preface to *Lyrical Ballads* (No. 3) defends poems which (the poet admits) are experimental in matter and manner and therefore, again, perhaps difficult of acceptance; and the letter to Fox (No. 5) urges their acceptability to a man of power who, Wordsworth thinks, is likely to be sympathetic to them. The *Essays upon Epitaphs* (No. 9), though often more general in scope than other Wordsworthian documents in that they deal with much material outside the Wordsworthian poetic canon, nevertheless defend Wordsworth's way of writing epitaphs and, on the whole, the way of Chiabrera whose epitaphs Wordsworth admired and translated. The Preface of 1815 (No. 11) and the sketch for it in the letter to Coleridge (No. 8) defend a particular arrangement of Wordsworth's poems, and the Preface goes on to expound two 'new' aesthetic concepts which are relevant to that arrangement and to the production of poetry generally. The Essay, Supplementary (No. 12) defends Wordsworth's poetry against the attacks of Francis Jeffrey and, implicitly and explicitly, all new poetry against the attacks of incompetent but powerful critics. The defensive stance of the letters to John Wilson, Lady Beaumont, and Catherine Clarkson (Nos 6, 7, 13) is obvious.

Although the defence or exposition thus arises, as it were, from the poet's private literary concerns, its argument usually draws upon, and often develops in a personal way, established ideas or ways of writing. The Preface to *The Borderers* draws upon a newish fashion of Shakespearean criticism developed more or less in Wordsworth's generation or just before (section II below). The Preface to *Lyrical Ballads* and its Appendix draw on commonplaces of primitivism and, especially in the version of 1802, on the concept of poetry as 'expression': ideas frequently combined in the Scottish 'common-sense' philosophers of the later eighteenth century and given a specifically literary turn by Scots such as Hugh Blair in his *Critical Dissertation on the Poems of Ossian* (1763) and his *Lectures on Rhetoric and Belles Lettres* (1783) (sections IV–IX below). The *Essays upon Epitaphs* draw to some extent on the crude theorizing of Wordsworth's main source-book, John Weever's *Ancient Funerall Monuments* (1631); they gain considerable critical impetus from Wordsworth's avowed intention to dispute Samuel Johnson's views on this poetic form which appear in the *Life of Pope*; and in their psychology of literary creation they may owe something to discussion with Coleridge on the faculty of Imagination (sections X–XII below). The Preface of 1815 draws specifically on Coleridge from time to time in its exposition of the distinction between Imagination and Fancy, and indirectly on Coleridge's predecessors in this distinction (section XIII below). The Essay, Supplementary, while it expounds Wordsworth's own views on the nature and likely progress of literary reputation, borrows heavily from many sources of historical information and literary judgment, and, overall, is a kind of parody of particular works by Francis Jeffrey, the target of its attack (section XIV below). Outside the texts printed in this book, Wordsworth's formal discourse on the aesthetics of natural scenery, the fragmentary essay on the *Sublime and the Beautiful* (*Prose*, ii. 349–60), and a good many parts of the *Guide to the Lakes* with which this fragment is connected, are closely aligned with the theories of Edmund Burke and of other writers on the sublime in eighteenth-century England.

That most of Wordsworth's theory is 'psychological', concerned to describe the making of poetry and the way in which the poet's mind works, is a tribute to the large gains in psychological theory made in Europe, and especially in Britain, during the eighteenth century. The same interest is reflected in the subject-matter of much of the verse written in the 'great decade': in the presentation of the mind of Oswald in *The Borderers* and in the curious probing into motive in other poems (usually unpublished) of the same period (see *PW*, i. Appendix, Poems, xv, xvi, xxx, xxxi); in the conscious analysis of 'the great and simple affections of our nature' (p. 72) in a good many of the *Lyrical Ballads* of 1798; above all, in the exposition of the making of Wordsworth's own mind in *The Prelude*. He scoffed at the possibility of precise analysis of his own or anyone's mind in that poem (ii. 208 ff.), yet forthwith proceeded to 'conjecture' how consciousness of self and how the co-operation of mind and environment are achieved in the infant (ii. 237 ff.); the whole poem is a 'history or science' (p. 97) of his own feelings; and much of the early books leans, not precisely on David Hartley's *Observations on Man* as Arthur Beatty wished to persuade us,[1] but upon the general ideas of associationist psychology begun, for our purposes, by John Locke and enlarged and refined by Hartley and others. Wordsworth moved beyond this to a Coleridgean view of a creative mind both in the poem and in the later critical writings, from the *Essays upon Epitaphs* onwards.

It is clear from what has been said above that, while the matter and the manner of proceeding in Wordsworth's criticism are often shared with the eighteenth and early nineteenth century, the occasion of Wordsworth's criticism is usually personal: he began to write criticism—in the sense of aesthetic theory—almost as soon as he began to write verse of substance and importance, and he continued to do so, sporadically, for nearly twenty years.[2] No one should believe that every poem Wordsworth wrote, or every word of criticism written in defence or explanation of his poetry, has some deep biographical implication beyond itself: it is nevertheless sometimes possible to detect, or to guess at, some personal pressures which suggested this or that poem or body of poetry, and hence this or that piece of related criticism.

The sequence begins in the 1790s, when Wordsworth's spirit appears to have undergone a particularly violent development which he describes, directly but not with complete clarity, in *The Prelude*, and indirectly in other places, such as the account of the Solitary in the early books of *The Excursion*. Like many Englishmen of his time, he saw the French Revolution in its early stages as a natural process: the kind of society it was expected to produce Wordsworth had already seen (he thought) in the egalitarian societies of the English Lake District and Cambridge (*Prel.* ix. 217 ff.). He thought he saw it again as he walked through France with Robert Jones in 1790 (*Prel.* vi. 352–70). The events in France, he says (*Prel.* ix. 252–3), 'Seemed nothing out of nature's certain course,/A gift that rather was come late than soon'. That a new society in France could be produced without difficulty and bloodshed he did not believe, as we can see from his hard-headed Leftish 'Letter to the Bishop of Llandaff' (1793), written 'by a Republican' and discreetly left unpublished by the author (*Prose*, i. 19–66). He accepted the execution of Louis as inevitable, and argued that the royal office was heavier than any man could bear. He was severely shocked by the British declaration of war against France in 1793, and confesses to satisfaction at British defeats (*Prel*. x. 228–75). But his opinions were changed, or at least disturbed, by events such as the September Massacres of 1792, which he came near to witnessing (*Prel*. x. 64–6), and the Terror, which he claims to have escaped by a fairly narrow margin (*Prel*. x. 189–97, 308 ff.); and by the aggressive tendencies of French military power which began to emerge about 1794 (*Prel*. x. 792 ff.). From his observation of such matters, he says, emerges the figure of Oswald/ Rivers in *The Borderers* (*PW*, i. 342–3):

> The study of human nature suggests . . . that . . . sin and crime are apt to start from their very opposite qualities, [and that] there are no limits to the hardening of the heart, and the perversion of the understanding to which they may carry their slaves. During my long residence in France, while the revolution was rapidly advancing to its extreme of wickedness, I had frequent opportunities of being an eye-witness of this process, and it was while that knowledge was fresh in my memory, that the Tragedy of 'The Borderers' was composed. . . .

> While I was composing this Play I wrote a short essay illustrative of that constitution and those tendencies of human nature which make the apparently *motiveless* actions of bad men intelligible to careful observers. This was . . . done . . . to preserve in my distinct remembrance what I had observed of transition in character, and the reflections I had been led to make during the time I was a witness of the changes through which the French Revolution passed.

As I observe below (p. 8), it is difficult to connect such accounts, or the play itself, with the recorded behaviour of leading French politicians, who, while they undertook the destruction or perversion, physical or moral, of colleagues and rivals, do not appear to have done so, as Oswald claims to do in the play, with the aim of educating their victims in the direction of intellectual freedom, but rather with a view to preserving the safety of the State, or of themselves under cover of preserving the safety of the State. Because of this difficulty, Oswald/Rivers has been seen, not so much as a Robespierre, as a Wordsworth as he was *in potentia* at the period which he describes in *The Prelude*, x. 806–905. Biography does not record that Wordsworth was guilty of any crime, voluntary or involuntary, of the enormity of that of which Oswald accuses himself in the play; the view that Oswald's desertion of the sea-captain stands for Wordsworth's seduction and desertion of Annette Vallon seems less popular now than it was forty years ago. Nevertheless it is possible to see, in the rationalizing of Oswald whereby he sheds a 'natural' remorse and reaches the conclusion that a crime is an intellectually liberating act, an enormous projection of that over-rational state of the mind which Wordsworth describes in *The Prelude* as 'that/ Which makes the human Reason's naked self/ The object of its fervour' (x. 817–19), when man has 'an independent intellect' (x. 830), and shall 'spread abroad the wings of Liberty,/ Lord of himself' (x. 838–9), attempting to achieve such a state 'by such means/ As did not lie in nature' (x. 843–4). We may suppose that Wordsworth was the better able to depict Oswald in both play and Preface because he had travelled at least part of Oswald's road himself.[3] Presumably he never reached that pitch of rationalized self-deception at which Oswald arrives; but it is possible to see Oswald as Wordsworth's conjecture, depicted with a kind of controlled horror, of what he might have become. Whatever point he reached, he passed through crisis to cure, as *The Prelude* describes it. He promises (*Prel.* x. 880–901) 'some dramatic Story' (perhaps *The Borderers*) which will show

> the errors into which I was betray'd
> By present objects, and by reasoning false
> From the beginning, inasmuch as drawn
> Out of a heart which had been turn'd aside
> From nature by external accidents,
> And which was thus confounded more and more,
> Misguiding and misguided. Thus I fared,
> Dragging all passions, notions, shapes of faith,
> Like culprits to the bar, suspiciously
> Calling the mind to establish in plain day
> Her titles and her honours, now believing,
> Now disbelieving, endlessly perplex'd
> With impulse, motive, right and wrong, the ground
> Of moral obligation, what the rule
> And what the sanction, till, demanding *proof*,
> And seeking it in everything, I lost

> All feeling of conviction, and, in fine,
> Sick, wearied out with contrarieties,
> Yielded up moral questions in despair.

Then, shifting his rationalizations from human nature to a more appropriate field, he applied them to the study of mathematics (x. 902–5); and from this fruitless occupation he turned, with the aid of his sister Dorothy, to 'nature' (x. 908 ff.), 'found/ Once more in Man an object of delight' (xii. 53–4), and perceived the positive value of what he and most people have regarded as normal in man's behaviour (xii. 82–7):

> A more judicious knowledge of what makes
> The dignity of individual Man,
> Of Man, no composition of the thought,
> Abstraction, shadow, image, but the man
> Of whom we read, the man whom we behold
> With our own eyes.

The Borderers and its Preface can be seen as a backward glance at what might have been, and a shudder of relief; *Lyrical Ballads* and its Preface celebrate, with vigour if not always with logic, Wordsworth's new or renewed enthusiasm for the normal and the permanent to which he is now able to attribute positive value: he seems actually to have believed in the primitivism of *Lyrical Ballads* and the Preface which attributes all normality and virtue, or all the normality and virtue we can hope for, to the rustic.[4]

No such prolonged spiritual development can be traced as background for the *Essays upon Epitaphs*, though the course of Wordsworth's aesthetic theory, expounded in sections X–XII below, is understandable. But a tenuous connection is perhaps to be seen between Wordsworth's interest in epitaphs and the next major emotional shock of his life, the death of his brother John by shipwreck in 1805. His correspondence, especially a notably frank letter to Sir George Beaumont written shortly after the event, shows the emotional pressure which urged him to write something to lament and praise John Wordsworth, and also the artistic conscience which prevented him from doing so at that time (*EY*, 586):

> At first I had a strong impulse to write a poem that should record my Brother's virtues and be worthy of his memory. I began to give vent to my feelings, with this view, but I was overpowered by my subject and could not proceed: I composed much, but it is

all lost except a few lines, as it came from me in such a torrent that I was unable to remember it; I could not hold the pen myself, and the subject was such, that I could not employ Mrs Wordsworth or my Sister as my amanuensis. This work must therefore rest awhile till I am something calmer, I shall, however never be at peace till, as far as in me lies, I have done justice to my departed Brother's memory.

It is not possible to demonstrate that Wordsworth looked for models, among them Chiabrera whose epitaphs are the nominal starting-point of the *Essays*, in these circumstances. Still, he looked at Chiabrera, for whatever reason, at some date before 1810; and there is at the beginning of Essay II a curious collection of references to shipwreck, and a quotation from a famous passage on the subject from Shakespeare's *Richard III* which had been used as a motto for a pamphlet describing the wreck of the *Earl of Abergavenny*, John Wordsworth's ship (*EY*, 565). The poems bearing on John Wordsworth which eventually came from Wordsworth's pen are not very like Chiabrera's epitaphs; but he learned something, for several of the portraits of characters, living or dead, in *The Excursion* (to which the first Essay was appended as a note) read very like the kind of character-sketch at which Chiabrera is expert and which Wordsworth admired (p. 158).

The only obvious motive behind the Preface of 1815 is aesthetic. One paragraph of the text records the sense of neglected merit which is the main theme of the companion Essay, Supplementary (p. 184: 'And if, bearing . . . remembrance'). It is perhaps worth noting that many of the ideas in this Preface had long been in Wordsworth's mind: there are definitions of Imagination and Fancy in the Note to 'The Thorn' of 1800 (p. 96); the summary of the activities of the Imagination (pp. 181–2: 'Thus far of images . . . new existence') is anticipated in the final book of *The Prelude* and drafts therefore earlier than 1805 (xiii. 74 ff. and textual notes); the classification of the poems by subject-matter is discussed in 1809 (No. 8), and by aesthetic faculty in 1812 (see p. 38).

The Essay, Supplementary, on the other hand, springs from resentment long felt against Francis Jeffrey and the *Edinburgh Review*. Jeffrey had made Wordsworth the butt of his criticism since he referred incidentally to *Lyrical Ballads* and the theories of its Preface in a review of Southey's *Thalaba* (*Edin. Rev.* i [1802]). The *Poems, in Two Volumes* (1807) were roughly handled (*Edin. Rev.* xi

[1807]); and for the next few years Jeffrey went out of his way to drag unfavourable references to Wordsworth into reviews where they had no marked relevance: of Crabbe (*Edin. Rev.* xii [1808]), of Cromek's *Reliques of Robert Burns* (*Edin. Rev.* xiii [1809]), and of Weber's edition of John Ford (*Edin. Rev.* xviii [1811]). These attacks reached their climax in the notorious account of *The Excursion*, beginning 'This will never do' (*Edin. Rev.* xxiv [1814]). At the date of this last, Wordsworth had in the press the collected *Poems* of 1815 (mainly a conflation of *Lyrical Ballads* and the *Poems* of 1807) and *The White Doe of Rylstone*; apart from a natural urge to retort to abuse long borne without public protest, it might well have occurred to Wordsworth that it would further his prestige and perhaps his financial interests if Jeffrey could be shamed into silence. The means by which he proposed to achieve this end are sketched in section XIV below.

II   Preface to *The Borderers*

The Preface to *The Borderers* is unique among Wordsworth's critical writings in that it is not concerned with *poetics*, with an account of the nature or the making of poetry. All Wordsworth's later formal critical utterances of major scope are so concerned; but the Preface to *The Borderers* is concerned with the analysis of a dramatic character whom the author feels to be potentially puzzling to the audience, and with an attempt to show that the character is psychologically credible in spite of contrary appearances. Elizabeth Threlkeld reported that 'the metaphysical obscurity of one character, was the great reason for [the play's] rejection' by Covent Garden in late 1797 (*EY*, 197 n.), and Wordsworth said much the same in 1843: 'while I was composing this Play I wrote a short essay illustrative of that constitution and those tendencies of human nature which make the apparently *motiveless* actions of bad men intelligible to careful observers' (*PW*, i. 343).

In the note just cited, and in another of approximately the same date (*PW*, i. 342), Wordsworth connects the character of Oswald/ Rivers with 'what I had observed of transition in character, and the reflections I had been led to make during the time I was a witness of the changes through which the French Revolution passed.' The relevance of this connection has been doubted, and various literary antecedents for the character of Oswald, in the works of William

Godwin and in 'Gothic' novels such as Mrs Radcliffe's, as well as possible semi-autobiographical analogues in Wordsworth's own experience, have been cited by critics.[5] Whatever the origin of the character, the resulting character-analysis has been recognized as acute; but the literary antecedents of the character-analysis, as distinct from the character, have been less usually noticed.

The critical approach used here by Wordsworth is that of character-analysis of Shakespearean characters, which was a comparatively recent invention in Wordsworth's day: 'The third quarter of the eighteenth century, and not the first quarter of the nineteenth, is the true period of transition in Shakespearian criticism . . . there is a far-reaching change in the literary appreciation of Shakespeare, which announces the school of Coleridge and Hazlitt: his characters now become the main topic of criticism.'[6] Nichol Smith's protagonists in this achievement were Joseph Warton, Lord Kames, William Richardson, Thomas Whately and, above all, Maurice Morgann. I do not know which of these Wordsworth might have read by 1797; but all were available to him, and those which seem most useful to our purpose, Warton, Morgann, and especially Richardson, share a common approach in that they are concerned, often or wholly, with unusual or problematic characters whose dramatic credibility it is their aim to defend. Thus Warton in *Adventurer* No. 97 is concerned to show that 'Shakespeare has wonderfully succeeded in his *Tempest* [in] the monster *Calyban*.'[7] Morgann's thesis, sustained through a whole book, is that Falstaff, contrary to the general impression and to some appearances in 1 *Henry IV*, is no coward. Richardson's, in his first and perhaps most notable essay, is to account for 'a very extraordinary change . . . a violent and total change'[8] in Macbeth's character during the course of the play: such a 'transition in character' as Wordsworth claims to have observed in revolutionary France.

Since the critical effort is to reconcile seeming inconsistencies or to make seeming improbabilities acceptable, the critic needs to identify a unifying element in the character in which the inconsistencies can be seen to be reconciled. Thus Richardson draws upon the eighteenth-century concept of a ruling passion: in the case of Macbeth, it is ambition, the degree of which, or the degree of ascendancy of which over repressive faculties, determines the behaviour of the character (Richardson, 45–6):

He is exhibited to us valiant, dutiful to his sovereign, mild, gentle, and ambitious: But ambitious without guilt. Soon after, we find him false, perfidious, barbarous, and vindictive. All the principles in his constitution seem to have undergone a violent and total change. Some appear to be altogether reduced or extirpated: Others monstrously overgrown. Ferocity is substituted instead of mildness, treasonable intentions instead of a sense of duty. His ambition, however, has suffered no diminution: On the contrary, by having become exceedingly powerful, and by rising to undue pretensions, it seems to have vanquished and suppressed every amiable and virtuous principle . . . the prevailing passion could [not] have been enabled to contend with virtue, without having gained, at some former period, an unlawful ascendency. Therefore, in treating the history of this revolution, we shall consider how the usurping principle became so powerful; how its powers were exerted in its conflict with opposing principles; and what were the consequences of its victory.

Likewise, in Wordsworth's Oswald/Rivers (pp. 59–63):

His master passions are pride and the love of distinction. . . . His feelings are interested in making him a moral sceptic, &, as his scepticism increases, he is raised in his own esteem. . . . Of actions, those are most attractive which best exhibit his own powers, partly from the original pride of his character, and still more because the loss of authority and influence which followed upon his crime was the first circumstance which impressed him with the magnitude of that crime. . . . The recovery of his original importance & the exhibition of his own powers are therefore in his mind almost identified with the extinction of those painful feelings which attend the recollection of his guilt. . . . If . . . I am asked what are Rivers's motives to the atrocity detailed in the drama? I answer: they are founded chiefly in the very constitution of his character; in his pride which borders even upon madness . . . in his perverted reason justifying his perverted instincts.

Ambition in Macbeth, or pride in Oswald, dictates the actions of the character and accounts for the 'violent and total change' in Macbeth or the 'transition in character' in Oswald.

Macbeth, or rather a generalized 'man of uncommon sensibility . . . misled by some pernicious appetite', is presented as 'reflecting on his own conduct' (Richardson, 74); as Oswald is concerned with, and concerned to shake off, 'the recollection of his guilt'. Such a man in such circumstances, according to Richardson, 'conceives a sentiment of universal hatred', as Oswald is 'in the habit of considering the world as a body which is in some sort at war with him [and] has a feeling borrowed from that habit which gives an additional zest to his hatred of those members of society whom he hates & to his contempt of those whom he despises'; and he is seen 'deliberately prosecuting the destruction of an amiable young man by the most atrocious means' (pp. 60–2).

As this last comparison indicates, the critic's observations tend to be generalized from the specific character under consideration, even to the extent of statements in the first person: behaviour is assumed to be credible because 'we' behave in the same or in a comparable fashion. 'Perfidious ourselves', says Richardson (p. 73), describing the decline of Macbeth,

> we repose no confidence in mankind, and are incapable of friendship. We are particularly fearful of all those to whom eminent virtue and integrity have given a strong sense of injustice. . . . Prompted by our fears, we hate every amiable and exalted character, we wage war with the virtuous, and endeavour, by their destruction, to prevent our own.

'It must be observed', says Wordsworth (pp. 62–3),

> that to make the non-existence of a common motive itself a motive to action is a practice which we are never so prone to attribute exclusively to madmen as when we forget ourselves. . . . We all know that the dissatisfaction accompanying the first impulses towards a criminal action, where the mind is familiar with guilt, acts as a stimulus to proceed in that action . . . in a course of criminal conduct every fresh step that we make appears a justification of the one that preceded it. . . . Every time we plan a fresh accumulation of our guilt, we have restored to us something like that original state of mind . . . which first made the crime attractive.

Thus the critic, by identifying a single intellectual trait to which the seemingly inconsistent aspects of the character's behaviour conform, and by insinuating that in any case his behaviour can be recognized in the behaviour of ourselves, attempts to persuade us that his behaviour is intelligible and dramatically probable.

III Note to 'The Thorn'

These pages contain one other specimen of Wordsworth's interest in the description of dramatic character: the Note to 'The Thorn' (No. 4), which attempts to suggest the narrator of the story of Martha Ray by conjuring up 'a Captain of a small trading vessel . . . who being past the middle age of life, had retired upon an annuity or small independent income to some village or country town of which he was not a native, or in which he had not been accustomed to live.' The presentation is obviously far less detailed than that of Oswald/ Rivers in the Preface to *The Borderers*, and a good many critics (though not the editor of this book) have been so far unconvinced by it as virtually to doubt the credibility of any narrator for the story except Wordsworth. We are not so much concerned with this point, however, as with the observation that, on a reduced scale, the presentation is comparable to that of Oswald in the Preface to *The Borderers*. It begins with the same kind of appeal to general experience as is implicit in the use of the first person pronoun in the Preface and in its antecedents such as Richardson: 'The character . . . is sufficiently common. The Reader will perhaps have a general notion of it, if he has ever known a man, a Captain of a small trading vessel for example,' etc. And shortly the sketch moves to the generalities and the ruling passion or psychological principle determining conduct which are typical of the Shakespearean critic: 'Such men . . . are prone to superstition. On which account it appeared to me proper to select a character like this to exhibit some of the general laws by which superstition acts upon the mind. Superstitious men are almost always men of slow faculties and deep feelings.' The interest of this note in the present context is that, after the miniature character-sketch in the manner of the Shakespearean critic, and of Wordsworth in the Preface to *The Borderers*, Wordsworth shifts his attention from the abstract conception of the character to the practical poetics of presenting it:

> while I adhered to the style in which such persons describe, [I had] to take care that words, which in their minds are impregnated with passion, should likewise convey passion to Readers who are not accustomed to sympathize with men feeling in that manner or using such language. It seemed to me that this might be done by calling in the assistance of Lyrical and rapid Metre.

The justification of this technique is provided in the next sentence; the following paragraph moves to a wider justification of verbal repetition in the credible presentation of dramatic character. Thus the Note to 'The Thorn' marks a significant shift in Wordsworth's critical approach: from his early interest in justifying dramatic probability to his later and fairly consistent interest in one or another aspect of the practical problem: how to write poetry of a specified kind—dramatic, in the case of 'The Thorn' itself; of other kinds in the related documents to which we now turn.

IV   Advertisement to *Lyrical Ballads*

Thus, as the Note to 'The Thorn' seeks to justify a particular characteristic of style—verbal repetition—in the portrayal of a particular sort of character, with the implication that the characteristic may also be of more general serviceability; so the Advertisement to *Lyrical Ballads* (No. 2) seeks to justify a generally defined style ('the language of conversation in the middle and lower classes of society') for 'the purposes of poetic pleasure'; and more precisely for the presentation of what the Preface to *Lyrical Ballads* will call general truth, and what the Advertisement itself calls, less succinctly, 'every subject which can interest the human mind'. The justification is given in no very direct terms and in nothing like the detail devoted to it in the Preface; but since the poems are called 'experiments', the reader is given to understand that the author concedes the possibility of failure. The motive for the experiment is implied to be reaction against 'the gaudiness and inane phraseology of many modern writers'; the concession of possible failure is minimized by an appeal to the readers' freedom from cant: 'they should ask themselves if [this book] contains a natural delineation of human passions, human characters, and human incidents; and if the answer be favorable to the author's wishes, that they should consent to be pleased in spite of that most dreadful enemy to our pleasures, our own pre-established codes of decision'; and by a similar appeal to a liberal and well-educated literary sensibility: 'It is apprehended, that the more conversant the reader is with our elder writers, and with those in modern times who have been the most successful in painting manners and passions, the fewer complaints [against over-familiarity and lack of dignity] will he have to make.' Why the style canvassed earlier should appeal to readers thus free from cant and thus educated in literature, and in the hard canons of taste proposed by Sir Joshua Reynolds which are also invoked, does not appear from this document: Wordsworth, in spite of the democratic implications of phrases like 'the human mind' and 'the middle and lower classes of society', proceeds by way of a snobbish winking at a hypothetical intelligentsia and a patronizing glance in the direction of 'the most inexperienced reader'.

The rest of the Advertisement is devoted to the explication of possible difficulties in particular poems: the credibility of 'Goody Blake' is justified by an appeal to 'well-authenticated fact'; the proper stance for reading 'The Thorn' is defined in terms which will be expanded in the Note of 1800; the style of 'The Ancient Mariner' is defined by tradition; and the occasion of 'Expostulation and Reply' and 'The Tables Turned' is given biographical authority. There is little literary criticism here, but the confident stance of the critic, and more important the pragmatic approach, the definition of a literary aim and a description of the means towards it, will be seen maintained and greatly developed in the Preface of 1800.

V Preface to *Lyrical Ballads*

The aim of *Lyrical Ballads*, and especially of the volume of 1798 to which the Preface is retrospectively mainly devoted, is clear enough, though clearer when the Preface is read in its earliest published form, that of 1800: it is to produce a poetry which escapes the ravages of time. *Permanence* is a quality highly valued by Wordsworth in various contexts: the stability of the natural scene; the comparative stability of a great city such as London; the stability of a social order such as that of the Lake District 'statesman' represented by Michael in the poem of that name; the stability of basic human feelings, codes of moral behaviour, and aesthetic taste.

> Several of my Friends are anxious for the success of these Poems from a belief, that, if the views with which they were composed were indeed realized, a class of Poetry would be produced, well adapted to interest mankind permanently, and not unimportant in the multiplicity, and in the quality of its moral relations.

A difficulty in the way of such a project is that literary history seems to suggest its impracticability: the expectations of readers which are roused by poetic styles have differed from age to age. The exponent or symbol held forth by metrical language must in different æras of literature have excited very different expectations: for example, in the age of Catullus, Terence and Lucretius, and that of Statius or Claudian; and in our own country, in the age of Shakespeare and Beaumont and Fletcher, and that of Donne and Cowley, or Dryden, or Pope.

How to eliminate the differences is the theme of much of the Preface.

The first approach is by way of subject-matter. If the poetry is to survive; if it is to have permanent appeal to the poet's and to future generations, 'well adapted to interest mankind permanently'; then the subject-matter had better be of that quality also. As Arnold put it in his Preface of 1853, probably echoing Wordsworth:[9]

> the eternal objects of Poetry, among all nations and at all times. . . . Those [actions] which most powerfully appeal to the great primary human affections: to those elementary feelings which subsist permanently in the race, and which are independent of time. Those feelings are permanent and the same; that which interests them is permanent and the same also.

In theory the critics were thoroughly in agreement, though (as Arnold's deprecatory remarks on *The Excursion* which follow indicate) they might well have failed to agree where the poet might find such 'actions'.

Wordsworth, with the primitivistic preconceptions of the later eighteenth century, and relying also, apparently, on his own observation of men in the 1790s as he reports it in *The Prelude*, Book xii, thought he could find them in the lives of men of 'Low and rustic life'. There follows a vision of the rustic as a kind of spiritual athlete, stripped of the sophistication of the city-dweller[10] and carrying the minimum of moral fat. In particular, the 'manners' of rural life are 'more durable', and 'in that condition the passions of men are incorporated with[11] the beautiful and permanent forms of nature.' The rustic is consequently a kind of linguistic athlete too: his passions 'speak a plainer and more emphatic language', his 'elementary feelings' are 'more forcibly communicated'; because he uses 'simple and unelaborated expressions', his language is 'a more permanent and far more philosophical[12] language, than that which is frequently substituted for it by Poets'. The emphasis is on simple intellectual efficiency matched by linguistic efficiency; a return to basic (and therefore permanent) requirements in thinking, feeling, and speaking.[13]

That the rustic of late eighteenth-century England was really such a figure as Wordsworth here conjures up has, of course, been doubted by many critics, and probably with justice; what is perhaps more important is that the Preface proceeds by assertion and analogy, not by way of the sociological evidence which the argument requires. It is asserted that the man close to the soil is purer (in a kind of chemical sense) or more ideal (in a kind of Platonic sense) than the townsman: 'men as they are men within themselves' is Wordsworth's own phrase in *The Prelude* (xii. 225). From the ideal man thus defined, an analogical extension is made to include his language: the ideal man speaks an ideal language. Or at least, the man and his language come as close to the ideal as imperfect humanity is likely to come in our experience. Even Wordsworth made concessions. The Preface itself concedes the need for the 'purification' of the rustic's language from 'its real defects, from all lasting and rational causes of dislike or disgust'; and five or six years later the fragmentary *Recluse* (*PW*, v. 325, lines 341–2 and textual n. 343–6) grants that

> That Shepherd's voice, it may have reached mine ear
> Debased and under profanation, made
> An organ for the sounds articulate
> Of ribaldry and blasphemy, and wrath
> When drunkenness hath kindled senseless frays.

And the same passage concedes that, however transparently the rustic reveals his feelings, they are not necessarily admirable:

> I came not dreaming of unruffled life,
> Untainted manners. . . . Pleased with the good,
> I shrink not from the evil with disgust,
> Or with immoderate pain,

and he found in Grasmere

> selfishness, and envy, and revenge . . .
> Flattery and double dealing, strife and wrong.

Nevertheless in this society he thought that there was (lines 402–6)

> An art, a music, and a strain of words
> That shall be life, the acknowledged voice of life,

Shall speak of what is done among the fields,
Done truly there, or felt, of solid good
And real evil, yet be sweet withal.

So the argument returns to 'the real language of men' which might also be the permanent language of poetry.

And this is indeed the major task of the Preface in its early form: to define a language for poetry which shall be permanent in its appeal. Towards this definition, it now appears, the rustic and his language formed only a partial, possible, or tentative step; for the argument now discards the rustic as a means of defining language. Rather than 'a selection of the real language of men in a state of vivid sensation' or 'the language of . . . men [of low and rustic life], purified . . . from . . . its real defects', the model for the poet's language in the next section of the Preface is 'the language of prose'. No definition of this model is offered; and though it is postulated that it must be 'well written' prose, no standards of good writing are offered either. No attempt is made, even, to show that the rustic of the earlier argument has, like Molière's M. Jourdain, spoken prose, aware or unaware of his achievement, for forty years or a lifetime.

Some hints towards a Wordsworthian definition of 'prose' can be had from the surrounding context, but they are slight and negative in tone. There will presumably be no 'personifications of abstract ideas', and there will be 'little of what is usually called poetic diction'. The italicized lines in Gray's sonnet to which Wordsworth gives grudging approval 'in no respect differ from [the language] of prose' except that they rhyme and use the Latinate idiom 'I fruitless mourn' rather than 'I mourn fruitlessly'. If we try to find out why this equation is made, we shall probably conclude that the approved lines do not, on the whole, use the explicit or implicit personifications of natural objects or phenomena which appear in the rest of the poem. A positive quality (if it can be so called) which the italicized lines have (but it is also the general strategy of the sonnet) is understatement: the poem, except in its title, never mentions the fact of death. Such understatement, or deliberately spare statement, is a characteristic of much of Wordsworth's most effective writing: the famous line from 'Michael', 'And never lifted up a single stone' (line 466), understates to the extent that the whole tragedy of a poem 500-odd lines long is implicit in its ten syllables. But beyond such slight inferences which we can draw from the context, Wordsworth's attempt to define the language of permanence as 'the language of prose' is no more successful than the linking of it with the (purified) speech of rustics.

It is probable that the attempt was futile from the outset; for language is not a phenomenon susceptible to such a definition. It is true that (to use Wordsworth's example) much of Chaucer is as readily intelligible to the twentieth or the eighteenth century as to the fourteenth; but much is not, as Wordsworth discovered in his attempts to modernize 'The Prioress's Tale' and *Troilus and Criseyde*; and much that seems so is not either, as the undergraduate discovers when he is faced with the pitfalls of shifting semantics in a vocabulary which often looks deceptively modern. Old English neither seems, nor is, intelligible without rigorous linguistic study, though much of its vocabulary and syntactical mechanism survives in modern English. A linguistic gloss is necessary for the intelligent reading of Spenser, Shakespeare, Milton, and even many eighteenth-century poets, and a stylistic commentary on all poets except, perhaps, those of the reader's own generation is a need for the reader and the aim of much literary study. In short, language in general survives in spite of, or because of, growth and change; and these are the very qualities which a permanent language has to avoid. There are some exceptions, such as classical Greek and Latin, as they survive in the exercises of schoolboys and undergraduates; but no one ever thought of calling these 'the real language of men'.

VI   Metre

In the Preface of 1800, Wordsworth now turns directly to meet possible objections to his argument which are related to the presence of metrical form in a poetry the language of which has just been defined as essentially that of well-written prose.[14] The first of these objections may be stated in this paraphrase of the text: since it is obvious from the presence of rhyme and metre in poetry that poetry is *not* prose, with what logic do you argue for the identity of the languages of poetry and prose? Does not the obvious difference in linguistic form at least suggest the possible propriety of a difference in linguistic texture? The second objection may be stated in Wordsworth's own phrase for the 'obvious question': 'Why, professing these opinions,[15] have I written in verse?'

As to the first objection: Wordsworth replies that the presence of metrical form has no bearing on the matter. For 'the distinction of [rhyme and (1800)] metre is regular and uniform'; that is, verse differs from prose, indeed, but differs by a constant factor;[16] because of its constancy, and because the reader is assured of its constancy, this factor can be ignored in the discussion of what is or may be variable in verse, namely its language, which is or may be 'arbitrary, and subject to infinite caprices upon which no calculation whatever can be made'. One could write metrically regular and rhymed verse in 'poetic diction' *or* in 'the language of prose', and the presence of rhyme and metre would not have any logical bearing on one's choice of language, which depends upon other factors.

Wordsworth's answer to the second objection is based upon what he considers the positive advantages of metrical form. His subject-matter, he grants, might 'be as vividly described in prose'; but by writing in verse he adds 'the charm which, by the consent of all nations, is acknowledged to exist in metrical language'. But (says the straw objector) you will upset conventional responses if you write in verse while you discard the 'artificial distinctions of style with which metre is usually accompanied', and the pleasurable bonus of metrical form will not compensate. It will (replies the theorist), as you can see from poems (presumably popular ballads) on 'more humble subjects, and in a more naked and simple style than I have aimed at, which poems have continued to give pleasure from genera-tion to generation'; that is, have achieved virtual permanence of appeal. *A fortiori*, my poems have an even better chance of success.

But this is only the basis of the answer; a more significant addendum follows: 'The end of Poetry is to produce excitement in co-existence with an overbalance of pleasure'. To an excessive 'excitement' produced by 'the words', Wordsworth opposes the *regularity* of metrical form; to the possibly *painful* nature of this excitement (as, perhaps, in tragic narratives)[17] he opposes the *pleasure* of metrical form. By a kind of arithmetical summing of the elements of excitement versus regularity, pain versus pleasure, we arrive at the required result: 'excitement in co-existence with an overbalance of pleasure'. How it is ensured that the 'overbalance' is necessarily 'of pleasure' is not explained; but two additions made in 1802 serve to clarify. The dilution or cancellation of 'pain' is ensured by the 'tendency of metre to divest language in a certain degree of its reality, and thus to throw a sort of half consciousness of un-substantial existence over the whole composition'; likewise the reader achieves, when reading the right kind of verse, 'an indistinct perception perpetually renewed of language closely resembling that of real life, and yet, in the circumstance of metre, differing from it so widely'. In short, the presence of metrical form guarantees that, though the reader might mistake the language for that of real life, and the poem, therefore, as a raw report of what Arnold in the Preface of 1853 calls a 'painful' as distinct from a 'tragic' situation, he will eventually be undeceived; and he will recognize that he has to do with a work of art, of which metrical form is the 'exponent or symbol'; or, in Coleridgean terms, with an imitation, not a copy, of real life.

Surprisingly, metre can (Wordsworth claims) have an effect virtually the opposite of 'tempering and restraining the passion': it can, 'if the Poet's words should be incommensurate with the passion, and inadequate to raise the Reader to a height of desirable excitement', 'greatly contribute to impart passion to the words, and to effect the complex end which the Poet proposes to himself.' How? we ask, especially when we observe that metre is 'something regular, something to which the mind has been accustomed in various moods and in a less excited state', or even 'accustomed when in an unexcited or a less excited state' (as the text of 1800 baldly puts it); and therefore, we might suppose, inevitably associated with 'tempering and restraining'. The answer seems to lie in 'the feeling, whether cheerful or melancholy, which [the Reader] has been accustomed to connect with that particular movement of metre'. A 'cheerful' metre will contribute 'cheerfulness' to a would-be cheerful poem, even though 'the Poet's words should be incommensurate with the passion'; a 'melancholy' metre will contribute 'melancholy' in a parallel situation. What is a 'cheerful' metre or a 'melancholy' metre? I do not know, and indeed Wordsworth's phrase 'the feeling . . . which he has been accustomed to connect with that particular movement of metre' indicates that such qualities are attributed to metre by virtue of arbitrary or conventional associations rather than for anything inherent in its metrical nature.

Nevertheless Wordsworth gives one specific instance where he attributes a particular quality to a particular metre: in his Note to 'The Thorn' he calls the metre of 'The Thorn' 'Lyrical and rapid' (p. 97). 'Lyrical' is vaguer than 'cheerful or melancholy', but 'rapid' seems to be intelligible. When is a line of English verse 'rapid'? When, perhaps, it avoids a spondaic movement and when it is 'short' compared with, say, that arbitrary but convenient norm of English verse, the iambic pentameter. The usual four-stress line of 'The Thorn' is of this nature; moreover, it is varied with a three-stress line, and a good many of the four-stress lines break firmly into half-lines of two stresses each, suggesting an even shorter line. Because most lines rhyme, the three unrhymed lines in each stanza direct the reader forward, seeking the rhyme which by analogy is expected, but which never arrives to satisfy the expectation. By such means, perhaps, Wordsworth ensures that the poem 'appear[s] to move quickly' when it 'in reality move[s] slowly': it moves slowly because the narrative is full of hesitations, circumlocutions, and repetitions, whereas the metre gives the impression of a speaker excited by his subject and talking rapidly in his excitement.

The language of 'The Thorn' is deliberately designed so that it may *not* 'convey passion to Readers who are not accustomed to sympathize with men feeling in that manner or using such language'; or, in the words of the Preface, so that it is 'incommensurate with the passion, and inadequate to raise the Reader to a height of desirable excitement'. In such a case (Wordsworth hopes) the metre may provide the necessary compensation; moreover, the general sense of 'pleasure' connected with metrical form contributes to 'an overbalance of pleasure' which is part of 'the complex end which the Poet proposes to himself'. The success of this strategy in the poem is a matter of individual judgment; at least the theory is clear.

VII 'Emotion recollected in tranquillity'

Embedded in Wordsworth's theory of metrical form, and resuming obscure hints given earlier in the Preface, is the famous Wordsworthian doctrine of poetry emerging from 'emotion recollected in tranquillity'. This and the related phrase, 'all good poetry is the spontaneous overflow of powerful feelings', repeated here from its earlier context (p. 72), require attention because of their obscurity and also because they introduce a concept of poetry not otherwise used in the Preface of 1800. The poet who draws his subject-matter from a particular social class which is not his own, and who adopts the language of this class rather than his own, is not, one would suppose, so much a man involved with (his own) powerful feelings, as an observer, reporter, or imitator of the habits, personal, social, and linguistic, of a body of society to which he does not belong. According to the Note to 'The Thorn', it is the habit of those who try 'to communicate impassioned feelings' to repeat themselves (p. 97); and again Wordsworth's stance is of the observer of men in general who, when he wishes to present such an attempt with dramatic credibility, draws upon his fund of observations and produces as convincing an imitation as he can, by (for instance) attributing repetitious language to the narrator of 'The Thorn'.

In short, the general argument of the Preface of 1800 is that of poetry as imitation, an argument descending from Plato and Aristotle, and urged by many theorists of the Renaissance and even of the eighteenth century; the two troublesome *obiter dicta* with which we are now concerned, however, postulate poetry as 'expression', as in some way the outpouring of the poet's own emotions, as his attempt to 'communicate [the] impassioned feelings', not of a dramatic character like the narrator of 'The Thorn', but of himself.

How is the attempt made? Two processes are described, the one general and preparatory to any poetry at all, the other particular and relating to the approach to the act of composition. The first is that by which the poet so disciplines his feelings that, when he has them, he is certain, or virtually certain, that they are worth having—that they are concerned with what the Preface calls 'important'. This appears to be the sense of the long and difficult sentence beginning 'For our continued influxes' (p. 72); where Wordsworth seems to be saying that the poet who thinks 'long and deeply' is introspectively *evaluating* his 'past feelings', and that, if he does this often enough ('by the repetition and continuance of this act'), he will build up habits of mind ensuring that any feeling which he entertains is connected with what is 'important' (and, presumably, that any concerned with what is not 'important' will not be entertained).

What, in such a context, is 'important'? Wordsworth offers no definition, but we may guess at one from his concern with the 'purpose' which he attributes to his poetry. This is defined at least twice; the more useful definition is the second: the purpose is 'to follow the fluxes and refluxes of the mind when agitated by the great and simple affections of our nature'. It is, in fact (as the illustrations show), to demonstrate the existence of what the text of 1802 calls 'truth . . . general, and operative'; indeed, to assert the persistence of this in cases where it might be doubted, as in 'The Idiot Boy' and 'The Mad Mother'. In short, 'what is really important to men' is 'the great and simple affections of our nature', the way men's minds and feelings work, so that poetry, which is a record or case-book of these affections, is, as the Note to 'The Thorn' puts it, a 'history or science of feelings'. To use a later jargon: it is important that men have, on the whole, a single psychology which is regarded as 'normal',

and that they should be aware, or be made aware by such media as
Wordsworth's poetry, that they share in this normality.

The second process described concerns the actual composition of
a poem; and it appears, contrary to what might have been supposed
from the earlier statement, now repeated: 'poetry is the spontaneous
overflow of powerful feelings', that poetry is not, or is not usually,
the result of an immediate verbal reaction to an emotional situation.
There is, indeed, powerful feeling, but it is neither the powerful
feeling generated directly by the original occasion, nor is it that feeling only. The sequence of the process appears to be: a state of
tranquillity; a recollection, in this state, of a previous occasion of
feeling, and a recreation of the emotion which replaces the tranquillity;[18] the beginning of composition in this state, presumably
the 'spontaneous overflow'; the continuing of composition in 'a mood
similar to this'. The operative qualification of the mere 'spontaneous
overflow' is contained in the differentiation of the mood in which the
poet starts from the mood in which he continues; and this difference
is defined (or at least this is the only definition offered) in the final
clauses of the sentence under consideration: 'the emotion, of whatever kind and in whatever degree, from various causes is qualified
by various pleasures, so that in describing any passions whatsoever,
which are voluntarily described, the mind will upon the whole be in
a state of enjoyment'. The indefinites 'of whatever kind and in whatever degree . . . any passions whatsoever' are intended to show
that the emotion/passion may be painful; whether it is or not, the
'various pleasures' are such that they will outweigh the pain, or add
to the pleasure, of the emotion which initiates composition.

The definition is deficient, in Wordsworthian terms, for lack of
specification of the 'various pleasures' which perform this function.
They obviously act in the same way as (or indeed they may include)
the pleasurable content which Wordsworth attributes to metrical
form; with this difference, that it appears to be the reader, rather
than the poet, who experiences the pleasures of metre. But clearly
the 'various pleasures' mentioned here belong to the composing poet
rather than to his reader. What are they? It is impossible to say for
certain, but two related utterances may throw some light. The more
obvious is a sonnet of 1820 which begins by asserting that 'There is
a pleasure in poetic pains' (*PW*, iii. 29–30). The drift of this poem is
the poet's search for the *mot juste*, which may long escape him: 'Yet
he repines not, if his thought stand clear,/ At last, of hindrance and
obscurity.' There is satisfaction (if that can be called pleasure) in

discovering what the third of the *Essays upon Epitaphs* calls the 'incarnation of the thought' (p. 154). Both this phrase and the sonnet distinguish thought from expression, as if thought can exist at some sub-verbal level, eluding expression, until the moment of clarity described in the sonnet, or the supreme intelligibility suggested by the prose phrase, arrives; until the poet, like the rest of us struggling for utterance, 'knows what he wants to say'. When does this moment arrive? Presumably (to draw upon our second utterance) when the poet sees the 'worthy purpose' for which he wrote his poem; when he perceives the connection of what he is talking about with 'truth . . . general, and operative'. He may do this before he actually writes, but he need not: 'Not that I mean to say, that I always began to write with a distinct purpose formally conceived.' And if not, then during, or after, composition; for at some point during or at the end of composition, if not before composition, the poet himself must recognize that his poem had a worthy purpose— that it was connected with what is 'important'; if he cannot do this, he might as well scrap the poem. In short, the writing of a poem is a means whereby the poet acquires a knowledge or an understanding (of the general relevance of the experience which the poem records) which he did not have before. The acquisition of such knowledge is, I believe, usually found pleasurable; indeed, the Preface of 1802 deals at length with the connection between knowledge and pleasure:[19]

> We have no knowledge . . . but what has been built up by pleasure, and exists in us by pleasure alone . . . the Poet, prompted by this feeling of pleasure which accompanies him through the whole course of his studies, converses with general nature with affections akin to those, which . . . the Man of Science has raised up in himself, by conversing with those particular parts of nature which are the objects of his studies. The knowledge both of the Poet and the Man of Science is pleasure.

It does not seem possible to discover more precise definitions of the 'various pleasures' with which the composition of Wordsworthian poetry is accompanied. Coleridge offers comparable statements in various places, but they do not usually assist any further than by suggesting that composition involves the total, articulated activity of the mind in its various relevant aspects, modes, or faculties.[20] Coleridge asserts that such activity is pleasurable, but he does not justify the assertion any more rigorously than Wordsworth justifies his in the Preface or in the various statements on the relation of knowledge and pleasure on which we have been drawing.

VIII The Preface of 1802

The ideas on the origins of poetry which we have just considered are implicit throughout the lengthy passage inserted into the text of the Preface in the edition of 1802. The insertion thus not only drifts towards a theory incongruous with the general argument of the Preface of 1800, but positively disturbs that argument at the point of insertion. For the original argument, as we saw, was concerned lest a justification should be found, in the presence of metrical form in verse, for 'other artificial distinctions' between 'metrical language [and] that of prose'. Although this concern still appears in the text of 1802, it is answered, not by the reply of 1800 (that metrical form is a constant factor which is to be ignored in merely linguistic problems), but by erecting a distinction between 'the language of such Poetry as I am recommending' and (not prose, but) 'the vulgarity and mean-ness of ordinary life' (meaning, evidently, the vulgarity and meanness of the language of ordinary life), not prose, which, when 'well written', can scarcely be characterized by 'vulgarity and meanness'.[21] The argument is still concerned to exclude 'artificial distinctions'; it differs from what precedes, however, in its notion of that from which the artificial distinctions are to be excluded. For, although the passage just examined suggests that we are now back in the world of a 'selection of the real language of men in a state of vivid sensation', or of the language of rustics 'purified . . . from all lasting and rational causes of dislike or disgust', what is now offered, and that on which 'selection' operates, is neither of these, but a language 'dignified and variegated . . . alive with metaphors and figures', which is 'the language of' passions to which the poet has been 'led' by a judiciously chosen subject. When the theorist talks in terms of the *language of passions* to which his subject *leads* him, or of a language 'which the passion *naturally suggests*', he is talking in terms of utterance which is a virtually automatic reaction to 'passion' and the authenticity of which is guaranteed by its origin. Such a language, though it may be attenuated for the purposes of pleasure by 'selec-tion', must not be amplified by the 'addition' of 'foreign splendour'.

This view of the poetics of 1802 is confirmed by what follows. The poet is defined, not as a close observer and reporter of mankind, but as 'a man speaking to men', presumably in his own voice and expressing his own thoughts and feelings. How, then, does he express the thoughts and feelings of others, a feat which Wordsworth attempts in a good many poems in *Lyrical Ballads*? How can an 'expressive' poet write dramatic poetry? By attempting

> to bring his feelings near to those of the persons whose feelings he describes, nay, for short spaces of time perhaps, to let himself slip into an entire delusion, and even confound and identify his own feelings with theirs; modifying only the language which is thus suggested to him, by a consideration that he describes for a particular purpose, that of giving pleasure.

He will not, that is to say, draw upon a fund of accumulated observations on the way in which men behave; he will, rather, empathically identify himself with his dramatic characters and then give utterance as a 'spontaneous overflow of powerful feelings' which, 'for short spaces of time perhaps', he has made his own. He will not need to draw on his recollection, for instance, that men under the stress of feeling repeat themselves: the repetition will come naturally to him, or be 'suggested' to him, in his temporarily achieved state of passion.

What, say imaginary objectors, happens in the intervals between the 'short spaces of time' during which this desirable state of mind persists? Should not the poet then 'substitute excellences of another kind for those which are unattainable by him'? No, says Wordsworth, one must keep trying: 'this would be to encourage idleness and unmanly despair'; for (he says after a lengthy digression) 'the dramatic parts of composition are defective, in proportion as they deviate from the real language of nature, and are coloured by a diction of the Poet's own'. The objection which led to the digression is not squarely answered: one must strive for adequate utterance, an inadequate utterance is 'defective', and 'excellences of another kind . . . transitory and accidental ornaments . . . a diction of the Poet's own', individual or traditional, are no compensation for the inadequacies—this is the extent of Wordsworth's answer.

The digression just mentioned is an eloquent defence of poetry as concerned with general truth (and therefore 'important'), with the 'knowledge which all men carry about with them, and . . . sympathies in which without any other discipline than that of our daily life we are fitted to take delight'. The acquisition of such knowledge is (as we saw earlier) accompanied by pleasure; those who acquire it are men *qua* men, not *qua* specially trained intellects; and the poet, being a man, is fitted to display such knowledge, for its acquisition and display require no further qualifications, apart from a heightening of certain qualities which the poet shares with 'men'. Unlike the biographer and historian, he requires no special training or special interest in particular bodies of information, any more than his audience does; his stance towards such knowledge is akin to that of the scientist towards his narrowly specialized field—which may indeed be included, eventually, in the poet's general one. The 'sublime notion of Poetry' which this passage gives should (Wordsworth claims) deter anyone who has it in mind to 'break in upon the sanctity and truth of his pictures by transitory and accidental ornaments, and endeavour to excite admiration of himself by arts, the necessity of which must manifestly depend upon the assumed meanness of his subject'.

The straw objector to Wordsworth's arguments throws in his final protest by urging that a 'distinction of language . . . still . . . may be proper and necessary where the Poet speaks to us in his own person and character'. The protest is rejected on the ground that the poet's subject is 'the general passions and thoughts and feelings of men . . . the sensations of other men, and the objects which interest them. . . . How, then, can his language differ in any material degree from that of all other men who feel vividly and see clearly?' Sensing, perhaps, a retort that one may indeed write about such things in the most contrived of poetic dictions, if one will and if one can find sufficient reason, Wordsworth adds that, even if one may, the need to communicate with one's audience forbids it, for 'Poets do not write for Poets alone, but for men, [and therefore the Poet] must express himself as other men express themselves.'

At this point the argument of 1802 reverts to the discussion of metre, involving that of 'emotion recollected in tranquillity', which we have already considered. Except to repeat the observation that that discussion now fails in its original purpose, which was to justify the use of metrical form when the language was that of 'prose', we need not consider this passage further.

The rest of the Preface, in either text, is of smaller interest. It makes one notable concession of possible failure: 'I am sensible that my associations must have sometimes been particular instead of general, and that, consequently, giving to things a false importance, sometimes from diseased impulses I may have written upon unworthy subjects' (p. 87); but Wordsworth is concerned less with this possible flaw than with lapses in linguistic taste, or what some readers might suppose were such. The passage quoted needs to be referred to the early discussion of the purpose of Wordsworth's poems and the formation of desirable habits of mind such that 'by obeying blindly and mechanically the impulses of those habits, we shall' compose valuable poems (p. 72). Wordsworth is now conceding that the evaluative processes obscurely described in the earlier passages may at times produce erroneous evaluations ('giving to things a false importance') which will result in 'the impulses of those habits' being 'diseased', that is, abnormal in the sense that particular rather than general truth is seen as valuable. That Wordsworth's verse does run the double risk which he here envisages has been a commonplace since Coleridge wrote in *Biographia Literaria* of the 'matter-of-factness' of Wordsworth's subjects and of the 'inconstancy' of his style.[22] It is not till the subtler analyses of some modern critics of the poet that the risks have been shown, implicitly, to be often as minimal as he made them himself in this passage.

Yet the risk is sometimes present. Supposing (what some critics have denied) that the object of 'The Thorn' is that which Wordsworth's Note to the poem describes, and that it is in a measure achieved, we may yet question whether the laws of superstition, at least as the poem exemplifies them, are sufficiently 'important' to justify the poem. The aim of 'Goody Blake' seems to have been a comparable study of what Wordsworth calls 'the power of the human imagination' (p. 86), or what a modern jargon might call the psychology of auto-suggestion; yet many find the poem effective, if at all, in its own terms, which are that, with or without a Coleridgean 'suspension of disbelief',[23] a curse works *qua* curse, not as an internally generated derangement of the victim's psyche. The extraordinary justification, in Wordsworth's letter to Lady Beaumont of May 1807 (No. 7), of the trivial incident which called forth a trivial sonnet, is an even more marked example of Wordsworth's failure to realize that not all operations of the mind are equally 'important', and that some are probably not important enough to warrant a poem. Thus, while we remain Wordsworth's debtors for his insistence on the importance of the normal and the commonplace in human psychology, we may sometimes regret that he gave to 'things a false importance' by an imprecise evaluation. The failure in such cases often occurs, not because the false importance is attributed to the 'particular', but because it is attributed to the general merely on the ground that it is general, rather than that it is at once general and generally important.

IX   Appendix to *Lyrical Ballads*

The Appendix to *Lyrical Ballads*, added in the edition of 1802, attempts to explain the origins of formal poetic diction in arguments commonplace in many theories of literature in the eighteenth century, which by a process of unwarranted historical extrapolation infer the intellectual attitudes and poetic practice of 'the earliest Poets of all nations'.[24] It is of course true that a particular style, diction, or rhetoric may gain prestige and hence be applied 'to feelings and ideas with which [it has] no natural connection whatsoever': the most notable instance in English is the spread of the Miltonic blank-verse manner to eighteenth-century verse on a variety of subjects widely removed from Milton's own heroic argument; and it is also true that, as used in *Paradise Lost*, Milton's language was 'daring, and figurative'. But that it sprang from 'passion excited by real events', and that Milton 'wrote naturally', in a Wordsworthian sense, seem improbable, in spite of Milton's own claim to the production of unpremeditated verse at the dictation of the heavenly Muse. Except in so far as Wordsworth's primitivistic theories are in obvious accord with his ideas on the virtues of 'Low and rustic life', and with those on poetry as 'the spontaneous overflow of powerful feelings',[25] this document is of small interest in the growth of Wordsworth's aesthetics.

X   Essays upon Epitaphs

The three *Essays upon Epitaphs* of 1810 resume the most significant arguments of the Preface to *Lyrical Ballads* and present them with greater clarity, arising from a firmer grasp of the topics actually handled and a discreet omission of some of the less satisfactory elements of the Preface.

The most obvious omission is of any sustained attempt to define a subject-matter and a language gathered from a particular social class. The corresponding attempt in the Preface of 1800 showed, or permitted, the poet to be a cool observer or reporter of men's behaviour, including their linguistic behaviour, and proposed the rustic as the model or epitome of men most practically available to him. To this attempt those parts of the 1800 Preface, and those additions of 1802, which deal with the concept of 'powerful feelings' as the basis of poetry, are not obviously relevant. Neither is the epitaph; for in Wordsworth's view the epitaph cannot effectively be written by a cool observer: emotional involvement with the subject is the prime basis for utterance. Moreover, since the subject, death and mourning, is of universal significance (for every man faces it at some time), every man is, in fact or potentially, the composer of an epitaph. Thus the form becomes a model of utterance for all poetry which can be construed to emerge from the more or less controlled expression of 'powerful feelings'. To this expression only the poet's own voice, not a voice borrowed from a rustic, is appropriate; of this subject-matter only the poet's own bosom, not the feelings of others in their 'more subtle windings', can be the source. True, the subject-matter is commonplace, and rightly so, as are the feelings listed in the Preface (p. 82); but it is a commonplace and a normality not to be sought in odd corners of experience but in everyone's; for it deals with 'truths whose very interest and importance have caused them to be unattended to, as things which could take care of themselves'.

For various reasons, the epitaph must seek the permanence at which Wordsworth aimed in *Lyrical Ballads*. The monument on which it is inscribed is designed to 'preserve [the] memory' of the deceased; and the wish to do this springs from 'the consciousness of a principle of immortality in the human soul'. That which preserves, and that which records immortality, must, obviously, approach as nearly as possible to a permanent record, or its purpose will not be served. How to achieve this? Wordsworth does not say, in positive terms, or such seemingly positive terms as his defence of the language of rustics or the language of prose. He repeats the observations of the Preface on changing tastes in literary style as indexes of impermanence, with the implication that datable fashions, the mannerisms which one generation invents, and the next drops, had better be avoided (pp. 153, 165–6):

The far-searching influence of . . . Taste, is in nothing more evinced than in the changeful character and complexion of [the epitaph]. . . .

A man called to a task in which he is not practised may have his expression thoroughly defiled and clogged by the style prevalent in his age . . . the favourite style of different ages is so different and wanders so far from propriety that . . . we might suppose that truth and nature were things not to be looked for in books.

What does the poet substitute for 'the style prevalent in his age'? We are not told, in linguistic or stylistic terms; rather, we have descriptions of the poet's state of mind which will ensure, on the whole, that the appropriate language will emerge (p. 154): 'those expressions which are not what the garb is to the body but what the body is to the soul, themselves a constituent part and power or function in the thought . . . an incarnation of the thought'. A major recommendation is that, though the epitaph flows from emotion, the flow should be considered and controlled. Hence the content of the epitaph must be 'liberated from that weakness and anguish of sorrow which is in nature *transitory*'. A thought in William Mason is 'too poignant and *transitory*' for an epitaph; of a line of Pope: 'in a *permanent* Inscription things only should be admitted that have an *enduring* place in the mind' (pp. 131, 153, 157; my italics). A certain reticence, therefore, is demanded if permanence is to be achieved; the monument on the tomb is the type of this (pp. 131–2):

> to raise a monument is a sober and a reflective act . . . the inscription which it bears is intended to be permanent, and for universal perusal . . . for this reason, the thoughts and feelings expressed should be permanent also. . . . The very form and substance of the monument which has received the inscription, and the appearance of the letters, testifying with what a slow and laborious hand they must have been engraven, might seem to reproach the author who had given way upon this occasion to transports of mind, or to quick turns of conflicting passion.

The 'naked names' of great men serve as a reticent yet adequate record, for they 'will continue to be known familiarly to latest posterity'.

XI Sincerity

The epitaph springs, or must seem to spring, from a 'spontaneous overflow of powerful feelings'; 'the writer who would excite sympathy is bound in this case, more than in any other, to give proof that he himself has been moved' (p. 131). Therefore Wordsworth is able to introduce, for the first time with any emphasis in English criticism[26] (p. 141),

a criterion of sincerity, by which a Writer may be judged. . . .
For, when a Man is treating an interesting subject, or one which
he ought not to treat at all unless he be interested, no faults have
such a killing power as those which prove that he is not in
earnest, that he is acting a part, has leisure for affectation, and feels
that without it he could do nothing.

Lack of sincerity 'is worse in a sepulchral inscription, precisely in
the same degree as that mode of composition calls for sincerity more
urgently than any other'. Its presence, on the other hand, will compensate for faults: 'errors of style or manner', or the excessive feeling
of Montrose on the death of Charles I. (It is also, we might interject,
an unreliable criterion; for Wordsworth's next instance of it, the
tribute to Philip Sidney which he attributes to a 'simple effusion of
the moment' on the part of John Weever, is neither Weever's nor a
simple effusion of the moment, but Philemon Holland's English
version of an elegant piece of Latin prose in William Camden's
Britannia.)[27]

This criterion is easily linked with that total approach of poet to
subject which we saw as the basis of Wordsworth's view of the
language of the epitaph. For sincerity is here connected not only
with the literary appeal of the poet.[28] Insincerity 'shocks the moral
sense. . . . Literature is . . . so far identified with morals, the
quality of the act so far determined by our notion of the aim and
purpose of the agent, that nothing can please us . . . if we are
persuaded that the primary virtues of sincerity, earnestness, and a
real interest in the main object are wanting' (pp. 141, 165).

Sincerity does not necessarily demand what an uninvolved
observer might suppose was the whole truth about the deceased.
The Preface to *Lyrical Ballads*, we recall, proposed an obscurely
defined 'selection' as a means of removing what might be 'painful or
disgusting in the passion' and what might, therefore, frustrate the
poet's general aim of ensuring the reader's pleasure (p. 78). The
epitaph likewise uses a kind of selection, 'that takes away, indeed,
but only to the end that the parts which are not abstracted may
appear more dignified and lovely; may impress and affect the more'
(p. 129). And if it should be objected that thus to excise is also to
distort, Wordsworth replies that the selected utterance

is truth, and of the highest order; for, though doubtless things
are not apparent which did exist; yet, the object being looked at
through this medium, parts and proportions are brought into

distinct view which before had been only imperfectly or unconsciously seen: it is truth hallowed by love.

For this is how the lamenting living see the lamented dead; and
since to present that vision is the aim of the epitaph, the aim is thus
fulfilled.

While this kind of selection excises, it does not necessarily
attenuate: on the contrary, it may, by removing the unfavourable
aspects of the deceased's character, heighten its virtues. Nevertheless
that kind of attenuation which the Preface attributes to 'selection' is
of service in ensuring that that proper reticence, associated with
reflection and permanence rather than with an immediate 'overflow'
of feeling which is necessarily transitory, is attained. Of this the
monument itself, which is 'presupposed' as the medium of the
epitaph rather than the written or printed page, is the type: we are
to imagine, or are not to disbelieve, that the 'writing' of an epitaph
involves its inscription on stone (pp. 131–2): 'The very form and substance of the monument . . . and the appearance of the letters,
testifying with what a slow and laborious hand they must have been
engraven, might seem to reproach the [overhasty] author.' The
monument is, comparatively, permanent; its arduous preparation
makes it an artefact, parallel in its restraining function to the artificial
nature of metrical form as that is discussed in the Preface to *Lyrical
Ballads*;[29] and likewise the grave itself 'is a tranquillising object:
resignation in course of time springs up from it'. None of these real
or figurative restraints, however, is to be taken to indicate that the
epitaph is a passionless utterance: 'The passions should be subdued,
the emotions controlled; strong, indeed, but nothing ungovernable
or wholly involuntary. Seemliness requires this, and truth requires
it also: for how can the narrator otherwise be trusted?' The process
can be assisted by casting the epitaph into the dramatic form in
which the deceased speaks in his own person, seemingly from a
certainty about his own state about which the narrator can only
guess and hope; yet this form is not to be preferred to a more
straightforward statement of the survivor's feelings, because its
artifice is too transparent and its deviation from the real state of
affairs too obvious; other controls on exuberant feelings are possible
and necessary. Even Chiabrera, Wordsworth's model in the epitaph,
occasionally fails to apply them (p. 160): he 'has here neglected to
ascertain whether the passions expressed were in kind and degree a
dispensation of reason or at least commodities issued under her

licence and authority.' In general (p. 154), 'the excellence of writing
. . . consists in a conjunction of Reason and Passion, a conjunction
which must be of necessity benign.'

Because death and the reaction of the survivors towards death are
among the great commonplaces of our experience, the epitaph, like
Lyrical Ballads, will be concerned with general truth—in that more
conventional sense in which it is not to be sought in odd corners or
with recherché emphases such as some of the *Lyrical Ballads* affect.
Thus (pp. 148–9)

> it is not only no fault but a primary requisite in an Epitaph that
> it shall contain thoughts and feelings which are in their substance
> common-place, and even trite. It is grounded upon the universal
> intellectual property of man;—sensations which all men have felt
> and feel in some degree daily and hourly;—truths whose very
> interest and importance have caused them to be unattended to,
> as things which could take care of themselves.

How to present the deceased in congruity with these ideas? By
presenting him as a man whose qualities are essentially those of all
men. Since it is by details that individuality is defined, it follows that
the epitaph should not be overburdened with details, especially
details placed, in the manner of Pope, in antithesis one to another
(p.128):

> to analyse the characters of others, especially of those whom
> we love, is not a common or natural employment of men at any
> time. . . . We shrink from the thought of placing [the] merits
> and defects [of friends and kindred] to be weighed against each
> other in the nice balance of pure intellect . . . least of all, do we
> incline to these refinements when under the pressure of sorrow,
> admiration, or regret, or when actuated by any of those feelings
> which incite men to prolong the memory of their friends and
> kindred, by records placed in the bosom of the all-uniting and
> equalising receptacle of the dead.

Yet, because a completely general statement would be an epitaph on
no one in particular, it is necessary to particularize: we require

> a due proportion of the common or universal feeling of humanity
> to sensations excited by a distinct and clear conception . . . of
> the individual . . . at least of his character as, after death, it
> appeared to those who loved him and lament his loss.

The general and the particular should 'temper, restrain, and exalt each other', with the emphasis on generality (p. 158): 'what was peculiar to the individual shall still be subordinate to a sense of what he had in common with the species.' On the other hand, excessive detail is a defect (p. 130): 'It suffices . . . that the trunk and the main branches of the worth of the deceased be boldly and unaffectedly represented. Any further detail, minutely and scrupulously pursued, especially if this be done with laborious and antithetic discriminations, must inevitably frustrate its own purpose.' It brands the author as insincere: 'the understanding having been so busy in its petty occupation, how could the heart of the mourner be other than cold?' And it is incongruous with the main emphasis of the epitaph, which is to generalize, not to particularize; to unify, not to contrast.

It follows that the manner of Pope and his school is grossly unsuited to the epitaph. That manner is apt for satire: for satire operates by contrast, norm contrasted with deviation; this is the reverse of the intent of the epitaph. The incongruity can be seen when, his sense of the fitting paralysed by the Augustan need to balance, and preferably to balance by antithesis, the poet balances in form only: ' "Here rests a Woman good without pretence/ Blest with plain reason"—from which, *sober sense* is not sufficiently distinguishable' (p. 147); or he balances and contrasts where no contrast is logically possible: 'So firm yet soft, so strong yet so refined'; 'Though meek, magnanimous; though witty, wise'. The first antithetical pair, 'firm . . . soft', makes nonsense; the others, Pope's or Lyttleton's, throw into contrast qualities which are not necessarily opposed. These sharp but just judgments make more convincing practical criticism of the Augustan manner than the vague accusations which the Preface to *Lyrical Ballads* and its Appendix offer against poetic diction.

The presentation of generality and particularity thus appropriately interwoven is better achieved, in Wordsworth's view, by a freshness which he defines in large rather than detailed terms: even though the epitaph deals in commonplaces, in 'truths whose very interest and importance have caused them to be unattended to, as things which could take care of themselves', yet (p. 149)

> it is required that these truths should be instinctively ejaculated, or should rise irresistibly from circumstances; in a word that they should be uttered in such connection as shall make it felt that they

are not adopted—not spoken by rote, but perceived in their whole compass with the freshness and clearness of an original intuition.

The last phrases quoted suggest that access of *knowledge* which, the Preface to *Lyrical Ballads* seems to suggest, is the achievement of the poet in successful creation. Or again:

The Writer must introduce the truth with such accompaniment as shall imply that he has mounted to the sources of things— penetrated the dark cavern from which the River that murmurs in every one's ear has flowed from generation to generation.

Such a view draws, again, upon that simple view of general truth which is the main theme of the Preface; it does not seek the more novel aspects of truth which are canvassed by Wordsworth elsewhere. For where other documents seek, in the words of the Essay, Supplementary to the Preface, new elements of the intellectual universe as the province of poetry, in the epitaph it is to 'universally received truths' that the poet gives 'a pathos and spirit which shall re-admit them into the soul like revelations of the moment' (p. 153).

XII Reconciliation of opposites

Wordsworth rejects the Augustan rhetoric of balance and antithesis; yet we have already seen that the epitaph necessarily involves at least one major antithesis: the general balanced by the particular. The difference is, of course, in the poet's operation upon the members of the antithesis: Pope's is to separate, Wordsworth's is to join, interweave, and unify: in short, to achieve a Coleridgean 're-conciliation of opposites'. The opposed attitudes of Wordsworth's two philosophers towards a dead body are thus seen not to be irreconcilable: which one is adopted depends upon whether the emphasis of one's respect falls on the mortal or the immortal part of man, and on the mortal as the 'habitation' of the immortal (p. 124):

Each of these Sages was in sympathy with the best feelings of our nature; feelings which, though they seem opposite to each other, have another and a finer connection than that of contrast.—It is a connection formed through the subtle progress by which, both in the natural and the moral world, qualities pass insensibly into their contraries, and things revolve upon each other.

So 'On a midway point . . . which commands the thoughts and feelings of the two Sages . . . does the Author of [epitaphs] take his stand.' He is in that state in which, in Coleridge's words, the mind endeavours 'to reconcile opposites and qualify contradictions, leaving a middle state of mind more strictly appropriate to the imagination than any other, when it is, as it were, hovering between images'.[30]

Such a 'middle state of mind' is seen again in the need to reconcile reason and passion, which is a means towards the reticence essential if the epitaph is to achieve, or approach, permanence. The dramatic form which Wordsworth somewhat grudgingly permits in the epitaph is a means whereby 'the reason may speak her own language earlier than she would otherwise have been enabled to do'. The 'excellence of writing . . . consists in a conjunction of Reason and Passion, a conjunction which must be of necessity benign' (p. 154); and where Chiabrera failed it was because he had 'neglected to ascertain whether the passions expressed were in kind and degree a dispensation of reason or at least commodities issued under her licence and authority' (p. 160).

As the poet's state of mind thus 'hovers between' reason and passion, so the presentation of the deceased hovers between the general and the particular (p. 129):

> a due proportion of the common or universal feeling of humanity to sensations excited by a distinct and clear conception . . . of the individual. . . . The general sympathy ought to be quickened, provoked, and diversified, by particular thoughts, actions, images. . . . The two powers should temper, restrain, and exalt each other.

Likewise the moral nature of the deceased as seen in the epitaph is a reconciliation of opposites: 'something midway between what he was on earth walking about with his living frailties, and what he may be presumed to be as a Spirit in heaven.' And the observer will balance the peaceful atmosphere of a country churchyard with what he knows or guesses about the moral turbulence of the occupants (pp. 134–7). The churchyard itself is 'a visible centre of a community of the living and the dead', a place of reconciliation of these opposites (p. 127).

The faculty which reconciles opposites is, in the language of Wordsworth and Coleridge, the Imagination. In fact the word occurs only once in such a context in the Essays;[31] but the concept is readily seen, especially in implicit contrast, anticipating the discussion in the Preface of 1815, with the Fancy. If the writer of Sir George Vane's epitaph was intent merely on making a pun (on 'Sir George/ St George'), he was using his Fancy only. Wordsworth concludes, however, that, given the social conventions of the time, the poet linked 'unaffectedly' 'the sense of worldly dignity associated with the title' and the 'saintly and chivalrous name' of St George; and that 'both were united and consolidated in the Author's mind' (p. 140). Unification and consolidation are the marks of the imaginative process. Likewise Montrose's epitaph on Charles I reconciles large and small (deluge and tears), fabulous and commonplace. 'Hyperbole in the language of Montrose is a *mean* instrument made *mighty* because wielded by an afflicted Soul, and *strangeness* is here the order of *Nature*' (p. 143; my italics).

This imaginative process is possible in the poet, or acceptable to the reader, because it springs from 'an afflicted Soul'. Conversely, when head rather than heart is involved (as in the adaptation of du Bellay's epitaph to the tomb of Sidney, p. 143), or when 'there is no undercurrent, no skeleton or stamina, of thought and feeling' (as in Lord Lyttleton's epitaph on his wife, p. 145), imagination fails. We have returned to the concept from which this discussion set out: that the epitaph, epitomizing the poem (or at least the Wordsworthian lyrical poem), depends for its authority on the emotional involvement of the poet.

XIII Preface of 1815

The ostensible purpose of the Preface of 1815 is to justify the classification of Wordsworth's poems into the titled groups which first appeared in the edition of 1815. Wordsworth's letter to Coleridge of May 1809 (No. 8) shows a tentative version of this classification; its main features are that it is based primarily on the subject-matter of the poems; that the topic-headings run approximately parallel to what the Preface calls 'the course of human life'; and that within each group the poems are so arranged that they 'ascend in a gradual scale of imagination' and that 'there should be a scale in each class and in the whole'.

In May 1812 Henry Crabb Robinson reports a new scheme, based not upon subject-matter but upon the psychological sources of the poems (*HCR*, 89): 'arranging the poems with some reference either to the fancy, imagination, reflection, or mere feeling contained in them'.

The scheme which actually appeared in the edition of 1815 uses elements of both these schemes and adds further classes which usually depend on characteristics of form and genre. The three criteria are summarized by Wordsworth in the Preface (p. 177); that three criteria are unlikely to provide a meaningful classification appears to have escaped Wordsworth, who proceeds to insist that the chronological parallel to 'the course of human life' (a characteristic of the scheme of 1809) is maintained, though it is clear that perhaps half the classes of 1815 have no necessary relevance to this parallel. A few instances can be found where poems appear to be ordered so as to maintain an ascending 'scale of imagination', but this principle of arrangement which is proposed in 1809 is not certainly preserved throughout the contents of the edition of 1815.

Obviously more important than the overall arrangement of the poems is the exposition of the faculties which Wordsworth and Coleridge called Imagination and Fancy. Setting aside a typical if rather outmoded[32] attempt to distinguish them which he found in William Taylor, Wordsworth proceeds to define the Imagination by a series of examples drawn from his own and other poetry. The early examples, from Virgil, Shakespeare, and Milton, are essentially a series demonstrating the effect of metaphor based upon, virtually, optical illusion: the sight reports, and the poet records, what the mind knows (presumably extrapolating from experience) cannot be the fact; yet the record (presumably because it seems to be an accurate report of sense-data) acts for 'the gratification of the mind'.[33]

The second set of examples draws on Wordsworth's own poems and on 'impressions . . . of sound'. They still deal with metaphor and related figures of speech,[34] but Wordsworth's explanations are more detailed, expounding the connotations of his figures so that their full effect becomes clear. The summarizing paragraph which follows is a generalized account of the working of metaphor; it concludes with the significant statement that the result of metaphor's compounding or abstracting processes is to produce novelty which, as well as being recognizably a product of its elements, has its own distinct being, so that it can 're-act upon the mind which hath performed the process, like a new existence'.

Proceeding towards greater complexity, the argument moves to 'images in a conjunction by which they modify each other'. Wordsworth's main example, the image of stone/sea-beast/old man from

'Resolution and Independence', is impressive as a poetic image and also in Wordsworth's exposition. More than in the Virgilian enhancement of the goat's danger by the goat-herd's security, we have here a thorough commingling: of the animate (the sea-beast) with the inanimate (the rock which might be mistaken for the sea-beast); so that the reader arrives at the 'intermediate image' of the old man 'not all alive or dead', or like the motionless horse in a fragment discarded from *The Prelude* (p. 624): 'A borderer dwelling betwixt life and death,/ A living statue or a statued life.' In the language of Imagination, Shakespeare's samphire-gatherer or Virgil's goat simply *hangs*, because that is the record of a simple 'appearance to the senses'; in this passage, the complexity of the image reflects, similarly, the complexity of the poet's perception of the old man, which is based partly (but not wholly or even mainly) on his 'appearance to the senses', but rather on a whole series of intellectual judgments by the poet.

The next and last major discussion of the Imagination concerns its creativity. Of this we have already had implicit instances: since the metaphorical construct reacts upon the poetic mind 'like a new existence', such a construct must demonstrate the Imagination's creativity. The Leech-gatherer is created, in the particular aspect which Wordsworth emphasizes, from (actual) stone and (imaginary) sea-beast so as to construct an 'intermediate image' which is neither (but also both), and also the old man 'not all alive or dead'. Wordsworth's own example of the process, from *Paradise Lost*, seems less fortunately chosen, for it is concerned mainly with a thoroughly commonplace intellectual act whereby a number of related ships is seen, as occasion requires, as a multeity or as a unity, the one denominated by plural nouns and pronouns, the other by the singular collective 'fleet'.[35] That this unification or disunification is an intellectual act which may be attributed to the Imagination is indeed to be granted; but it is to be attributed, not specifically to the poet's Imagination, but (as the general currency of the noun 'fleet' indicates) to the Imagination of all of us, or to what Coleridge in his famous definition (*Biog. Lit.* i. 202) called the primary Imagination. The briefly treated Miltonic example which follows, involving the transformation of the Messiah and his saints into the 'indefinite abstraction "His coming!"', seems a much more remarkable instance, primarily because Milton's collective 'coming' (unlike 'fleet') is perpetually a 'new existence', never used before, and never to be used again except as a plagiarism.

It is a curiosity of this Preface that it declines to discuss a characteristic (perhaps *the* characteristic) mode of the Wordsworthian Imagination except in a brief reference and by citing a definition (brilliant, to be sure) of the faculty from Charles Lamb's essay on Hogarth. Wordsworth's poetry at its finest, in poems like 'Nutting', 'Tintern Abbey', 'The Simplon Pass', *The Ruined Cottage*, achieves its power not because it draws upon metaphor or other figures (though these may be present), but because the poet's vision 'draws all *things* to one', in Lamb's phrase; because scenic details are shown to be at once themselves and also types of abstractions, of ideas, like 'Eternity' in 'The Simplon Pass'; achieving the status of a Coleridgean 'symbol'[36] or, as Crabb Robinson's groping attempt to understand Wordsworth on this topic puts it (*HCR*, 93), 'the capacity of the *sensible* produced to represent and stand in the place of the abstract intellectual conception'. Of this distinctively Wordsworthian *poiesis* the Preface says virtually nothing.

Wordsworth's account of the Fancy is deliberately less rigorous than Coleridge's, and Coleridge in *Biographia Literaria* (i. 193–4) took it upon himself to correct Wordsworth, especially in the matter of the interaction between the two faculties. There are a few Wordsworthian observations which can be seen as parallel to the fairly rigid distinction which Coleridge usually makes: the definitions in the Note to 'The Thorn' (p. 96), and the claim in the Preface itself that the poems are classified 'according to the powers of mind, in the Author's conception, predominant in the production of them; *predominant*, which implies the exertion of other faculties in less degree. Where there is more imagination than fancy in a poem, it is placed under the head of imagination, and *vice versâ*.' If 'more imagination than fancy' can be detected, the faculties must be readily distinguishable.

But more often Wordsworth talks, in the Preface and elsewhere, a language suggestive of twentieth-century critics of Coleridge who allege that the distinction is meaningless, and that we are concerned only with what T. S. Eliot, among such critics, called 'degrees of imaginative success'.[37] Such is the proposal of 1809 that the poems should 'ascend in a scale of imagination . . . in each class and in the whole', as if all Wordsworth's poems, including those later called 'Poems of the Fancy', could be arranged according to 'degrees of imaginative success'. The passage to which Coleridge specifically objected was the claim that 'To aggregate and to associate, to evoke and to combine, belong as well to the Imagination as to the Fancy.' Wordsworth, says Coleridge, has 'mistaken the co-presence of fancy with imagination for the operation of the latter singly'. For, according to Coleridge (*Table Talk*, 20 August 1833), 'imagination must have fancy' if it is to function at all, and wherever we can detect the working of Imagination we must also recognize the prior (logically prior) working of Fancy, though the reverse is not true. In instances where Fancy has aggregated and associated in order that Imagination may then build, Wordsworth has attributed the whole effort to Imagination rather than to the joint efforts of the two faculties. So that, while it would be true to Coleridge that 'Imagination stoops to work with the materials of Fancy', it would not be true in Wordsworth's sense, which is that this happens in unusual, borderline instances; to Coleridge, this is the normal and indeed invariable procedure; and it could not be true that 'Fancy ambitiously aims at a rivalship with Imagination', or that Fancy is a 'creative faculty'. In all these disagreements, it is clear that Wordsworth is approaching dangerously close to the doctrine of a single creative faculty whose more and less intense efforts can be called imaginative and fanciful respectively.

In spite of these divergences from the comparatively rigorous theory of Coleridge, the Wordsworthian Fancy does exist in practice and is quite recognizable; and Wordsworth was competent to recognize the Fancy in other poets. It is well described in one of the sentences which distinguishes it from Imagination: 'Fancy depends upon the rapidity and profusion with which she scatters her thoughts and images; trusting that their number, and the felicity with which they are linked together, will make amends for the want of individual value'; and such a way of proceeding is well illustrated by Cotton's 'Winter', more especially by the description of Winter's army which Wordsworth summarizes than by the stanzas on wine and drinking which he actually quotes. In Wordsworth's own poems, the characteristic mode is perhaps best illustrated by the second poem addressed to the Daisy ('With little here to do or see'). This poem has a subject but virtually no argument. It proceeds by way of a series of similes in which the poet is obviously aware of 'the want of individual value': he confesses to 'play[ing] with similes,/ Loose types of things', and to giving to the daisy 'many a fond and idle name . . ./ As is the humour of the game'; he glosses (by anticipation) the Preface's description of Fancy's way of proceeding last quoted when he observes that 'That thought comes next—and instantly/ The freak is over,/ The shape will vanish'. The last stanza of the poem is a formal conclusion, but it is, rather than an elevated climax, a reversion to 'the language of prose' with which the poem began, casting aside the inflated trifling of the body of the poem and using instead the plain language of 'Bright *Flower*!'

The fanciful poem is thus a series: of alternatives, lacking the inevitability of the image or poem of Imagination, to which belongs a growing 'sense of the truth of the likeness'. Rather than being convinced that A is like B for reasons c, d, e . . . , the reader is showered with assertions that A is like B *or* like C *or* like D . . . , and the assertions are offered so rapidly that the reader gives no more than a nodding assent to each equivalence. The poet is entirely aware that such is the mode of his thinking: that his relation to his subject is such that he can validly see it from numerous viewpoints, none of which is more (or less) appropriate to it than any other. Consequently, any one of the similes proposed for the daisy is as effective as any other, and any one could be excised from the series without marked damage to the whole, since the series does not depend on interrelation between its members, and since it leads to no particular conclusion. It would be possible to excise this or that image, likewise, from an imaginative series such as that in 'The Simplon Pass'; yet, because in such a series any image is related to any other, and because each adds weight to the single conclusion (the making palpable of the concept of eternity) towards which all point, the poem would to that extent lose something of its power.

There is, then, a distinction between the imaginative and the fanciful Wordsworthian poem. The Preface hints, rather than fully succeeds, at a definition of the distinction. As for the classification of poems based on the distinction, it is useful in a poet as prolific as Wordsworth. So he thought himself, when in 1826 he was under the criticism of Lamb and Crabb Robinson for persisting in it: 'Miscellaneous poems ought not to be jumbled together at *random* . . . as to the classification of Imagination &c—it is of slight importance as matter of Reflection, but of great as matter of *feeling* for the Reader by making one Poem smooth the way for another.'[38] With this modest statement it is easier to agree than with the theoretical basis of the whole complex scheme of 1815.

XIV Essay, Supplementary to the Preface

The Essay, Supplementary to the Preface (1815) is basically a document of controversy rather than of literary criticism. Aimed at

Francis Jeffrey, who since 1802, and more especially since his review of Wordsworth's *Poems, in Two Volumes* (1807) in the *Edinburgh Review* (xi [1807], 214–31), had lost no opportunity of castigating Wordsworth and his verse, the Essay proceeds, by what I believe is intended as a subtle imitation of Jeffrey's manner, to beat him with his own rod and to insist, in a kind of parody of an *Edinburgh* argument, on the ultimate recognition of the merits of Wordsworth's poetry by the body which Wordsworth calls 'the people' as opposed to 'the public'. It purports to show that good poets are neglected, or, if admired, admired for the wrong reasons, in their own time, and that literary history shows an inevitable time-lag between the appearance of an original poet and the establishment of a just reputation for him; whence it seems to follow (though the conclusion is formally fallacious) that Wordsworth's poetry, neglected in its own time, is likely to have permanent merit. The basic form of the Essay, a historical survey of the repute of various authors, good and bad, is borrowed, I believe, from Jeffrey's review of Henry Weber's edition of John Ford (*Edin. Rev.* xviii [1811], 275–304); the basic philosophy, that good poetry is appreciated only by a minority, is likewise from Jeffrey's review of Scott's *Lady of the Lake* (*Edin. Rev.* xvi [1810], 263–93), slightly modified so that Jeffrey's argument can be turned against him.[39]

The Wordsworths evidently expected the Essay to be recognized as a blow damaging to Jeffrey's prestige;[40] I find no evidence that it was so received, by Jeffrey or the public, and it is probable that Wordsworth's procedure was too subtle to be effective. That Wordsworth himself recognized this is suggested by the much more vigorous statement of his contempt for Jeffrey in his *Letter to a Friend of Robert Burns* (1816), a work which roused Hazlitt to a sneer, John Wilson to an ingeniously dishonest account of the work in *Blackwood's*, and Jeffrey himself to a published rebuke.[41]

As literary criticism, apart from the incidental comments on this author or that into which the historical survey leads Wordsworth, the Essay begins to acquire interest in some remarkable and often difficult paragraphs towards its conclusion. They take their origin from the judgment which Wordsworth attributes to a 'philosophical Friend', namely Coleridge, that 'every author, as far as he is great and at the same time *original*, has had the task of *creating* the taste by which he is to be enjoyed' (p. 210; cf. No. 7, p. 115). This proposition, which is no doubt usually true, and could hardly be false if an ordinary sense is given to 'original', is scarcely true in the particular context of the Essay, which postulates that the creation of new taste requires time, and is marked by the ultimate and usually distant approval of 'the people': a postulate which the case of Thomson as presented in the Essay virtually disproves, and which might be disproved by other poets such as the Metaphysical school, who seem to have been popular in their own as well as in the twentieth century. If we set aside this element of Wordsworth's argument as unessential to its general truth (though especially pertinent to the particular situation of Wordsworth in 1815), we may find a good deal of interest, and some obscurity, in his statement of 'the real difficulty of creating that taste by which a truly original poet is to be relished'.

What is the difficulty? 'Is it in breaking the bonds of custom, in overcoming the prejudices of false refinement, and displacing the aversions of inexperience?' Or does it lie in the task of inducing the reader to perceive general truth, the resemblances rather than the differences between man and man?[42] Not, Wordsworth replies to his own questions, 'If these ends are to be attained by the mere communication of *knowledge*.' Indeed (he digresses), the word 'taste', suggesting the passive reception of art by its audience, is an inappropriate figure; for the reception of art requires an active response: 'without the exertion of a co-operating *power* in the mind of the Reader, there can be no adequate sympathy with' what Wordsworth calls 'the pathetic and the sublime'.[43] Wordsworth is here approaching (but only approaching) a statement of a distinction between the Literature of Knowledge and the Literature of Power, attributed to him by De Quincey and expanded, in De Quincey's third 'Letter to a Young Man whose Education has been neglected' (1823) and his article on Pope (1848),[44] on the basis of 'many years' conversation with Mr. Wordsworth'.

The distinction is easy in essentials: it is between informational writing and imaginative literature. It differs from the Horatian *prodesse aut delectare* in that, while the Literature of Knowledge conveys useful information, imaginative literature conveys *power* rather than Horace's *pleasure*; it *moves* rather than *teaches*, though it may teach by moving; it reveals 'emotions which ordinary life rarely or never supplies occasions for exciting', or it provides '*power*, that is, exercise and expansion of your own latent capacity of sympathy with the infinite'; and it has permanent value, since it cannot be superseded or modified, whereas informational literature is always capable of obsolescence and supersession.[45]

These distinctions are readily paralleled in Wordsworth's criticism:

the distinction between 'Poetry and Matter of Fact, or Science' is already in the Preface to *Lyrical Ballads* (p. 95); the Horatian *delectare*, though echoed in that Preface as a general motive as well as an aim of poetry, has virtually disappeared by 1815 in favour of the emphasis on *power*; the major distinction between *knowledge* and *power* is, as we have just seen, more than implicit in the Essay; the Essay also concedes, like De Quincey, that 'knowledge is the effect' of power. De Quincey's observations on the rarer emotions will appear in our discussion of Wordsworth's use of John Dennis's distinction between 'ordinary' and 'enthusiastic' passions; while De Quincey's claim for the survival of the Literature of Power appears especially in the final paragraphs of the Essay (though Wordsworth's antithesis is here 'vicious poetry', not the literature of knowledge), and is indeed the general drift of the whole Essay.

A major difficulty in Wordsworth's argument both in the Essay and in its presentation by De Quincey lies in the obscurity of the word 'power', which appears without any of the defining contexts of ordinary English idiom. In the Essay we have two clear instances, and a probable third, of this usage: power is a quality which the poet 'calls forth' from the reader, which he 'communicates' to the reader, and which he 'bestows' on the reader (pp. 211–12); in the third instance, power is 'exerted' in the reader's mind (p. 211).[46] Power is thus a quality both subjective and objective: it is added to, but also emanates from, the mind of the reader, and its operations are governed by the Wordsworthian concept of 'action from within and from without'.[47] It is thus an aspect of the Wordsworthian concept of mutual adaptation of, and co-operation between, creative mind and active universe canvassed in a good many places in Wordsworth.[48]

The exertion and the calling forth of power are described in various incidents in *The Prelude*, where the troublesome usage of the unqualified noun is likewise to be seen. At the moment of his first entry into London, Wordsworth experienced 'weight and power,/ Power growing with the weight' (viii. 705–6). The 'spot of time' which occurred on his visit to the site of the gibbet on the Penrith Beacon 'left behind' power (xi. 325–6), and an early manuscript (V) of the poem dealing with the ensuing episode of waiting for the horses asserts that that experience left 'a kindred power/ Implanted in my mind' (*Prel.* p. 450). The comparable childhood episodes of Book i (especially), though they are not called 'spots of time' neither do they contain the word 'power' in this usage, are clearly similar. In other episodes, the feeling of power is connected with large physical objects: the Wanderer in *The Excursion*, here obviously a Wordsworthian *persona*, 'saw the hills/ Grow larger in the darkness', and[49]

> In such communion, not from terror free, . . .
> Had he perceived the presence and the power
> Of greatness; and deep feelings had impressed
> So vividly great objects that they lay
> Upon his mind like substances.

The physical largeness of London, the 'great City . . . that vast Metropolis . . . That great Emporium' (*Prel.* viii. 693, 746, 749), obviously contributes to its power. 'Simplicity', meaning simplicity of shape, is another characteristic associated with power in a notable passage at the end of Book vii.[50] The experience of power is accompanied by strong feeling: 'a swell of feeling' (*Prel.* viii. 743), as Wordsworth entered London; more often a sense of fear or awe, as in the experience on the Penrith Beacon and the Wanderer's observation of 'great objects'.

The most instructive passage in *The Prelude* on the effect of power is perhaps this account of Wordsworth in London (viii. 754-9):[51]

> I sought not then
> Knowledge; but craved for power, and power I found
> In all things; nothing had a circumscribed
> And narrow influence; but all objects, being
> Themselves capacious, also found in me
> Capaciousness and amplitude of mind.

This passage is useful since it emphasizes the reciprocity of the process of perceiving power; it is both active and passive, 'action from within and from without'; and more especially we see, in the verbal parallels in the early text and in the word 'correspondent' in the later text, that the process involved is one of sympathetic adaptation of mind to object; an enlargement of the mind in its effort to match the largeness of the object. Indeed, from the passage which introduces the 'spots of time' (xi. 258-75), we learn that the mind may pass beyond such an identification to a complete domination of the environment, so that it becomes 'lord and master' and imposes its own quality (in this case, terror) on the place of the gibbet, and transforms what the poem confesses to be 'An ordinary sight' into a 'visionary dreariness' impossible to describe (xi. 309, 311).

Most of the characteristics just mentioned are readily recognizable as commonplaces of eighteenth-century discussions of the Sublime, headed by Edmund Burke's *Philosophical Enquiry into the Origin of our Ideas of the Sublime and Beautiful* (1757); and we now have at our disposal a Wordsworthian text which, though it exists only as a fragment, draws together the scattered hints, in *The Prelude* and in other works such as the *Guide to the Lakes*, that Wordsworth in this matter thought in the tradition, and developed the ideas, of eighteenth-century theorists such as Burke. This is the fragment now published under the title of *The Sublime and the Beautiful*.[52] This fragment is especially noteworthy in its discussion of the sublime in natural scenery for its emphasis on the quality of power as one of three aspects of the sublime in nature.[53] Thus it is 'impressions of power to a sympathy with & participation of which the mind must be elevated—or to a dread and awe of which, as existing out of itself, it must be subdued'—rather than a sympathy with a more broadly defined 'sublime'. It is power that is manifested by various aspects of the natural scene: 'the abrupt and the precipitous' (suggestive of danger to the observer); a wave-like outline 'infinitely continuous and without cognizable beginning' (suggestive of infinity); torrents, clouds, height, storms (physical size and physical energy); scenic outlines suggestive of parts of a living body 'which are dignified in our estimation as being the seats & instruments of active force'. None of these manifestations, obviously, is a manifestation without the co-operation of the observing mind, whether the co-operation appears as empathic identification with the object, as awe before the object which discourages such identification, or (as two later passages in the fragment propose) as a will to resist the object, or as appreciation of a comparable resistance (illustrated by the fall of the Rhine at Schaffhausen) in the natural scene (*Prose*, ii. 351–7).

The analogy between these theoretical considerations and those of Wordsworth's poems which deal specifically with sublime natural scenes is obvious, whether the scene seems to be presented for its own sake (the glaciers at Chamonix, for instance, *Prel.* vi. 456–60); or as a background of imaginative experience (the pursuing mountain of the stolen-boat episode, *Prel.* i. 372–427); or as a type of a philosophical idea (the Ravine of Gondo as a type of Eternity, *Prel.* vi. 556–72; the Welsh cloudscape as a type of Imagination, *Prel.* xiii. 40–119). In such cases the poem can be seen, at one level of appeal, as a verbal rendering of the visual impact of power and of the imaginative response which the impact evokes. Less obvious, but probably

as real, is the analogy between the notion of power and Wordsworth'
presentation of certain human figures and the situations in which
they are involved. Such are Michael, the leech-gatherer of 'Resolution
and Independence', the soldier of *The Prelude*, Book iv, and, probably,
the women of 'Beggars' and 'The Sailor's Mother'. As the rock in the
Rhine at Schaffhausen offers a seemingly eternal resistance to the
assault of the waterfall, thereby manifesting power (to resist) and
duration (in resisting), so these figures seem to offer an eternal resistance to the assault of tragic circumstances, like that of a natural
object to the forces of decay; or when, as in the case of Michael, the
resistance is broken, we are nevertheless left with a sense that the
resistance was powerful and long-sustained.

What are the qualities of 'an original writer' which make it more
difficult for him to communicate power of this sort than for a classic?
The answer is not immediately obvious, especially as Wordsworth
proceeds to defer an immediate answer by distinguishing three kinds
of poetic occasion: the 'simple and direct' pathetic, the 'complex and
revolutionary' pathetic, and the sublime. As we noted above, by the
pathetic he means literature or an occasion of literature concerned
with the emotions;[54] and his division of the pathetic into 'simple'
and 'complex' is based on his reading of John Dennis's distinction
between 'ordinary' and 'enthusiastic' passions.[55] For the communication of 'simple' passions Wordsworth foresees no difficulty:
'all men, possessed of competent knowledge of the facts and circumstances [are] instantaneously affected.' He means that there are
situations the emotional implications of which are so obvious that a
mere statement of the situation will be sufficient to impress the
reader.[56] It is harder to discover examples of what Wordsworth calls
the 'complex and revolutionary' pathetic or 'meditative passion' (p.
212), or of what Dennis calls enthusiasms or enthusiastic passions, of
which the 'Cause is not clearly understood by him who feels them'
(Dennis, i. 216–17). Wordsworth's letter to Mrs Clarkson offers one
half-hearted example, the Solitary of *The Excursion* in his 'quarrel
with his own conscience'. The point of distinction seems to be that
the Solitary's involvement with revolutionary France is an involvement with ideas rather than with people and feelings; when this
involvement is shown to have been mistaken he flees from it, and
from all involvements (such as those with his family), without
making any honest admission of his error. Since this crisis arises
from a particular historical situation rather than from the readily
accepted general truth of Ellen's anger, the reader may need to

engage in intellectual manoeuvres (what Wordsworth calls 'treading the steps of thought') before he can fully grasp the significance of the Solitary's situation.

Somewhat similar manoeuvres are involved in some instances which Wordsworth lists in the letter to Mrs Clarkson where he foresees that communication may be impossible or difficult. If the reader has not shared certain childhood feelings with Wordsworth, he 'cannot understand' the 'Ode: Intimations of Immortality'. If he has not 'heard the echoes of the flying Raven's voice in a mountainous Country, as described at the close of the 4th Book [of *The Excursion*, he] will not perhaps be able to relish that illustration'. Wordsworth made this kind of concession once before, in the Preface to *Lyrical Ballads*, where he thought that 'my associations must have sometimes been particular instead of general, and that, consequently, giving to things a false importance, sometimes from diseased impulses I may have written upon unworthy subjects' (p. 87). The difference is that, in 1815, while Wordsworth is willing to allow a difficulty, he is much less willing than in 1800 to confess a fault. The deficiency is in the reader's ignorance rather than, or as much as, the poet's use of the particular and the private; and the resulting barrier is unfortunate, but inevitable. But not insuperable; for (the letter continues) 'every one must have been in the way of perceiving similar effects from different causes'. By analogy, by imaginative effort, the willing reader can co-operate with the poet, if only to the extent of seeing that what the poet is talking about—notions of immortality, emotional involvement with political movements, the effect of a raven's cry—is 'something like' something in the reader's experience the significance of which he knows.

This being so, it is clear that such an effort is demanded especially, Wordsworth says, by the 'original' poet. The reader's responses to the traditional poet (whether he is ancient or modern) are reliable merely because they are traditional; because the reader has made them often before. Not so when the critic defines genius as 'the *widening* the sphere of human sensibility . . . the introduction of a *new* element into the intellectual universe . . . the application of powers to objects *on which they had not before been exercised*' (pp. 211–12; my italics). *Ex hypothesi*, such an art must present an initial barrier, if only of unfamiliarity, to its audience.

How readily, and (from the point of view of Wordsworth's general argument) how soon, such a barrier can be overcome, must surely differ from poet to poet and subject to subject. We might risk generalizing and say that, if that which is new is nevertheless a part of 'general truth', excluded from regular treatment by mere familiarity: 'truths whose very interest and importance have caused them to be unattended to, as things which could take care of themselves' (p. 149)—or by convention (as in the anti-Petrarchan erotic verse of Donne and his like); or perhaps by both (as in the exposure of moral and social evil by Blake's *Songs of Experience*)—then acceptance may be easy and rapid. But if the novelty lies in the personal, the private, perhaps the unique experience, the effort of acceptance must be the greater, and the general acceptance the longer delayed if it is achieved at all. Wordsworth's adoption of Dennis's theory of ordinary and enthusiastic passions is an attempt to describe the two fates of novelty which have just been indicated. As the 'complex and revolutionary' pathetic risks a failure of communication, since it raises the possibility that its validity can never be tested on the pulse of the audience's experience; so, *a fortiori*, of the sublime: 'if we consider . . . how remote is the practice and the course of life from the sources of sublimity, in the soul of Man, can it be wondered that there is little existing preparation for a poet charged with a new mission to extend its kingdom, and to augment and spread its enjoyments?' Whence it follows that the Wordsworthian 'spots of time' tend to be ultimately indefinable in their significance, even though the power which resides in them and which links them with the sublime can be felt by most experienced readers of the poet.

XV

In my *Wordsworth as Critic* (229–30) I described the progress of Wordsworth's critical ideas as a progress

> by instalments . . . whereby a concept hinted at in an early work is more fully developed in a later, and (if necessary) irrelevances, difficulties, and inconsistencies are silently abandoned. What is gained in one document, as it were by the way, and as if the author were aware of it . . . as a 'natural,' instinctive way of talking about poetry, becomes in a later document consolidated and expounded as a formal critical concept.

Thus the second version of the Preface to *Lyrical Ballads* (1802) stresses an emotional involvement of poet with subject which was not fully envisaged in the version of 1800. The concept of emotional involvement is fully developed in the *Essays upon Epitaphs*, which in turn introduce by way of novelty the concepts of reconciled opposites and the reconciling Imagination. The Preface of 1815 expounds the concept of Imagination and, more briefly, the complementary concept of Fancy. The Essay, Supplementary, in its operative parts, introduces, without adequate formal definition, the concept of *power* in literature which has obvious connections with the Imagination and somewhat dimmer analogues in other fields of aesthetics which are outside the scope of this book.

Sections II and III of this Introduction describe an earlier step in this progress. The critic moves from a traditional (though not very old) approach to drama (the analysis of character) in the Preface to *The Borderers* to an account, in the Note to 'The Thorn', of the practical means of character-presentation, from the viewpoint of Aristotelean mimesis rather than of a Coleridgean projection of self and the utilization of the 'all in each' in the conception of a credible dramatic character. This stance is the principal stance of the Preface of 1800; by 1802 the progress towards expressive poetics and away from drama which I described in 1969 is well under way. But the same step-by-step procedure can be seen: drama is the starting-point of Wordsworth's career as critic, but becomes less and less relevant to his criticism, as does drama itself in his creative output; and expressive poetics and expressive poetry go hand in hand, on the whole, from this point onward in Wordsworth's career.

XVI Conclusion: Values

Wordsworth's critical ideas were not so much adopted by a school as passed into common currency. The famous phrases 'Poetry is the spontaneous overflow of powerful feelings: it takes its origin from emotion recollected in tranquillity' (p. 85) must have been repeated in text-book after text-book on the nature of poetry. As well as being parroted they have been misunderstood, by such a notable critic, for instance, as T. S. Eliot in his almost equally famous 'Tradition and the Individual Talent', where he manages virtually to repeat Wordsworth's sense while proposing to correct him on the psychology of poetic creation.[57] Since the *Essays upon Epitaphs* have been almost unknown and unread until comparatively recent years, it would be difficult to show that that catch-all virtue of literature, Sincerity, instilled into every schoolboy for generations as the correct thing to say about a poem when he wishes to praise it without having the least idea why it should be praised, was derived from Wordsworth; but Wordsworth's is probably the earliest full-scale statement of it in English criticism. The distinction between Imagination and Fancy has likewise been thrust upon generations of students in university schools of English Literature, usually in terms of Coleridge's definitions, from which some, at least, have turned with relief to Wordsworth's often clearer and better-exemplified expositions.

Details of his work have sometimes been taken up by particular critics. De Quincey expounded at length the concept of style as an 'incarnation of the thought' (p. 154; see *Prose*, ii. 114–15) and the distinction between the literature of knowledge and the literature of power (see section XIV). There are probably echoes of Wordsworthian ideas in Shelly's compilation of critical ideas from all literary quarters, the *Defence of Poetry* (1821);[58] and I believe that Arnold's Preface of 1853 on the need for permanent themes in poetry echoes Wordsworth in the Preface to *Lyrical Ballads* (see p. 15).

None of these uses of Wordsworth's ideas improves much upon his original statements of them; for the best of them emerge from Wordsworth's own experience as a poet. Of this nature are such deviations from the commonplace as the admission, in the midst of a fairly conventional account of the need for the would-be dramatic poet to identify himself with his fictional characters, that such an identification can be sustained only 'for short spaces of time' (p. 78). He had probably found it so from experience, as is suggested, not so much by the partial identification of Oswald in *The Borderers* with an aspect of Wordsworth himself, as by the rather awkward attempts at dramatization in a short poem like 'The Thorn' or in the various voices of *The Excursion*, and by various *obiter dicta* which suggest that, on the whole, Wordsworth moved uneasily in the dramatic mode.[59] The account in the Preface to *Lyrical Ballads* of the effects of metrical form in poetry and the proposition about the metre of 'The Thorn' (pp. 84–5, 97) suggest careful attention to this matter and close meditation on his own technical problems. The notion of poetry as a 'spontaneous overflow of powerful feelings' is commonplace by 1800, but the modification in the direction of 'emotion recollected in tranquillity' is rare enough at that date to suggest, as does what we know of the composition of a good many of his poems, that this was the Wordsworthian experience (p. 85).[60] The need for a statement which should blend the pain of loss with the calm of resignation in the epitaph may well have arisen from his own experience in the death of John Wordsworth, and may have led him to the praise of such epitaphs, by Chiabrera and others, as he found satisfying in their successful reconciliation of these opposites. The experience of the poet in analysing his own achievement, in terms of both practical and theoretical criticism, is writ large in the Preface of 1815, and what Henry Crabb Robinson called his 'pain' and his 'manly avowal of his sense of his own poetic merits' (see *Prose*, iii. 85) in the Essay, Supplementary. And the two documents mentioned earlier, the *Guide to the Lakes* and the fragmentary *Sublime and the Beautiful* connected with it, reflect the modification of conventional eighteenth-century aesthetics by Wordsworth's personal experience of the English scenery which he knew better than anyone else of his generation. It is for this kind of hard-won expertise in the field of criticism and aesthetics that we value Wordsworth as critic in this century.

NOTES

1 *William Wordsworth: His Mind and Art in their Historical Relations*, Madison, 1922, 1927, *passim*.

2 Even the early and immature *Descriptive Sketches* (1793) mentions in its apparatus the aesthetic theory of the Picturesque (*PW*, i. 62).

3 The state of mind described in *The Prelude* is commonly ascribed to Wordsworth's acquaintance with William Godwin's *Political Justice* (1793), and with Godwin himself, who records in his diary meetings with Wordsworth during 1795. Certainly 'the Philosophy/That promised to abstract [i.e. remove] the hopes of man/Out of his feelings, to be fix'd henceforth/For ever in a purer element' (x. 807–10) sounds like a description of Godwin's philosophy. *Prel.* x. 829–30 repeats *The Borderers*, 1495–6, nearly verbatim. The Solitary in *The Excursion*, who obviously records some aspects of Wordsworth's disappointment with the Revolution, is also obviously a pallid version of Oswald; and *Exc.* iii. 700–1 (of the Solitary) repeats *Borderers*, 1774–5 (of Oswald). The word 'nature' in the contexts cited usually means 'natural, normal human behaviour'.

4 See sections V–VII.

5 See the introduction to this text in *Prose*, i. 69–74.

6 *Eighteenth Century Essays on Shakespeare*, ed. D. Nichol Smith, 2nd ed., Oxford, 1963, xxxii.

7 *Shakespeare Criticism: A Selection*, ed. D. Nichol Smith, London, 1946, 53–4.

8 William Richardson, *Essays on Shakespeare's Dramatic Characters of Macbeth, Hamlet, Jacques, and Imogen*, 4th ed., London, 1785, 44–5. Cited below as 'Richardson'.

9 *Poetical Works of Matthew Arnold*, eds C. B. Tinker and H. F. Lowry, London, 1950, xix–xx.

10 The comparatives 'better . . . less . . . plainer and more emphatic . . . greater . . . more accurately . . . more forcibly . . . more easily . . . more durable' are never resolved by a 'than'; but the general primitivistic tone must imply the townsman as the other member of the comparison.

11 The meaning seems to be 'are associated with', 'are in close accord with'.

12 The meaning is 'precise', 'adequate to the expression of the thought'.

13 Likewise 'the language adopted in ["The Ancient Mariner"] has been equally intelligible for these three last centuries' (p. 66); and 'the affecting parts of Chaucer are almost always expressed in language pure and universally intelligible even to this day.'

14 The text of 1800 proceeds after 'I answer that' (p. 76) to 'the distinction of [rhyme and (1800)] metre is regular and uniform' (p. 83), and omits the whole of the passage intervening in the text of 1802–5.

15 The wording is the same in both texts here, and in 1800 'these opinions' means, clearly, 'these opinions about the linguistic identity of verse and prose'. In the text of 1802, 'these opinions' ought to mean the same, since virtually the same answer to the question is given as in 1800. But in 1802 the theory of the language of prose has long been forgotten, and Wordsworth is now, as far as he is discussing language at all, discussing neither 'the language of prose' nor the language of rustics, but a virtually new entity called the language of men, a concept which has not been heard of since the opening paragraph of either text.

16 In the English heroic couplet, for instance, the line is constantly of ten syllables, and the odd-numbered line constantly rhymes with the even-numbered line immediately following.

17 The examples proposed are Richardson's *Clarissa* and Edward Moore's domestic tragedy *The Gamester*, in prose, as opposed to 'the most pathetic scenes' in Shakespeare's verse-drama.

18 These steps are familiar: I recall a loss and my sorrow is renewed; I recall an insult and my anger is renewed; and so forth.

19 In youth, says *The Prelude* (ii. 306), 'all knowledge is delight'.

20 See especially *Shakespearean Criticism*, ed. T. M. Raysor, London, 1960, i. 147–8, a passage obviously drawing in its early sentences on Wordsworth's Preface.

21 The 'distinction' is to be achieved by the virtually undefined process called 'selection', which 'will entirely separate the composition from the vulgarity and meanness of ordinary life', and also assist the poet in

'removing what would otherwise be painful or disgusting in the passion'; and these operations, or at any rate the second, are undertaken 'for a particular purpose, that of giving pleasure', the poet's overriding aim. How this process operates is not explained in detail, but, since it 'removes', it appears to complement the function assigned to metre, which is to 'superadd the charm which . . . is acknowledged to exist in metrical language', or to 'impart . . . a pleasure to mankind': metre adds pleasure, selection subtracts what might be displeasing. Wordsworth calls it 'the principle on which I have so much insisted', though the word or its cognates occur only five times before this reference and only eight times in the whole Preface. For an analysis of a (probably unique) specimen of its workings, see my *Wordsworth as Critic*, 80–3.

22 *Biog. Lit.* ii. 97, 101.

23 Ibid. 6.

24 It does not seem to have occurred to Wordsworth, or to the many theorists whose ideas he is here rather blindly following, that, in the absence of written records of primitive literature, no conclusions about its qualities can be drawn. The 'early' poetries of Europe which happen to survive, for instance Homeric Greek and Old English, are marked by well-established formal dictions, the origins of which can only be guessed. For an account of analogues and probable sources for Wordsworth's primitivistic speculations, see my *Wordsworth's Preface to Lyrical Ballads*, 192–4.

25 Even so, there are discrepancies. The language of primitive poets is 'daring, and figurative', and therefore much more like the language of the successful dramatic poet of 1802, whose language is 'dignified and variegated, and alive with metaphors and figures', than that of rustics, who 'convey their feelings and notions in simple and unelaborated expressions' (pp. 71, 77). And the primitive poet 'wrote from passion excited by real events . . . when he had been affected by the events which he described', rather than in a state of 'emotion recollected in tranquillity'.

26 See David Perkins, *Wordsworth and the Poetry of Sincerity*, Cambridge, Mass., 1964, *passim*.

27 See *Prose*, ii. 110.

28 For adumbrations of this view see Preface to *Lyrical Ballads*, pp. 69, 77.

29 But hardly at all in these Essays, which dismiss metrical form as a by no means essential decoration; a view hinted at but rapidly abandoned in the Preface.

30 Raysor, op. cit. ii. 103.

31 The fictional epitaph in which the deceased speaks from the tomb employs 'the intervention of the imagination in order that the reason may speak her own language earlier than she would otherwise have

been enabled to do. This shadowy interposition also harmoniously unites the two worlds of the living and the dead by their appropriate affections' (p. 132).

32 It is clear that the usage of Wordsworth and Coleridge had been proposed by psychologists, especially of the Scottish school, before Wordsworth and Coleridge adopted it. See *Prose*, iii. 44–6, 49.

33 Wordsworth offers no explanation of this gratification, but probably it resides in the satisfaction in the seeming accuracy, modified by a tension between that and the known inaccuracy. We have here, as in all metaphor, an instance of the aesthetic principle of 'similitude in dissimilitude' which is briefly canvassed in the Preface to *Lyrical Ballads* (p. 85).

34 'Broods' means 'incubates' and 'meditates'; the first sense, literal in itself, is metaphorical as applied to 'voice'; the second is metaphorical in itself, but more readily applied to 'voice' than is the first sense. In addition, the word retains most of the onomatopoeic effect of 'coo'. And so forth.

35 Cf. the discussion of the sonnet 'With ships the sea was scattered', in No. 7, pp. 113–14.

36 See *The Statesman's Manual*, in *Lay Sermons*, ed. R. J. White, London and Princeton, 1972, 30.

37 *The Use of Poetry and the Use of Criticism*, London, 1933, 79.

38 *Correspondence of Henry Crabb Robinson with the Wordsworth Circle*, ed. E. J. Morley, Oxford, 1927, 161.

39 For documentation of these views see W. J. B. Owen, 'Wordsworth and Jeffrey in Collaboration', *RES*, NS xv (1964), 161–7; and for Wordsworth's growing irritation and diminishing confidence under Jeffrey's attacks see the introduction to this text in *Prose*, iii. 55–60.

40 See the remarks of Dorothy Wordsworth in *MY*, ii. 200, 206.

41 See *Prose*, iii. 111–13.

42 Wordsworth is echoing, in particular, the stated aims of *Lyrical Ballads*; see pp. 65, 71, 79.

43 His own glosses on these nouns are given just before: the 'pathetic' has to do with feeling, the sublime with 'the lofty and universal in thought and imagination'.

44 *Collected Writings*, ed. D. Masson, Edinburgh, 1889–90, x. 46 ff. and xi. 54 ff.

45 Ibid. x. 46–9; xi. 54–9.

46 The phrase 'a co-operating *power*' may mean merely 'power to co-operate' with the poet; I believe, however, that the usage is the same as in the other two instances.

47 See p. 166; *Prel*. xii. 377.

48 In the documents collected here, see especially pp. 80, 173; elsewhere, *Prel*. ii. 237 ff.

49 *Exc.* i. 127 ff.; cf. ii. 864–9, iii. 881–4.

50 *Prel.* vii. 720; more fully treated in the text of 1850, vii. [740] ff.

51 The text of 1850 modifies the emphasis on knowledge:

> seeking knowledge at that time
> Far less than craving power; yet knowledge came
> Sought or unsought, and influxes of power
> Came, of themselves, or at her call derived . . .
> From all sides, when whate'er was in itself
> Capacious found, or seemed to find, in me
> A correspondent amplitude of mind.

52 *Prose*, ii. 349–60. For fuller discussion see my *Wordsworth as Critic*, 203–10; W. J. B. Owen, 'The Sublime and the Beautiful in *The Prelude*', *The Wordsworth Circle*, 4 (1973), 67–86.

53 The other two are 'individual form' and 'duration'. 'Power' is a concept found in Burke; see the edition of J. T. Boulton, London, 1958; Notre-Dame, 1968, 64 ff.

54 See above, n. 43. The relation of the sublime, defined as the 'lofty and universal in thought and imagination', to the sublime of formal Burkean and Wordsworthian aesthetics of landscape, is not made clear at either mention of it in the Essay.

55 See *Prose*, iii. 104–5; W. J. B. Owen, 'Wordsworth, the Problem of Communication, and John Dennis', in *Wordsworth's Mind and Art*, ed. A. W. Thomson, Edinburgh, 1969, 140–56.

56 In his letter to Catherine Clarkson (No. 13), in which he writes in terms of the same distinction borrowed from Dennis, he lists several situations of this kind. The most striking is perhaps that of Ellen in *The Excursion*, Book vi, who, confronted and insulted by the unseemly haste of the party attending her child's funeral, demonstrates what Dennis calls 'Anger . . . moved by an Affront that is offer'd us in our presence', an example of 'ordinary Passion, whose Cause is clearly comprehended by him who feels it' (Dennis, i. 216, 338).

57 *Selected Essays*, London, 1946, 20–1.

58 See *Shelley's Critical Prose*, ed. B. R. McElderry, Jr, Lincoln, Neb., 1967, xvi–xvii.

59 Wordsworth says this himself on various occasions, claiming that he is better equipped to see the resemblances between men than the differences on which the dramatist dwells. See my *Wordsworth as Critic*, 100–1.

60 For an account of an aesthetically disastrous 'overflow of powerful feelings', see Wordsworth's letter to Sir George Beaumont, cited above, pp. 6–7.

Preface to *The Borderers*
1796-7

Written, according to Wordsworth's own account, when he was
composing the play which it expounds, i.e. in late 1796 or early 1797
(*PW*, i. 343-4). The Preface survives in two manuscripts preserved
in the Wordsworth Library, Grasmere, both probably to be dated
about 1800. An inaccurately transcribed text, based on one of the
manuscripts, was printed by Ernest de Selincourt in *Nineteenth
Century and After*, c (1926), 723-41, and reprinted in his *Oxford
Lectures on Poetry*, Oxford, 1934, 157-79. A slightly improved text
appears in *PW*, i. 345-9. The text given here is from *Prose*, i. 76-80.
For details see the apparatus there printed, the textual introduction
(*Prose*, i. 75), and the commentary (*Prose*, i. 81-6).

Let us suppose a young man of great intellectual powers, yet without
any solid principles of genuine benevolence.[1] His master passions are
pride and the love of distinction—He has deeply imbibed a spirit of
enterprize in a tumultuous age. He goes into the world and is
betrayed into a great crime.—That influence on which all his
happiness is built immediately deserts him. His talents are robbed
of their weight—his exertions are unavailing, and he quits the world
in disgust, with strong misanthropic feelings. In his retirement, he
is impelled to examine the reasonableness of established opinions,
& the force of his mind exhausts itself in constant efforts to
separate the elements of virtue and vice. It is his pleasure & his
consolation to hunt out whatever is bad in actions usually esteemed
virtuous, & to detect the good in actions which the universal sense
of mankind teaches us to reprobate. While the general exertion of
his intellect seduces him from the remembrance of his own crime,
the particular conclusions to which he is led have a tendency to
reconcile him to himself. His feelings are interested in making him
a moral sceptic, &, as his scepticism increases, he is raised in his own

esteem. After this process has been continued some time, his natural energy & restlessness impel him again into the world. In this state, pressed by the recollection of his guilt, he seeks relief from two sources, action & meditation. Of actions, those are most attractive which best exhibit his own powers, partly from the original pride of his character, and still more because the loss of authority and influence which followed upon his crime was the first circumstance which impressed him with the magnitude of that crime, & brought along with it those tormenting sensations by which he is assailed. The recovery of his original importance & the exhibition of his own powers are therefore in his mind almost identified with the extinction of those painful feelings which attend the recollection of his guilt. Perhaps there is no cause which has greater weight in preventing the return of bad men to virtue than that good actions being for the most part in their nature silent & regularly progressive, they do not present those sudden results which can afford a sufficient stimulus to a troubled mind. In processes of vice the effects are more frequently immediate, palpable, and extensive. Power is much more easily manifested in destroying than in creating. A child, Rousseau has observed, will tear in pieces fifty toys before he will think of making one.[2] From these causes, assisted by disgust and misanthropic feeling, the character we are now contemplating will have a strong tendency to vice. His energies are most impressively manifested in works of devastation. He is the Orlando of Ariosto, the Cardenio of Cervantes, who lays waste the groves that should shelter him.[3] He has rebelled against the world & the laws of the world, & he regards them as tyrannical masters; convinced that he is right in some of his conclusions, he nourishes a contempt for mankind the more dangerous because he has been led to it by reflexion. Being in the habit of considering the world as a body which is in some sort at war with him, he has a feeling borrowed from that habit which gives an additional zest to his hatred of those members of society whom he hates & to his contempt of those whom he despises. Add to this, that a mind fond of nourishing sentiments of contempt will be prone to the admission of those feelings which are considered under any uncommon bond of relation (as must be the case with a man who has quarrelled with the world), the feelings will mutually strengthen each other. In this morbid state of mind he cannot exist without occupation, he requires constant provocatives, all his pleasures are prospective, he is perpetually chasing a phantom, he commits new crimes to drive away the memory of the past. But the lenitives of his pain are twofold: meditation as well as action. Accordingly, his reason is almost exclusively employed in justifying his past enormities & in enabling him to commit new ones. He is perpetually imposing upon himself, he has a sophism for every crime. The *mild* effusions of thought, the milk of human reason, are unknown to him. His imagination is powerful, being strengthened by the habit of picturing possible forms of society where his crimes would be no longer crimes, and he would enjoy that estimation to which, from his intellectual attainments, he deems himself entitled. The nicer shades of manners he disregards, but whenever, upon looking back upon past ages, or in surveying the practices of different countries in the age in which he lives, he finds such contrarieties as seem to affect the principles of *morals*, he exults over his discovery, and applies it to his heart as the dearest of his consolations. Such a mind cannot but discover some truths, but he is unable to profit by them, and in his hands they become instruments of evil.

He presses truth and falshood into the same service. He looks at society through an optical glass of a peculiar tint; something of the forms of objects he takes from objects, but their colour is exclusively what he gives them; it is one, and it is his own. Having indulged a habit, dangerous in a man who has fallen, of dallying with moral calculations, he becomes an empiric, and a daring & unfeeling empiric. He disguises from himself his own malignity by assuming the character of a speculator in morals, and one who has the hardihood to realize his speculations.

It will easily be perceived that to such a mind those enterprizes which are the most extraordinary will in time appear the most inviting. His appetite from being exhausted becomes unnatural. Accordingly, he will struggle so [   ]⁴ to characterize & to exalt actions, little and contemptible in themselves, by a forced greatness of *manner*, and will chequer & degrade enterprizes great in their atrocity by grotesque littleness of manner, and fantastic obliquities. He is like a worn out voluptuary—he finds his temptation in strangeness, he is unable to suppress a low hankering after the *double entendre* in vice; yet his thirst after the extraordinary buoys him up, and, supported by a habit of constant reflexion, he frequently breaks out into what has the appearance of greatness; and, in sudden emergencies, when he is called upon by surprize & thrown out of the path of his regular habits, or when dormant associations are awakened tracing the revolutions through which his character has passed, in painting his former self he really *is* great.

Benefits conferred on a man like this will be the seeds of a worse feeling than ingratitude. They will give birth to positive hatred. Let him be deprived of power, though by means which he despises, & he will never forgive. It will scarcely be denied that such a mind, by very slight external motives, may be led to the commission of the greatest enormities. Let its malignant feelings be fixed on a particular object, & the rest follows of itself.

Having shaken off the obligations of religion & morality in a dark and tempestuous age, it is probable that such a character will be infected with a tinge of superstition. The period in which he lives teems with great events, which he feels he cannot controul. That influence which his pride makes him unwilling to allow to his fellow-men he has no reluctance to ascribe to invisible agents: his pride impels him to superstition and shapes out the nature of his belief: his creed is his own: it is made & not adopted.

A character like this, or some of its features at least, I have attempted to delineate in the following drama. I have introduced him deliberately prosecuting the destruction of an amiable young man by the most atrocious means, & with a pertinacity, as it should seem, not to be accounted for but on the supposition of the most malignant injuries. No such injuries, however, appear to have been sustained. What are, then, his motives? First, it must be observed that to make the non-existence of a common motive itself a motive to action is a practice which we are never so prone to attribute exclusively to madmen as when we forget ourselves. Our love of the marvellous is not confined to external things. There is no object on which it settles with more delight than on our own minds. This habit is in the very essence of the habit which we are delineating.[5]

But there are particles of that poisonous mineral of which Iago speaks gnawing his inwards,[6] his malevolent feelings are excited, & he hates the more deeply because he feels he ought not to hate.

We all know that the dissatisfaction accompanying the first impulses towards a criminal action, where the mind is familiar with guilt, acts as a stimulus to proceed in that action. Uneasiness must be driven away by fresh uneasiness, obstinacy, waywardness, & wilful blindness are alternatives resorted to, till there is an universal insurrection of every depraved feeling of the heart.

Besides, in a course of criminal conduct every fresh step that we make appears a justification of the one that preceded it, it seems to bring back again the moment of liberty and choice; it banishes the idea of repentance, and seems to set remorse at defiance. Every time we plan a fresh accumulation of our guilt, we have restored to us something like that original state of mind, that perturbed pleasure, which first made the crime attractive.

If, after these general remarks, I am asked what are Rivers's[7] motives to the atrocity detailed in the drama? I answer: they are founded chiefly in the very constitution of his character; in his pride which borders even upon madness, in his restless disposition, in his disturbed mind, in his superstition, in irresistible propensities to embody in practical experiments his worst & most extravagant speculations, in his thoughts & in his feelings, in his general habits & his particular impulses, in his perverted reason justifying his perverted instincts. The general moral intended to be impressed by the delineation of such a character is obvious: it is to shew the dangerous use which may be made of reason when a man has committed a great crime.

There is a kind of superstition which makes us shudder when we find moral sentiments to which we attach a sacred importance applied to vicious purposes. In real life this is done every day, and we do not feel the disgust. The difference is here. In works of imagination we see the motive and the end. In real life we rarely see either the one or the other; and, when the distress comes, it prevents us from attending to the cause. This superstition of which I have spoken is not without its use; yet it appears to be one great source of our vices; it is our constant engine in seducing each other. We are lulled asleep by its agency, and betrayed before we know that an attempt is made to betray us.

I have endeavoured to shake this prejudice, persuaded that in so doing I was well employed. It has been a further object with me to shew that, from abuses interwoven with the texture of society, a bad man may be furnished with sophisms in support of his crimes which it would be difficult to answer.

One word more upon the subject of motives. In private life what is more common than, when we hear of law-suits prosecuted to the utter ruin of the parties, and the most deadly feuds in families, to find them attributed to trifling and apparently inadequate sources? But when our malignant passions operate, the original causes which called them forth are soon supplanted, yet when we account for the effect we forget the immediate impulse, and the whole is attributed to the force from which the first motion was received. The vessel keeps sailing on, and we attribute her progress in the voyage to the ropes which first towed her out of harbour.

To this must be added that we are too apt to apply our own moral sentiments as a measure of the conduct of others. We insensibly suppose that a criminal action assumes the same form to the agent as to ourselves. We forget that his feelings and his reason are equally busy in contracting its dimensions and pleading for its necessity.

A Tragedy

On human actions reason though you can,
It may be reason, but it is not man;
His principle of action once explore,
That instant 'tis his principle no more.

Pope.[8]

NOTES

1 For parallels between the Preface and *The Borderers*, and discussion of difficult passages, see *Prose*, i. 81–6.
2 See *Emilius . . . Translated from the French by Mr. Nugent*, London, 1763, i. 57–8: 'A child wants to throw whatever he sees into disorder and confusion; he breaks every thing he can lay his hands on; he seizes a bird just in the same manner as he would grasp a stone, and squeezes it to death, without knowing what he does. . . . And if he seems to have a greater bent to destroy, it is not through perverseness; but because the action that creates or forms, is slow; and that which destroys, being more rapid, is better suited to his vivacity.'
3 *Orlando Furioso*, xxiii. 131–5; cf. *Don Quixote*, Book III, chs 9–10.
4 In both manuscripts a blank space appears after 'so', apparently for the insertion of a word on which the author had not decided or which the scribes had failed to read in their exemplar. The sentence as it stands is complete without 'so'.
5 The sense is doubtful, and probably the second 'habit' has been written for some now irrecoverable word such as 'man' or 'character'.
6 *Othello*, II. i. 308–9: 'the thought . . ./ Doth like a poisonous mineral gnaw my inwards.'
7 Rivers is the name given to Oswald in the play as represented by de Selincourt's manuscript B of the play, of which one manuscript version of the Preface forms a part: see *PW*, i. 343–4.
8 Pope, 'Epistle to Cobham', 35–8.

2 Advertisement to *Lyrical Ballads* 1798

Published for the first and only time in *Lyrical Ballads* (1798). The date of composition cannot be discovered more precisely than summer 1798. *Lyrical Ballads* was in active preparation by March or April of that year, and was 'printed, but not published' on 13 September (*EY*, 216, 227; see also my edition of *Lyrical Ballads 1798*, vii–xx). The text given here is from *Lyrical Ballads, with a Few Other Poems*, London, 1798, i–v, with editorial insertion of one punctuation mark.

ADVERTISEMENT.

It is the honourable characteristic of Poetry that its materials are to be found in every subject which can interest the human mind. The evidence of this fact is to be sought, not in the writings of Critics, but in those of Poets themselves.

The majority of the following poems are to be considered as experiments. They were written chiefly with a view to ascertain how far the language of conversation in the middle and lower classes of society is adapted to the purposes of poetic pleasure. Readers accustomed to the gaudiness and inane phraseology of many modern writers, if they persist in reading this book to its conclusion, will perhaps frequently have to struggle with feelings of strangeness and aukwardness: they will look round for poetry, and will be induced to enquire by what species of courtesy these attempts can be permitted to assume that title. It is desirable that such readers, for their own sakes, should not suffer the solitary word Poetry, a word of very disputed meaning, to stand in the way of their gratification; but that, while they are perusing this book, they should ask themselves if it contains a natural delineation of human passions, human characters, and human incidents; and if the answer be favorable to the author's wishes, that they should consent to be pleased in spite of that most dreadful enemy to our pleasures, our own pre-established codes of decision.

Readers of superior judgment may disapprove of the style in which many of these pieces are executed: it must be expected that many lines and phrases will not exactly suit their taste. It will perhaps appear to them, that wishing to avoid the prevalent fault of the day, the author has sometimes descended too low, and that many of his expressions are too familiar, and not of sufficient dignity. It is apprehended, that the more conversant the reader is with our elder writers,[1] and with those in modern times who have been the most successful in painting manners and passions,[2] the fewer complaints of this kind will he have to make.

An accurate taste in poetry, and in all the other arts, Sir Joshua Reynolds has observed, is an acquired talent, which can only be produced by severe thought, and a long continued intercourse with the best models of composition.[3] This is mentioned not with so ridiculous a purpose as to prevent the most inexperienced reader from judging for himself; but merely to temper the rashness of decision, and to suggest that if poetry be a subject on which much time has not been bestowed, the judgment may be erroneous, and that in many cases it necessarily will be so.

The tale of Goody Blake and Harry Gill is founded on a well-authenticated fact which happened in Warwickshire.[4] Of the other poems in the collection, it may be proper to say that they are either absolute inventions of the author, or facts which took place within his personal observation or that of his friends. The poem of the Thorn, as the reader will soon discover, is not supposed to be spoken in the author's own person: the character of the loquacious narrator will sufficiently shew itself in the course of the story.[5] The Rime of the Ancyent Marinere was professedly written in imitation of the *style*, as well as of the spirit of the elder poets; but with a few exceptions, the Author believes that the language adopted in it has been equally intelligible for these three last centuries. The lines entitled Expostulation and Reply, and those which follow, arose out of conversation with a friend who was somewhat unreasonably attached to modern books of moral philosophy.[6]

NOTES

1 Ballad writers? See the account of 'The Ancient Mariner' in the final paragraph, below.
2 Burns and Cowper are likely to have been in Wordsworth's mind.

3 A commonplace in Reynolds's *Discourses*: see his *Works*, London, 1798, i. 11. 25–6, 29, 222–3, ii. 95 (Discourses i, ii, vii, xii); and *Prose*, i. 186.

4 Wordsworth borrowed the story from Erasmus Darwin's *Zoonomia*, London, 1796; see my edition of *Lyrical Ballads 1798*, 132.

5 See the Note of 1800 (No. 4 below).

6 Usually stated to be William Hazlitt, who, according to his 'My First Acquaintance with Poets', in 1798 'got into a metaphysical argument with Wordsworth . . . in which we neither of us succeeded in making ourselves perfectly clear and intelligible'.

3 Preface and Appendix to *Lyrical Ballads*

1800, 1802

The shorter, early version of the Preface (1800) was written probably in the late summer of 1800, certainly in September, and on 1 October Dorothy Wordsworth 'corrected the last sheet' of the manuscript (*Journals*, i. 61–2; the manuscript is preserved, in part, in Yale University Library). *Lyrical Ballads* actually appeared in January 1801, and by June of that year had sold well enough to enable Longman, its publisher, to call for a new edition; this was in print by April 1802, and to it Wordsworth contributed an enlarged version of the Preface and the Appendix on poetic diction: see *EY*, 337; *The Library*, 5th Series, xii (1957), 94. Some of the new material in the expanded Preface suggests that the revision took place in the early months of 1802: see *Prose*, i. 112. Wordsworth reprinted the Preface, more or less in this enlarged form, and the Appendix in all later collected editions of his poems; in the edition of 1836–7 he cut the Preface somewhat and made stylistic revisions, especially by removing the pronoun 'I' as far as possible. Because the material cut in 1836–7 is important in the understanding of this document, I have preferred to print here, not Wordsworth's final text of 1849–50, but the full second version of the Preface, and in the text of *Lyrical Ballads* (1805), in which some differences of pointing and spelling from that of 1802 (there are no verbal revisions) suggest that Wordsworth looked over the copy or proofs of this edition with a view to establishing a text authoritative for the time being. Details of the important differences between the texts of 1800 and 1802–5 can be found in *Prose*, i. 118–59, my *Wordsworth's Preface to Lyrical Ballads*, 143–51, or my edition of *Lyrical Ballads 1798*, 153–79; my annotations to the present text indicate the broad lines of Wordsworth's revisions. My text, as indicated above, is based on *Lyrical Ballads, with Pastoral and Other Poems*, London, 1805, i. i–lxiv (for the Preface), and ii. 237–47 (for the Appendix).

PREFACE.

The first Volume of these Poems has already been submitted to general perusal.[1] It was published, as an experiment, which, I hoped, might be of some use to ascertain, how far, by fitting to metrical arrangement a selection of the real language of men in a state of vivid sensation, that sort of pleasure and that quantity of pleasure may be imparted, which a Poet may rationally endeavour to impart.

I had formed no very inaccurate estimate of the probable effect of those Poems: I flattered myself that they who should be pleased with them would read them with more than common pleasure: and, on the other hand, I was well aware, that by those who should dislike them they would be read with more than common dislike. The result has differed from my expectation in this only, that I have pleased a greater number, than I ventured to hope I should please.

For the sake of variety, and from a consciousness of my own weakness, I was induced to request the assistance of a Friend,[2] who furnished me with the Poems of the ANCIENT MARINER, the FOSTER-MOTHER'S TALE, the NIGHTINGALE, and the Poem entitled LOVE. I should not, however, have requested this assistance, had I not believed that the Poems of my Friend would in a great measure have the same tendency as my own, and that, though there would be found a difference, there would be found no discordance in the colours of our style; as our opinions on the subject of poetry do almost entirely coincide.

Several of my Friends are anxious for the success of these Poems from a belief, that, if the views with which they were composed were indeed realized, a class of Poetry would be produced, well adapted to interest mankind permanently, and not unimportant in the multiplicity, and in the quality of its moral relations: and on this account they have advised me to prefix a systematic defence of the theory upon which the poems were written. But I was unwilling to undertake the task, because I knew that on this occasion the Reader would look coldly upon my arguments, since I might be suspected of having been principally influenced by the selfish and foolish hope of *reasoning* him into an approbation of these particular Poems: and I was still more unwilling to undertake the task, because, adequately to display my opinions, and fully to enforce my arguments, would require a space wholly disproportionate to the nature of a preface. For to treat the subject with the clearness and coherence, of which I believe it susceptible, it would be necessary to give a full account of the present state of the public taste in this country, and to determine how far this taste is healthy or depraved; which, again, could not be determined, without pointing out, in what manner language and the human mind act and re-act on each other, and without retracing the revolutions, not of literature alone, but likewise of society itself. I have therefore altogether declined to enter regularly upon this defence; yet I am sensible, that there would be some impropriety in abruptly obtruding upon the Public, without a few words of introduction, Poems so materially different from those, upon which general approbation is at present bestowed.

It is supposed, that by the act of writing in verse an Author makes a formal engagement that he will gratify certain known habits of association; that he not only thus apprizes the Reader that certain classes of ideas and expressions will be found in his book, but that others will be carefully excluded. This exponent or symbol held forth by metrical language must in different æras of literature have excited very different expectations: for example, in the age of Catullus, Terence and Lucretius, and that of Statius or Claudian;[3] and in our own country, in the age of Shakespeare and Beaumont and Fletcher, and that of Donne and Cowley,[4] or Dryden, or Pope. I will not take upon me to determine the exact import of the promise which by the act of writing in verse an Author, in the present day, makes to his Reader; but I am certain, it will appear to many persons that I have not fulfilled the terms of an engagement thus voluntarily contracted. They who have been accustomed to the gaudiness and inane phraseology of many modern writers, if they persist in reading this book to its conclusion, will, no doubt, frequently have to struggle with feelings of strangeness and aukwardness: they will look round for poetry, and will be induced to inquire by what species of courtesy these attempts can be permitted to assume that title. I hope therefore the Reader will not censure me, if I attempt to state what I have proposed to myself to perform; and also, (as far as the limits of a preface will permit) to explain some of the chief reasons which have determined me in the choice of my purpose: that at least he may be spared any unpleasant feeling of disappointment, and that I myself may be protected from the most dishonourable accusation which can be brought against an Author, namely, that of an indolence which prevents him from endeavouring to ascertain what is his duty, or, when his duty is ascertained, prevents him from performing it.

The principal object, then, which I proposed to myself in these

Poems was[5] to choose incidents and situations from common life, and to relate or describe them, throughout, as far as was possible, in a selection of language really used by men; and, at the same time, to throw over them a certain colouring of imagination, whereby ordinary things should be presented to the mind in an unusual way; and, further, and above all, to make these incidents and situations interesting[5] by tracing in them, truly though not ostentatiously, the primary laws of our nature: chiefly, as far as regards the manner in which we associate ideas in a state of excitement. Low and rustic life was generally chosen, because in that condition, the essential passions of the heart find a better soil in which they can attain their maturity, are less under restraint, and speak a plainer and more emphatic language; because in that condition of life our elementary feelings co-exist in a state of greater simplicity, and, consequently, may be more accurately contemplated, and more forcibly communicated; because the manners of rural life germinate from those elementary feelings; and, from the necessary character of rural occupations, are more easily comprehended; and are more durable; and lastly, because in that condition the passions of men are incorporated with the beautiful and permanent forms of nature. The language, too, of these men is adopted (purified indeed from what appear to be its real defects, from all lasting and rational causes of dislike or disgust) because such men hourly communicate with the best objects from which the best part of language is originally derived; and because, from their rank in society and the sameness and narrow circle of their intercourse, being less under the influence of social vanity they convey their feelings and notions in simple and unelaborated expressions. Accordingly, such a language, arising out of repeated experience and regular feelings, is a more permanent, and a far more philosophical[6] language, than that which is frequently substituted for it by Poets, who think that they are conferring honour upon themselves and their art, in proportion as they separate themselves from the sympathies of men, and indulge in arbitrary and capricious habits of expression, in order to furnish food for fickle tastes, and fickle appetites, of their own creation.[7]

I cannot, however, be insensible of the present outcry against the triviality and meanness both of thought and language, which some of my contemporaries have occasionally introduced into their metrical compositions; and I acknowledge that this defect, where it exists, is more dishonourable to the Writer's own character than false refinement or arbitrary innovation, though I should contend at the same time that it is far less pernicious in the sum of its consequences. From such verses the Poems in these volumes will be found distinguished at least by one mark of difference, that each of them has a worthy *purpose*. Not that I mean to say, that I always began to write with a distinct purpose formally conceived; but I believe that my habits of meditation have so formed my feelings, as that my descriptions of such objects as strongly excite those feelings, will be found to carry along with them a *purpose*. If in this opinion I am mistaken, I can have little right to the name of a Poet. For all good poetry is the spontaneous overflow of powerful feelings: but though this be true, Poems to which any value can be attached, were never produced on any variety of subjects but by a man, who being possessed of more than usual organic sensibility, had also thought long and deeply. For our continued influxes of feeling are modified and directed by our thoughts, which are indeed the representatives of all our past feelings; and, as by contemplating the relation of these general representatives to each other we discover what is really important to men, so, by the repetition and continuance of this act,[8] our feelings will be connected with important subjects,[8] till at length, if we be originally possessed of much sensibility, such habits of mind will be produced, that, by obeying blindly and mechanically the impulses of those habits, we shall describe objects, and utter sentiments, of such a nature and in such connection with each other, that the understanding of the being to whom we address ourselves, if he be in a healthful state of association, must necessarily be in some degree enlightened, and his affections ameliorated.

I have said that each of these poems has a purpose. I have also informed my Reader what this purpose will be found principally to be: namely, to illustrate the manner in which our feelings and ideas are associated in a state of excitement. But, speaking in language somewhat more appropriate, it is to follow the fluxes and refluxes of the mind when agitated by the great and simple affections of our nature. This object I have endeavoured in these short essays to attain by various means; by tracing the maternal passion through many of its more subtile windings, as in the poems of the IDIOT BOY and the MAD MOTHER;[9] by accompanying the last struggles of a human being, at the approach of death, cleaving in solitude to life and society, as in the Poem of the FORSAKEN INDIAN; by showing, as in the Stanzas entitled WE ARE SEVEN, the perplexity and obscurity which in childhood attend our notion of death, or rather our utter inability to admit that notion; or by displaying the strength of fraternal, or to speak more philosophically, of moral attachment when early associated with the great and beautiful objects of nature, as in THE BROTHERS; or, as in the Incident of SIMON LEE, by placing my Reader in the way of receiving from ordinary moral sensations another and more salutary impression than we are accustomed to receive from them. It has also been part of my general purpose to attempt to sketch characters under the influence of less impassioned feelings, as in the TWO APRIL MORNINGS, THE FOUNTAIN, THE OLD MAN TRAVELLING, THE TWO THIEVES, &c. characters of which the elements are simple, belonging rather to nature than to manners,[10] such as exist now, and will probably always exist, and which from their constitution may be distinctly and profitably contemplated. I will not abuse the indulgence of my Reader by dwelling longer upon this subject; but it is proper that I should mention one other circumstance which distinguishes these Poems from the popular Poetry of the day; it is this, that the feeling therein developed gives importance to the action and situation, and not the action and situation to the feeling. My meaning will be rendered perfectly intelligible by referring my Reader to the Poems entitled POOR SUSAN and the CHILDLESS FATHER; particularly to the last Stanza of the latter Poem.

I will not suffer a sense of false modesty to prevent me from asserting, that I point my Reader's attention to this mark of distinction, far less for the sake of these particular Poems than from the general importance of the subject. The subject is indeed important! For the human mind is capable of being excited without the application of gross and violent stimulants; and he must have a very faint perception of its beauty and dignity who does not know this, and who does not further know, that one being is elevated above another, in proportion as he possesses this capability. It has therefore appeared to me, that to endeavour to produce or enlarge this capability is one of the best services in which, at any period, a Writer can be engaged; but this service, excellent at all times, is especially so at the present day. For a multitude of causes, unknown to former times, are now acting with a combined force to blunt the discriminating powers of the mind, and unfitting it for all voluntary exertion to reduce it to a state of almost savage torpor. The most effective of these causes are the great national events which are daily taking place,[11] and the increasing accumulation of men in cities, where the uniformity of their occupations produces a craving for extraordinary incident, which the rapid communication of intelligence hourly gratifies. To this tendency of life and manners the literature and theatrical exhibitions of the country have conformed themselves. The invaluable works of our elder writers, I had almost said the works of Shakespear and Milton, are driven into neglect by frantic novels, sickly and stupid German Tragedies, and deluges of idle and extravagant stories in verse.[12]—When I think upon this degrading thirst after outrageous stimulation, I am almost ashamed to have spoken of the feeble effort with which I have endeavoured to counteract it; and, reflecting upon the magnitude of the general evil, I should be oppressed with no dishonorable melancholy, had I not a deep impression of certain inherent and indestructible qualities of the human mind, and likewise of certain powers in the great and permanent objects that act upon it, which are equally inherent and indestructible; and did I not further add to this impression a belief, that the time is approaching when the evil will be systematically opposed, by men of greater powers, and with far more distinguished success.

Having dwelt thus long on the subjects and aim of these Poems, I shall request the Reader's permission to apprize him of a few circumstances relating to their *style*, in order, among other reasons, that I may not be censured for not having performed what I never attempted. The Reader will find that personifications of abstract ideas rarely occur in these volumes; and, I hope, are utterly rejected as an ordinary device to elevate the style, and raise it above prose. I have proposed to myself to imitate, and, as far as is possible, to adopt the very language of men; and assuredly such personifications do not make any natural or regular part of that language. They are, indeed, a figure of speech occasionally prompted by passion, and I have made use of them as such; but I have endeavoured utterly to reject them as a mechanical device of style, or as a family language which Writers in metre seem to lay claim to by prescription. I have wished to keep my Reader in the company of flesh and blood, persuaded that by so doing I shall interest him. I am, however, well aware that others who pursue a different track may interest him likewise; I do not interfere with their claim, I only wish to prefer a different claim of my own. There will also be found in these volumes little of what is usually called poetic diction; I have taken as much pains to avoid it as others ordinarily take to produce it; this I have done for the reason already alleged, to bring my language near to the language of men, and further, because the pleasure which I have proposed to myself to impart is of a kind very different from that which is supposed by many persons to be the proper object of poetry. I do not know how, without being culpably particular, I can give my Reader a more exact notion of the style in which I wished these poems to be written, than by informing him that I have at all times endeavoured to look steadily at my subject, consequently, I hope that there is in these Poems little falsehood of description, and that my ideas are expressed in language fitted to their respective importance. Something I must have gained by this practice, as it is friendly to one property of all good poetry, namely, good sense; but it has necessarily cut me off from a large portion of phrases and figures of speech which from father to son have long been regarded as the common inheritance of Poets. I have also thought it expedient to restrict myself still further, having abstained from the use of many expressions, in themselves proper and beautiful, but which have been foolishly repeated by bad Poets, till such feelings of disgust are connected with them as it is scarcely possible by any art of association to overpower.

If in a poem there should be found a series of lines, or even a single line, in which the language, though naturally arranged, and according to the strict laws of metre, does not differ from that of prose, there is a numerous class of critics, who, when they stumble upon these prosaisms, as they call them, imagine that they have made a notable discovery, and exult over the Poet as over a man ignorant of his own profession. Now these men would establish a canon of criticism which the Reader will conclude he must utterly reject, if he wishes to be pleased with these volumes. And it would be a most easy task to prove to him, that not only the language of a large portion of every good poem, even of the most elevated character, must necessarily, except with reference to the metre, in no respect differ from that of good prose, but likewise that some of the most interesting parts of the best poems will be found to be strictly the language of prose, when prose is well written. The truth of this assertion might be demonstrated by innumerable passages from almost all the poetical writings, even of Milton himself. I have not space for much quotation; but, to illustrate the subject in a general manner, I will here adduce a short composition of Gray, who was at the head of those who, by their reasonings, have attempted to widen the space of separation betwixt Prose and Metrical composition, and was more than any other man curiously elaborate in the structure of his own poetic diction.[13]

> In vain to me the smiling mornings shine,
> And reddening Phœbus lifts his golden fire:
> The birds in vain their amorous descant join,

Or cheerful fields resume their green attire.
These ears, alas! for other notes repine;
A different object do these eyes require;
My lonely anguish melts no heart but mine;
And in my breast the imperfect joys expire;
Yet morning smiles the busy race to cheer,
And new-born pleasure brings to happier men;
The fields to all their wonted tribute bear;
To warm their little loves the birds complain.
I fruitless mourn to him that cannot hear,
And weep the more because I weep in vain.

It will easily be perceived that the only part of this Sonnet which is of any value is the lines printed in Italics: it is equally obvious, that, except in the rhyme, and in the use of the single word 'fruitless' for fruitlessly, which is so far a defect, the language of these lines does in no respect differ from that of prose.

By the foregoing quotation I have shown that the language of Prose may yet be well adapted to Poetry; and I have previously asserted that a large portion of the language of every good poem can in no respect differ from that of good Prose. I will go further. I do not doubt that it may be safely affirmed, that there neither is, nor can be, any essential difference between the language of prose and metrical composition. We are fond of tracing the resemblance between Poetry and Painting, and, accordingly, we call them Sisters: but where shall we find bonds of connection sufficiently strict to typify the affinity betwixt metrical and prose composition? They both speak by and to the same organs; the bodies in which both of them are clothed may be said to be of the same substance, their affections are kindred, and almost identical, not necessarily differing even in degree; Poetry[14] sheds no tears 'such as Angels weep,'[15] but natural and human tears; she can boast of no celestial Ichor that distinguishes her vital juices from those of prose; the same human blood circulates through the veins of them both.

If it be affirmed that rhyme and metrical arrangement of themselves constitute a distinction which overturns what I have been saying on the strict affinity of metrical language with that of prose, and paves the way for other artificial distinctions which the mind voluntarily admits, I answer that[16] the language of such Poetry as I am recommending is, as far as is possible, a selection of the language really spoken by men; that this selection, wherever it is made with true taste and feeling, will of itself form a distinction far greater than would at first be imagined, and will entirely separate the composition from the vulgarity and meanness of ordinary life; and, if metre be superadded thereto, I believe that a dissimilitude will be produced altogether sufficient for the gratification of a rational mind. What other distinction would we have? Whence is it to come? And where is it to exist? Not, surely, where the Poet speaks through the mouths of his characters: it cannot be necessary here, either for elevation of style, or any of its supposed ornaments: for, if the Poet's subject be judiciously chosen, it will naturally, and upon fit occasion, lead him to passions the language of which, if selected truly and judiciously, must necessarily be dignified and variegated, and alive with metaphors and figures. I forbear to speak of an incongruity which would shock the intelligent Reader, should the Poet interweave any foreign splendour of his own with that which the passion naturally suggests: it is sufficient to say that such addition is unnecessary. And, surely, it is more probable that those passages, which with propriety abound with metaphors and figures, will have their due effect, if, upon other occasions where the passions are of a milder character, the style also be subdued and temperate.

But, as the pleasure which I hope to give by the Poems I now present to the Reader must depend entirely on just notions upon this subject, and, as it is in itself of the highest importance to our taste and moral feelings, I cannot content myself with these detached remarks. And if, in what I am about to say, it shall appear to some that my labour is unnecessary, and that I am like a man fighting a battle without enemies, I would remind such persons, that, whatever may be the language outwardly holden by men, a practical faith in the opinions which I am wishing to establish is almost unknown. If my conclusions are admitted, and carried as far as they must be carried if admitted at all, our judgments concerning the works of the greatest Poets both ancient and modern will be far different from what they are at present, both when we praise, and when we censure: and our moral feelings influencing, and influenced by these judgments will, I believe, be corrected and purified.

Taking up the subject, then, upon general grounds, I ask what is meant by the word Poet? What is a Poet? To whom does he address himself? And what language is to be expected from him? He is a man speaking to men: a man, it is true, endued with more lively sensibility, more enthusiasm and tenderness, who has a greater knowledge of human nature, and a more comprehensive soul, than are supposed to be common among mankind; a man pleased with his own passions and volitions, and who rejoices more than other men in the spirit of life that is in him; delighting to contemplate similar volitions and passions as manifested in the goings-on of the Universe, and habitually impelled to create them where he does not find them. To these qualities he has added a disposition to be affected more than other men by absent things as if they were present; an ability of conjuring up in himself passions, which are indeed far from being the same as those produced by real events, yet (especially in those parts of the general sympathy which are pleasing and delightful) do more nearly resemble the passions produced by real events, than any thing which, from the motions of their own minds merely, other men are accustomed to feel in themselves; whence, and from practice, he has acquired a greater readiness and power in expressing what he thinks and feels, and especially those thoughts and feelings which, by his own choice, or from the structure of his own mind, arise in him without immediate external excitement.

But, whatever portion of this faculty we may suppose even the greatest Poet to possess, there cannot be a doubt but that the language which it will suggest to him, must, in liveliness and truth, fall far short of that which is uttered by men in real life, under the actual pressure of those passions, certain shadows of which the Poet thus produces, or feels to be produced, in himself. However exalted a notion we would wish to cherish of the character of a Poet, it is obvious, that, while he describes and imitates passions, his situation is altogether slavish and mechanical, compared with the freedom and power of real and substantial action and suffering. So that it will be the wish of the Poet to bring his feelings near to those of the persons whose feelings he describes, nay, for short spaces of time perhaps, to let himself slip into an entire delusion, and even confound and identify his own feelings with theirs; modifying only the language which is thus suggested to him, by a consideration that he describes for a particular purpose, that of giving pleasure. Here, then, he will apply the principle on which I have so much insisted, namely, that of selection; on this he will depend for removing what would otherwise be painful or disgusting in the passion; he will feel that there is no necessity to trick out or to elevate nature:[17] and, the more industriously he applies this principle, the deeper will be his faith that no words, which his fancy or imagination can suggest, will be to be compared with those which are the emanations of reality and truth.

But it may be said by those who do not object to the general spirit of these remarks, that, as it is impossible for the Poet to produce upon all occasions language as exquisitely fitted for the passion as that which the real passion itself suggests, it is proper that he should consider himself as in the situation of a translator, who deems himself justified when he substitutes excellences of another kind for those which are unattainable by him; and endeavours occasionally to surpass his original, in order to make some amends for the general inferiority to which he feels that he must submit. But this would be to encourage idleness and unmanly despair. Further, it is the language of men who speak of what they do not understand; who talk of Poetry as of a matter of amusement and idle pleasure; who will converse with us as gravely about a *taste* for Poetry, as they express it, as if it were a thing as indifferent as a taste for Rope-dancing, or Frontiniac or Sherry. Aristotle, I have been told, hath said, that Poetry is the most philosophic of all writing:[18] it is so: its object is truth, not individual and local, but general, and operative; not standing upon external testimony, but carried alive into the heart by passion; truth which is its own testimony, which gives strength and divinity to the tribunal to which it appeals, and receives them from the same tribunal. Poetry is the image of man and nature. The obstacles which stand in the way of the fidelity of the Biographer and Historian, and of their consequent utility, are incalculably greater than those which are to be encountered by the Poet who has an adequate notion of the dignity of his art. The Poet writes under one restriction only, namely, that of the necessity of giving immediate pleasure to a human Being possessed of that information which may be expected from him, not as a lawyer, a physician, a mariner, an astronomer or a natural philosopher, but as a Man. Except this one restriction, there is no object standing between the Poet and the image of things; between this, and the Biographer and Historian there are a thousand.

Nor let this necessity of producing immediate pleasure be considered as a degradation of the Poet's art. It is far otherwise. It is an acknowledgment of the beauty of the universe, an acknowledgment the more sincere, because it is not formal, but indirect; it is a task light and easy to him who looks at the world in the spirit of love: further, it is a homage paid to the native and naked dignity of man, to the grand elementary principle of pleasure, by which he knows, and feels, and lives, and moves. We have no sympathy but what is propagated by pleasure: I would not be misunderstood; but wherever

we sympathize with pain it will be found that the sympathy is produced and carried on by subtle combinations with pleasure. We have
no knowledge, that is, no general principles drawn from the contemplation of particular facts, but what has been built up by
pleasure, and exists in us by pleasure alone. The Man of Science,
the Chemist and Mathematician, whatever difficulties and disgusts
they may have had to struggle with, know and feel this. However
painful may be the objects with which the Anatomist's knowledge is
connected, he feels that his knowledge is pleasure; and where he has
no pleasure he has no knowledge. What then does the Poet? He considers man and the objects that surround him as acting and re-acting
upon each other, so as to produce an infinite complexity of pain and
pleasure; he considers man in his own nature and in his ordinary life
as contemplating this with a certain quantity of immediate knowledge, with certain convictions, intuitions, and deductions which by
habit become of the nature of intuitions; he considers him as looking
upon this complex scene of ideas and sensations, and finding every
where objects that immediately excite in him sympathies which,
from the necessities of his nature, are accompanied by an overbalance of enjoyment.

To this knowledge which all men carry about with them, and to
these sympathies in which without any other discipline than that of
our daily life we are fitted to take delight, the Poet principally directs
his attention. He considers man and nature as essentially adapted to
each other, and the mind of man as naturally the mirror of the fairest
and most interesting qualities of nature. And thus the Poet, prompted
by this feeling of pleasure which accompanies him through the whole
course of his studies, converses with general nature with affections
akin to those, which, through labour and length of time, the Man of
Science has raised up in himself, by conversing with those particular
parts of nature which are the objects of his studies. The knowledge
both of the Poet and the Man of Science is pleasure; but the knowledge of the one cleaves to us as a necessary part of our existence, our
natural and unalienable inheritance; the other is a personal and
individual acquisition, slow to come to us, and by no habitual and
direct sympathy connecting us with our fellow-beings. The Man of
Science seeks truth as a remote and unknown benefactor; he
cherishes and loves it in his solitude: the Poet, singing a song in
which all human beings join with him, rejoices in the presence of
truth as our visible friend and hourly companion. Poetry is the
breath and finer spirit of all knowledge; it is the impassioned expres-

sion which is in the countenance of all Science. Emphatically may it be said of the Poet, as Shakespeare hath said of man, 'that he looks before and after.'[19] He is the rock of defence of human nature; an upholder and preserver, carrying every where with him relationship and love. In spite of difference of soil and climate, of language and manners, of laws and customs, in spite of things silently gone out of mind and things violently destroyed, the Poet binds together by passion and knowledge the vast empire of human society, as it is spread over the whole earth, and over all time. The objects of the Poet's thoughts are every where; though the eyes and senses of man are, it is true, his favourite guides, yet he will follow wheresoever he can find an atmosphere of sensation in which to move his wings. Poetry is the first and last of all knowledge—it is as immortal as the heart of man. If the labours of Men of Science should ever create any material revolution, direct or indirect, in our condition, and in the impressions which we habitually receive, the Poet will sleep then no more than at present, but he will be ready to follow the steps of the Man of Science, not only in those general indirect effects, but he will be at his side, carrying sensation into the midst of the objects of the Science itself. The remotest discoveries of the Chemist, the Botanist, or Mineralogist, will be as proper objects of the Poet's art as any upon which it can be employed, if the time should ever come when these things shall be familiar to us, and the relations under which they are contemplated by the followers of these respective Sciences shall be manifestly and palpably material to us as enjoying and suffering beings. If the time should ever come when what is now called Science, thus familiarized to men, shall be ready to put on, as it were, a form of flesh and blood, the Poet will lend his divine spirit to aid the transfiguration, and will welcome the Being thus produced, as a dear and genuine inmate of the household of man.—It is not, then, to be supposed that any one, who holds that sublime notion of Poetry which I have attempted to convey, will break in upon the sanctity and truth of his pictures by transitory and accidental ornaments, and endeavour to excite admiration of himself by arts, the necessity of which must manifestly depend upon the assumed meanness of his subject.

What I have thus far said applies to Poetry in general; but especially to those parts of composition where the Poet speaks through the mouths of his characters; and upon this point it appears to have such weight that I will conclude, there are few persons of good sense, who would not allow that the dramatic parts of composition are defective, in proportion as they deviate from the real language of nature, and are coloured by a diction of the Poet's own, either peculiar to him as an individual Poet, or belonging simply to Poets in general, to a body of men who, from the circumstance of their compositions being in metre, it is expected will employ a particular language.

It is not, then, in the dramatic parts of composition that we look for this distinction of language; but still it may be proper and necessary where the Poet speaks to us in his own person and character. To this I answer by referring my Reader to the description which I have before given of a Poet. Among the qualities which I have enumerated as principally conducing to form a Poet, is implied nothing differing in kind from other men, but only in degree. The sum of what I have there said is, that the Poet is chiefly distinguished from other men by a great promptness to think and feel without immediate external excitement, and a greater power in expressing such thoughts and feelings as are produced in him in that manner. But these passions and thoughts and feelings are the general passions and thoughts and feelings of men. And with what are they connected? Undoubtedly with our moral sentiments and animal sensations, and with the causes which excite these; with the operations of the elements and the appearances of the visible universe; with storm and sun-shine, with the revolutions of the seasons, with cold and heat, with loss of friends and kindred, with injuries and resentments, gratitude and hope, with fear and sorrow. These, and the like, are the sensations and objects which the Poet describes, as they are the sensations of other men, and the objects which interest them. The Poet thinks and feels in the spirit of the passions of men. How, then, can his language differ in any material degree from that of all other men who feel vividly and see clearly? It might be *proved* that it is impossible. But supposing that this were not the case, the Poet might then be allowed to use a peculiar language when expressing his feelings for his own gratification, or that of men like himself. But Poets do not write for Poets alone, but for men. Unless therefore we are advocates for that admiration which depends upon ignorance, and that pleasure which arises from hearing what we do not understand, the Poet must descend from this supposed height, and, in order to excite rational sympathy, he must express himself as other men express themselves. To this it may be added, that while he is only selecting from the real language of men, or, which amounts to the same thing, composing accurately in the spirit of such selection, he is treading upon safe ground, and we know what we are to expect from him. Our feelings are the same with respect to metre; for, as it may be proper to remind the Reader,[16] the distinction of metre[20] is regular and uniform, and not like that which is produced by what is usually called poetic diction, arbitrary, and subject to infinite caprices upon which no calculation whatever can be made. In the one case, the Reader is utterly at the mercy of the Poet respecting what imagery or diction he may choose to connect with the passion, whereas, in the other, the metre obeys certain laws, to which the Poet and Reader both willingly submit because they are certain, and because no interference is made by them with the passion but such as the concurring testimony of ages has shown to heighten and improve the pleasure which co-exists with it.

It will now be proper to answer an obvious question, namely, Why, professing these opinions, have I written in verse? To this, in addition to such answer as is included in what I have already said, I reply in the first place, Because, however I may have restricted myself, there is still left open to me what confessedly constitutes the most valuable object of all writing, whether in prose or verse, the great and universal passions of men, the most general and interesting of their occupations, and the entire world of nature, from which I am at liberty to supply myself with endless combinations of forms and imagery. Now, supposing for a moment that whatever is interesting in these objects may be as vividly described in prose, why am I to be condemned, if to such description I have endeavoured to superadd the charm which, by the consent of all nations, is acknowledged to exist in metrical language? To this, by such as are unconvinced by what I have already said, it may be answered, that a very small part of the pleasure given by Poetry depends upon the metre, and that it is injudicious to write in metre, unless it be accompanied with the other artificial distinctions of style with which metre is usually accompanied, and that by such deviation more will be lost from the shock which will be thereby given to the Reader's associations, than will be counterbalanced by any pleasure which he can derive from the general power of numbers. In answer to those who still contend for the necessity of accompanying metre with certain appropriate colours of style in order to the accomplishment of its appropriate end, and who also, in my opinion, greatly underrate the power of metre in itself, it might perhaps, as far as relates to these Poems, have been almost sufficient to observe, that poems are extant, written upon more humble subjects, and in a more naked and simple style than I have aimed at, which poems have continued to give pleasure from generation to generation. Now, if nakedness and simplicity be a defect, the fact here mentioned affords a strong presumption that poems somewhat less naked and simple are capable of affording pleasure at the present day; and, what I wished *chiefly* to attempt, at present, was to justify myself for having written under the impression of this belief.

But I might point out various causes why, when the style is manly, and the subject of some importance, words metrically arranged will long continue to impart such a pleasure to mankind as he who is sensible of the extent of that pleasure will be desirous to impart. The end of Poetry is to produce excitement in co-existence with an overbalance of pleasure. Now, by the supposition, excitement is an unusual and irregular state of the mind; ideas and feelings do not in that state succeed each other in accustomed order. But, if the words by which this excitement is produced are in themselves powerful, or the images and feelings have an undue proportion of pain connected with them, there is some danger that the excitement may be carried beyond its proper bounds. Now the co-presence of something regular, something to which the mind has been accustomed in various moods and in a less excited state,[21] cannot but have great efficacy in tempering and restraining the passion by an intertexture of ordinary feeling,[22] and of feeling not strictly and necessarily connected with the passion. This is unquestionably true, and hence, though the opinion will at first appear paradoxical, from the tendency of metre to divest language in a certain degree of its reality, and thus to throw a sort of half consciousness of unsubstantial existence over the whole composition, there can be little doubt but that more pathetic situations and sentiments, that is, those which have a greater proportion of pain connected with them, may be endured in metrical composition, especially in rhyme, than in prose. The metre of the old ballads is very artless; yet they contain many passages which would illustrate this opinion, and, I hope, if the following Poems be attentively perused, similar instances will be found in them.[22] This opinion may be further illustrated by appealing to the Reader's own experience of the reluctance with which he comes to the re-perusal of the distressful parts of Clarissa Harlowe, or the Gamester.[23] While Shakespeare's writings, in the most pathetic scenes, never act upon us as pathetic beyond the bounds of pleasure —an effect which, in a much greater degree than might at first be imagined, is to be ascribed to small, but continual and regular impulses of pleasurable surprise from the metrical arrangement.—On the other hand (what it must be allowed will much more frequently happen) if the Poet's words should be incommensurate with the passion, and inadequate to raise the Reader to a height of desirable excitement, then, (unless the Poet's choice of his metre has been grossly injudicious) in the feelings of pleasure which the Reader has been accustomed to connect with metre in general, and in the feeling, whether cheerful or melancholy, which he has been accustomed to connect with that particular movement of metre, there will be found something which will greatly contribute to impart passion to the words, and to effect the complex end which the Poet proposes to himself.

If I had undertaken a systematic defence of the theory upon which these poems are written, it would have been my duty to develope the various causes upon which the pleasure received from metrical language depends. Among the chief of these causes is to be reckoned a principle which must be well known to those who have made any of the Arts the object of accurate reflection; I mean the pleasure which the mind derives from the perception of similitude in dissimilitude.[24] This principle is the great spring of the activity of our minds, and their chief feeder. From this principle the direction of the sexual appetite, and all the passions connected with it, take their origin: it is the life of our ordinary conversation; and upon the accuracy with which similitude in dissimilitude, and dissimilitude in similitude are perceived, depend our taste and our moral feelings. It would not have been a useless employment to have applied this principle to the consideration of metre, and to have shown that metre is hence enabled to afford much pleasure, and to have pointed out in what manner that pleasure is produced. But my limits will not permit me to enter upon this subject, and I must content myself with a general summary.

I have said that Poetry is the spontaneous overflow of powerful feelings: it takes its origin from emotion recollected in tranquillity: the emotion is contemplated till by a species of reaction the tranquillity gradually disappears, and an emotion, kindred to that which was before the subject of contemplation, is gradually produced, and does itself actually exist in the mind. In this mood successful composition generally begins, and in a mood similar to this it is carried on; but the emotion, of whatever kind and in whatever degree, from various causes is qualified by various pleasures, so that in describing any passions whatsoever, which are voluntarily described, the mind will upon the whole be in a state of enjoyment. Now, if Nature be thus cautious in preserving in a state of enjoyment a being thus employed, the Poet ought to profit by the lesson thus held forth to him, and ought especially to take care, that whatever passions he communicates to his Reader, those passions, if his Reader's mind be sound and vigorous, should always be accompanied with an over-balance of pleasure. Now the music of harmonious metrical language, the sense of difficulty overcome, and the blind association of pleasure which has been previously received from works of rhyme or metre of the same or similar construction,[25] an indistinct perception perpetually renewed of language closely resembling that of real life, and yet, in the circumstance of metre, differing from it so widely,[25] all these imperceptibly make up a complex feeling of delight, which is of the most important use in tempering the painful feeling which will always be found intermingled with powerful descriptions of the deeper passions. This effect is always produced in pathetic and impassioned poetry; while, in lighter compositions, the ease and gracefulness with which the Poet manages his numbers are themselves confessedly a principal source of the gratification of the Reader. I might perhaps include all which it is *necessary* to say upon this subject by affirming, what few persons will deny, that, of two descriptions, either of passions, manners, or characters, each of them equally well executed, the one in prose and the other in verse, the verse will be read a hundred times where the prose is read once. We see that Pope, by the power of verse alone, has contrived to render the plainest common sense interesting, and even frequently to invest it with the appearance of passion. In consequence of these convictions I related in metre the Tale of GOODY BLAKE and HARRY GILL, which is one of the rudest of this collection. I wished to draw attention to the truth, that the power of the human imagination is sufficient to produce such changes even in our physical nature as might almost appear miraculous. The truth is an important one; the fact (for it is a *fact*) is a valuable illustration of it.[26] And I have the satisfaction of knowing that it has been communicated to many hundreds of people who would never have heard of it, had it not been narrated as a Ballad, and in a more impressive metre than is usual in Ballads.

Having thus explained a few of the reasons why I have written in verse, and why I have chosen subjects from common life, and endeavoured to bring my language near to the real language of men, if I have been too minute in pleading my own cause, I have at the same time been treating a subject of general interest; and it is for this reason that I request the Reader's permission to add a few words with reference solely to these particular poems, and to some defects which will probably be found in them. I am sensible that my associations must have sometimes been particular instead of general, and that, consequently, giving to things a false importance, sometimes from diseased impulses I may have written upon unworthy subjects; but I am less apprehensive on this account, than that my language may frequently have suffered from those arbitrary connections of feelings and ideas with particular words and phrases, from which no man can altogether protect himself. Hence I have no doubt, that, in some instances, feelings even of the ludicrous may be given to my Readers by expressions which appeared to me tender and pathetic. Such faulty expressions, were I convinced they were faulty at present, and that they must necessarily continue to be so, I would willingly take all reasonable pains to correct. But it is dangerous to make these alterations on the simple authority of a few individuals, or even of certain classes of men; for where the understanding of an Author is not convinced, or his feelings altered, this cannot be done without great injury to himself: for his own feelings are his stay and support, and, if he sets them aside in one instance, he may be induced to repeat this act till his mind loses all confidence in itself, and becomes utterly debilitated. To this it may be added, that the Reader ought never to forget that he is himself exposed to the same errors as the Poet, and perhaps in a much greater degree: for there can be no presumption in saying, that it is not probable he will be so well acquainted with the various stages of meaning through which words have passed, or with the fickleness or stability of the relations of particular ideas to each other; and above all, since he is so much less interested in the subject, he may decide lightly and carelessly.

Long as I have detained my Reader, I hope he will permit me to caution him against a mode of false criticism which has been applied to Poetry in which the language closely resembles that of life and nature. Such verses have been triumphed over in parodies of which Dr. Johnson's stanza is a fair specimen.[27]

> 'I put my hat upon my head,
> And walk'd into the Strand,
> And there I met another man
> Whose hat was in his hand.'

Immediately under these lines I will place one of the most justly admired stanzas of the '*Babes* in the Wood.'[28]

'These pretty Babes with hand in hand
Went wandering up and down;
But never more they saw the Man
Approaching from the Town.'

In both these stanzas the words, and the order of the words, in no respect differ from the most unimpassioned conversation. There are words in both, for example, 'the Strand,' and 'the Town,' connected with none but the most familiar ideas; yet the one stanza we admit as admirable, and the other as a fair example of the superlatively contemptible. Whence arises this difference? Not from the metre, not from the language, not from the order of the words; but the *matter* expressed in Dr. Johnson's stanza is contemptible. The proper method of treating trivial and simple verses, to which Dr. Johnson's stanza would be a fair parallelism, is not to say, This is a bad kind of poetry, or This is not poetry; but This wants sense; it is neither interesting in itself, nor can *lead* to any thing interesting; the images neither originate in that sane state of feeling which arises out of thought, nor can excite thought or feeling in the Reader. This is the only sensible manner of dealing with such verses. Why trouble yourself about the species till you have previously decided upon the genus? Why take pains to prove that an ape is not a Newton, when it is self-evident that he is not a man?

I have one request to make of my Reader, which is, that in judging these Poems he would decide by his own feelings genuinely, and not by reflection upon what will probably be the judgment of others. How common is it to hear a person say, 'I myself do not object to this style of composition, or this or that expression, but to such and such classes of people it will appear mean or ludicrous.' This mode of criticism, so destructive of all sound unadulterated judgment, is almost universal: I have therefore to request, that the Reader would abide independently by his own feelings, and that if he finds himself affected he would not suffer such conjectures to interfere with his pleasure.

If an Author by any single composition has impressed us with respect for his talents, it is useful to consider this as affording a presumption, that, on other occasions where we have been displeased, he nevertheless may not have written ill or absurdly; and, further, to give him so much credit for this one composition as may induce us to review what has displeased us with more care than we should otherwise have bestowed upon it. This is not only an act of justice, but, in our decisions upon poetry especially, may conduce in a high degree to the improvement of our own taste: for an *accurate* taste in poetry, and in all the other arts, as Sir Joshua Reynolds has observed, is an *acquired* talent, which can only be produced by thought, and a long continued intercourse with the best models of composition.[29] This is mentioned, not with so ridiculous a purpose as to prevent the most inexperienced Reader from judging for himself, (I have already said that I wish him to judge for himself;) but merely to temper the rashness of decision, and to suggest, that, if Poetry be a subject on which much time has not been bestowed, the judgment may be erroneous; and that in many cases it necessarily will be so.

I know that nothing would have so effectually contributed to further the end which I have in view, as to have shown of what kind the pleasure is, and how that pleasure is produced, which is confessedly produced by metrical composition essentially different from that which I have here endeavoured to recommend: for the Reader will say that he has been pleased by such composition; and what can I do more for him? The power of any art is limited; and he will suspect, that, if I propose to furnish him with new friends, it is only upon condition of his abandoning his old friends. Besides, as I have said, the Reader is himself conscious of the pleasure which he has received from such composition, composition to which he has peculiarly attached the endearing name of Poetry; and all men feel an habitual gratitude, and something of an honorable bigotry for the objects which have long continued to please them; we not only wish to be pleased, but to be pleased in that particular way in which we have been accustomed to be pleased. There is a host of arguments in these feelings; and I should be the less able to combat them successfully, as I am willing to allow, that, in order entirely to enjoy the Poetry which I am recommending, it would be necessary to give up much of what is ordinarily enjoyed. But, would my limits have permitted me to point out how this pleasure is produced, I might have removed many obstacles, and assisted my Reader in perceiving that the powers of language are not so limited as he may suppose; and that it is possible that poetry may give other enjoyments, of a purer, more lasting, and more exquisite nature. This part of my subject I have not altogether neglected;[30] but it has been less my present aim to prove, that the interest excited by some other kinds of poetry is less vivid, and less worthy of the nobler powers of the mind, than to offer reasons for presuming, that, if the object which I have proposed to myself were adequately attained, a species of poetry would be produced, which is genuine poetry; in its nature well adapted to interest mankind permanently, and likewise important in the multiplicity and quality of its moral relations.

From what has been said, and from a perusal of the Poems, the Reader will be able clearly to perceive the object which I have proposed to myself: he will determine how far I have attained this object; and, what is a much more important question, whether it be worth attaining: and upon the decision of these two questions will rest my claim to the approbation of the public.

APPENDIX.

See Preface, page 83—'by what is usually called Poetic Diction.'

As perhaps I have no right to expect from a Reader of an Introduction to a volume of Poems that attentive perusal without which it is impossible, imperfectly as I have been compelled to express my meaning, that what I have said in the Preface should throughout be fully understood, I am the more anxious to give an exact notion of the sense in which I use the phrase *poetic diction;*[1] and for this purpose I will here add a few words concerning the origin of the phraseology which I have condemned under that name.—The earliest Poets of all nations generally wrote from passion excited by real events; they wrote naturally, and as men: feeling powerfully as they did, their language was daring, and figurative. In succeeding times, Poets, and men ambitious of the fame of Poets, perceiving the influence of such language, and desirous of producing the same effect, without having the same animating passion, set themselves to a mechanical adoption of those figures of speech, and made use of them, sometimes with propriety, but much more frequently applied them to feelings and ideas with which they had no natural connection whatsoever. A language was thus insensibly produced, differing materially from the real language of men in *any situation*. The Reader or Hearer of this distorted language found himself in a perturbed and unusual state of mind: when affected by the genuine language of passion he had been in a perturbed and unusual state of mind also: in both cases he was willing that his common judgment and understanding should be laid asleep, and he had no instinctive and infallible perception of the true to make him reject the false; the one served as a passport for the other. The agitation and confusion of mind were in both cases delightful, and no wonder if he confounded the one with the other, and believed them both to be produced by the same, or similar causes. Besides, the Poet spake to him in the character of a man to be looked up to, a man of genius and authority. Thus, and from a variety of other causes, this distorted language was received with admiration; and Poets, it is probable, who had before contented themselves for the most part with misapplying only expressions which at first had been dictated by real passion, carried the abuse still further, and introduced phrases composed apparently in the spirit of the original figurative language of passion, yet altogether of their own invention, and distinguished by various degrees of wanton deviation from good sense and nature.

It is indeed true that the language of the earliest Poets was felt to differ materially from ordinary language, because it was the language of extraordinary occasions; but it was really spoken by men, language which the Poet himself had uttered when he had been affected by the events which he described, or which he had heard uttered by those around him. To this language it is probable that metre of some sort or other was early superadded. This separated the genuine language of Poetry still further from common life, so that whoever read or heard the poems of these earliest Poets felt himself moved in a way in which he had not been accustomed to be moved in real life, and by causes manifestly different from those which acted upon him in real life. This was the great temptation to all the corruptions which have followed: under the protection of this feeling succeeding Poets constructed a phraseology which had one thing, it is true, in common with the genuine language of poetry, namely, that it was not heard in ordinary conversation; that it was unusual. But the first Poets, as I have said, spake a language which, though unusual, was still the language of men. This circumstance, however, was disregarded by their successors; they found that they could please by easier means: they became proud of a language which they themselves had invented, and which was uttered only by themselves; and, with the spirit of a fraternity, they arrogated it to themselves as their own. In process of time metre became a symbol or promise of this unusual language, and whoever took upon him to write in metre, according as he possessed more or less of true poetic genius, introduced less or more of this adulterated phraseology into his compositions, and the true and the false became so inseparably interwoven that the taste of men was gradually perverted; and this language was received as a natural language; and at length, by the influence of books upon men, did to a certain degree really become so. Abuses of this kind were imported from one nation to another, and with the progress of refinement this diction became daily more and more corrupt, thrusting out of sight the plain humanities of nature by a motley masquerade of tricks, quaintnesses, hieroglyphics, and enigmas.

It would be highly interesting to point out the causes of the pleasure given by this extravagant and absurd language: but this is not the place; it depends upon a great variety of causes, but upon none perhaps more than its influence in impressing a notion of the peculiarity and exaltation of the Poet's character, and in flattering the Reader's self-love by bringing him nearer to a sympathy with that character; an effect which is accomplished by unsettling ordinary habits of thinking, and thus assisting the Reader to approach to that perturbed and dizzy state of mind in which if he does not find himself, he imagines that he is *balked* of a peculiar enjoyment which poetry can, and ought to bestow.

The sonnet which I have quoted from Gray, in the Preface, except the lines printed in Italics, consists of little else but this diction, though not of the worst kind; and indeed, if I may be permitted to say so, it is far too common in the best writers, both antient and modern. Perhaps I can in no way, by positive example, more easily give my Reader a notion of what I mean by the phrase *poetic diction* than by referring him to a comparison between the metrical paraphrases which we have of passages in the old and new Testament, and those passages as they exist in our common Translation. See Pope's 'Messiah' throughout, Prior's 'Did sweeter sounds adorn my flowing tongue,'[1] &c. &c. 'Though I speak with the tongues of men and of angels,' &c. &c. See 1st Corinthians, chapter xiiith. By way of immediate example, take the following of Dr. Johnson:[2]

> 'Turn on the prudent Ant thy heedless eyes,
> Observe her labours, Sluggard, and be wise;
> No stern command, no monitory voice,
> Prescribes her duties, or directs her choice;
> Yet, timely provident, she hastes away
> To snatch the blessings of a plenteous day;
> When fruitful Summer loads the teeming plain,
> She crops the harvest and she stores the grain.
> How long shall sloth usurp thy useless hours,
> Unnerve thy vigour, and enchain thy powers?
> While artful shades thy downy couch enclose,
> And soft solicitation courts repose,

Amidst the drowsy charms of dull delight,
Year chases year with unremitted flight,
Till want now following, fraudulent and slow,
Shall spring to seize thee, like an ambushed foe.'

From this hubbub of words pass to the original. 'Go to the Ant, thou Sluggard, consider her ways, and be wise: which having no guide, overseer, or ruler, provideth her meat in the summer, and gathereth her food in the harvest. How long wilt thou sleep, O Sluggard? when wilt thou arise out of thy sleep? Yet a little sleep, a little slumber, a little folding of the hands to sleep. So shall thy poverty come as one that travaileth, and thy want as an armed man.' Proverbs, chap. vith.

One more quotation and I have done. It is from Cowper's verses supposed to be written by Alexander Selkirk:[3]

'Religion! what treasure untold
Resides in that heavenly word!
More precious than silver and gold,
Or all that this earth can afford.
But the sound of the church-going bell
These valleys and rocks never heard,
Ne'er sighed at the sound of a knell,
Or smiled when a sabbath appeared.

Ye winds, that have made me your sport,
Convey to this desolate shore
Some cordial endearing report
Of a land I must visit no more.
My Friends, do they now and then send
A wish or a thought after me?
O tell me I yet have a friend,
Though a friend I am never to see.'

I have quoted this passage as an instance of three different styles of composition. The first four lines are poorly expressed; some Critics would call the language prosaic; the fact is, it would be bad prose, so bad, that it is scarcely worse in metre. The epithet 'church-going' applied to a bell, and that by so chaste a writer as Cowper, is an instance of the strange abuses which Poets have introduced into their language till they and their Readers take them as matters of course, if they do not single them out expressly as objects of admiration. The two lines 'Ne'er sigh'd at the sound,' &c. are, in my opinion, an instance of the language of passion wrested from its proper use, and, from the mere circumstance of the composition being in metre, applied upon an occasion that does not justify such violent expressions; and I should condemn the passage, though perhaps few Readers will agree with me, as vicious poetic diction. The last stanza is throughout admirably expressed: it would be equally good whether in prose or verse, except that the Reader has an exquisite pleasure in seeing such natural language so naturally connected with metre. The beauty of this stanza tempts me here to add a sentiment which ought to be the pervading spirit of a system, detached parts of which have been imperfectly explained in the Preface,—namely, that in proportion as ideas and feelings are valuable, whether the composition be in prose or in verse, they require and exact one and the same language.

NOTES

Preface

1 Volume i of *Lyrical Ballads*, 1800–5, is very similar in content to *Lyrical Ballads*, 1798.
2 Coleridge.
3 Terence (195–159 B.C.) is older by a century than Lucretius (95–52 B.C.) and Catullus (87–47 B.C.); Statius (A.D. 61–96) by three centuries than Claudian (*fl.* A.D. 400).
4 Wordsworth thinks of Donne (1571–1631) as of the seventeenth century, rather than as a contemporary of Shakespeare.
5 Text of 1800 reads, 'to make the incidents of common life interesting'.
6 Precise, adequate to the subject matter.
7 It is worth while here to observe that the affecting parts of Chaucer are almost always expressed in language pure and universally intelligible even to this day. [Wordsworth's note.]
8 Text of 1800 reads, 'feelings connected with important subjects will be nourished'.
9 Now without formal title and known as 'Her eyes are wild'.
10 'Nature' = inherent human characteristics; 'manners' = acquired aspects of social behaviour.
11 Primarily the fortunes of the French war; see also *Prose*, i. 172.
12 'Gothic' novels (such as Mrs Radcliffe's); German tragedies (such as Kotzebue's, frequently translated into English at this time); the 'stories' are not certainly identifiable.
13 'Sonnet on the Death of Richard West'. Gray in a letter of 1742 alleged that 'the language of the age is never the language of poetry': *Correspondence*, ed. P. Toynbee and L. Whibley, Oxford, 1935, 192–3.

14 I here use the word 'Poetry' (though against my own judgment) as opposed to the word Prose, and synonymous with metrical composition. But much confusion has been introduced into criticism by this contradistinction of Poetry and Prose, instead of the more philosophical one of Poetry and Matter of Fact, or Science. The only strict antithesis to Prose is Metre; nor is this, in truth, a *strict* antithesis; because lines and passages of metre so naturally occur in writing prose, that it would be scarcely possible to avoid them, even were it desirable. [Wordsworth's note.]

15 *Paradise Lost*, i. 620.

16 From 'the language of' down to 'remind the Reader', (p. 83) was inserted into the Preface in the edition of 1802.

17 I.e. natural utterance.

18 Aristotle, *Poetics*, 1451. b. 5–7, misreported: he says that poetry is more philosophical (i.e., more logical, more obviously governed, in its plots, by cause and effect) than history. See *Prose*, i. 179.

19 *Hamlet*, IV. iv. 37.

20 Text of 1800 reads, 'of rhyme and metre'. The long insertion made in 1802 ends at 'remind the Reader'.

21 Text of 1800 reads, 'accustomed when in an unexcited or a less excited state'.

22 The passage 'and of feeling . . . found in them' was added in 1802.

23 Samuel Richardson, *Clarissa Harlowe* (1747–8); Edward Moore, *The Gamester* (1753), a domestic tragedy in prose.

24 An eighteenth-century commonplace, anticipating Coleridge's distinction between 'copy' and 'imitation'. See *Prose*, i. 184.

25 The passage 'an indistinct . . . so widely' was added in 1802.

26 See No. 2, n. 4 (p. 67).

27 See Johnson's *Poems*, eds D. Nichol Smith and E. L. McAdam, Oxford, 1941, 157–8.

28 A traditional ballad, found in Percy's *Reliques of Ancient English Poetry*, 1765, etc., but not in Wordsworth's version. See *Prose*, i. 186.

29 See No. 2, n. 3 (p. 67).

30 Text of 1800 reads, 'But this part of my subject I have been obliged altogether to omit'.

Appendix

1 Matthew Prior, 'Charity. A Paraphrase on the Thirteenth Chapter of the First Epistle to the Corinthians', in *Poems on Several Occasions*, ed. A. R. Waller, Cambridge, 1905, 204–6.

2 'The Ant', in Johnson, op. cit., 151–2.

3 *Poems*, ed. H. S. Milford, London, 1926, 312.

4 Note to 'The Thorn'

1800

An expansion of the account of 'The Thorn' in the Advertisement to *Lyrical Ballads* (1798). The date of composition is unknown; its proximity to the Preface to *Lyrical Ballads* (1800) in the Yale manuscript (see headnote to No. 3 above) suggests that it may be contemporary with the Preface (late summer 1800). My text is from *Lyrical Ballads, with Other Poems*, London, 1800, i. 211–14.

This Poem ought to have been preceded by an introductory Poem, which I have been prevented from writing by never having felt myself in a mood when it was probable that I should write it well.—The character which I have here introduced speaking is sufficiently common. The Reader will perhaps have a general notion of it, if he has ever known a man, a Captain of a small trading vessel for example, who being past the middle age of life, had retired upon an annuity or small independent income to some village or country town of which he was not a native, or in which he had not been accustomed to live. Such men having little to do become credulous and talkative from indolence; and from the same cause, and other predisposing causes by which it is probable that such men may have been affected, they are prone to superstition. On which account it appeared to me proper to select a character like this to exhibit some of the general laws by which superstition acts upon the mind. Superstitious men are almost always men of slow faculties and deep feelings; their minds are not loose but adhesive; they have a reasonable share of imagination, by which word I mean the faculty which produces impressive effects out of simple elements; but they are utterly destitute of fancy, the power by which pleasure and surprize are excited by sudden varieties of situation and by accumulated imagery.

It was my wish in this poem to shew the manner in which such men cleave to the same ideas; and to follow the turns of passion, always different, yet not palpably different, by which their conversation is swayed. I had two objects to attain; first, to represent a picture which should not be unimpressive yet consistent with the character that should describe it, secondly, while I adhered to the style in which such persons describe, to take care that words, which in their minds are impregnated with passion, should likewise convey passion to Readers who are not accustomed to sympathize with men feeling in that manner or using such language. It seemed to me that this might be done by calling in the assistance of Lyrical and rapid Metre. It was necessary that the Poem, to be natural, should in reality move slowly; yet I hoped, that, by the aid of the metre, to those who should at all enter into the spirit of the Poem, it would appear to move quickly. The Reader will have the kindness to excuse this note as I am sensible that an introductory Poem is necessary to give this Poem its full effect.

Upon this occasion I will request permission to add a few words closely connected with THE THORN and many other Poems in these Volumes. There is a numerous class of readers who imagine that the same words cannot be repeated without tautology: this is a great error: virtual tautology is much oftener produced by using different words when the meaning is exactly the same. Words, a Poet's words more particularly, ought to be weighed in the balance of feeling and not measured by the space which they occupy upon paper. For the Reader cannot be too often reminded that Poetry is passion: it is the history or science of feelings: now every man must know that an attempt is rarely made to communicate impassioned feelings without something of an accompanying consciousness of the inadequateness of our own powers, or the deficiencies of language. During such efforts there will be a craving in the mind, and as long as it is unsatisfied the Speaker will cling to the same words, or words of the same character. There are also various other reasons why repetition and apparent tautology are frequently beauties of the highest kind. Among the chief of these reasons is the interest which the mind attaches to words, not only as symbols of the passion, but as *things*, active and efficient, which are of themselves part of the passion. And further, from a spirit of fondness, exultation, and gratitude, the mind luxuriates in the repetition of words which appear successfully to communicate its feelings. The truth of these remarks might be shewn by innumerable passages from the Bible and from the impassioned poetry of every nation.

'Awake, awake Deborah: awake, awake, utter a song:
Arise Barak, and lead thy captivity captive, thou Son of
   Abinoam.
'At her feet he bowed, he fell, he lay down: at her feet he
   bowed, he fell; where he bowed there he fell down dead.
'Why is his Chariot so long in coming? Why tarry the Wheels
   of his Chariot?'
            Judges, Chap. 5th. Verses 12th, 27th, and part of 28th.

See also the whole of that tumultuous and wonderful Poem.

5 Letter to Charles James Fox
1801

One of several letters covering complimentary copies of *Lyrical Ballads* (1800) sent to 'the Dutchess of Devonshire, Sir Bland Burgess, Mrs Jordan, Mr Fox, Mr Wilberforce, & 2 or 3 others'; all composed by Coleridge except this to Fox, which is Wordsworth's own composition (*CL*, ii. 665). The manuscript of the letter is in the Huntington Library; my text is from *EY*, 312–15. For Fox's reply see *Prose Works of William Wordsworth*, ed. A. B. Grosart, London, 1876, ii. 205–6.

Grasmere, Westmorland January 14th 1801

Sir,[1]

It is not without much difficulty, that I have summoned the courage to request your acceptance of these Volumes. Should I express my real feelings, I am sure that I should seem to make a parade of diffidence and humility.

Several of the poems contained in these Volumes are written upon subjects, which are the common property of all Poets, and which, at some period of your life, must have been interesting to a man of your sensibility, and perhaps may still continue to be so. It would be highly gratifying to me to suppose that even in a single instance the manner in which I have treated these general topics should afford you any pleasure; but such a hope does not influence me upon the present occasion; in truth I do not feel it. Besides, I am convinced that there must be many things in this collection, which may impress you with an unfavorable idea of my intellectual powers. I do not say this with a wish to degrade myself; but I am sensible that this must be the case, from the different circles in which we have moved, and the different objects with which we have been conversant.

Being utterly unknown to you as I am, I am well aware, that if I am justified in writing to you at all, it is necessary, my letter should

99

be short; but I have feelings within me which I hope will so far shew themselves in this letter, as to excuse the trespass which I am afraid I shall make. In common with the whole of the English people I have observed in your public character a constant predominance of sensibility of heart. Necessitated as you have been from your public situation to have much to do with men in bodies, and in classes, and accordingly to contemplate them in that relation, it has been your praise that you have not thereby been prevented from looking upon them as individuals, and that you have habitually left your heart open to be influenced by them in that capacity. This habit cannot but have made you dear to Poets; and I am sure that, if since your first entrance into public life there has been a single true poet living in England, he must have loved you.

But were I assured that I myself had a just claim to the title of a Poet, all the dignity being attached to the word which belongs to it, I do not think that I should have ventured for that reason to offer these volumes to you: at present it is solely on account of two poems in the second volume, the one entitled 'The Brothers,' and the other 'Michael,' that I have been emboldened to take this liberty.

It appears to me that the most calamitous effect, which has followed the measures which have lately been pursued in this country, is a rapid decay of the domestic affections among the lower orders of society. This effect the present Rulers of this country are not conscious of, or they disregard it. For many years past, the tendency of society amongst almost all the nations of Europe has been to produce it. But recently by the spreading of manufactures through every part of the country, by the heavy taxes upon postage, by work-houses, Houses of Industry, and the invention of Soup-shops &c. &c. superadded to the encreasing disproportion between the price of labour and that of the necessaries of life, the bonds of domestic feeling among the poor, as far as the influence of these things has extended, have been weakened, and in innumerable instances entirely destroyed. The evil would be the less to be regretted, if these institutions were regarded only as palliatives to a disease; but the vanity and pride of their promoters are so subtly interwoven with them, that they are deemed great discoveries and blessings to humanity. In the mean time parents are separated from their children, and children from their parents; the wife no longer prepares with her own hands a meal for her husband, the produce of his labour; there is little doing in his house in which his affections can be interested, and but little left in it which he can love. I have two neighbours, a man and his wife, both upwards of eighty years of age; they live alone; the husband has been confined to his bed many months and has never had, nor till within these few weeks has ever needed, any body to attend to him but his wife. She has recently been seized with a lameness which has often prevented her from being able to carry him his food to his bed; the neighbours fetch water for her from the well, and do other kind offices for them both, but her infirmities encrease. She told my Servant two days ago that she was afraid they must both be boarded out among some other Poor of the parish (they have long been supported by the parish) but she said, it was hard, having kept house together so long, to come to this, and she was sure that 'it would burst her heart.' I mention this fact to shew how deeply the spirit of independence is, even yet, rooted in some parts of the country. These people could not express themselves in this way without an almost sublime conviction of the blessings of independent domestic life. If it is true, as I believe, that this spirit is rapidly disappearing, no greater curse can befal a land.

I earnestly entreat your pardon for having detained you so long. In the two Poems, 'The Brothers' and 'Michael' I have attempted to draw a picture of the domestic affections as I know they exist amongst a class of men who are now almost confined to the North of England. They are small independent *proprietors* of land here called statesmen, men of respectable education who daily labour on their own little properties. The domestic affections will always be strong amongst men who live in a country not crowded with population, if these men are placed above poverty. But if they are proprietors of small estates, which have descended to them from their ancestors, the power which these affections will acquire amongst such men is inconceivable by those who have only had an opportunity of observing hired labourers, farmers, and the manufacturing Poor. Their little tract of land serves as a kind of permanent rallying point for their domestic feelings, as a tablet upon which they are written which makes them objects of memory in a thousand instances when they would otherwise be forgotten. It is a fountain fitted to the nature of social man from which supplies of affection, as pure as his heart was intended for, are daily drawn. This class of men is rapidly disappearing. You, Sir, have a consciousness, upon which every good man will congratulate you, that the whole of your public conduct has in one way or other been directed to the preservation of this class of men, and those who hold similar situations. You have felt that the most sacred of all property is the property of the Poor. The two poems which I have mentioned were written with a view to shew that men who do not wear fine cloaths can feel deeply. 'Pectus enim est quod disertos facit, et vis mentis. Ideoque imperitis quoque, si modo sint aliquo affectu concitati, verba non desunt.'[2] The poems are faithful copies from nature; and I hope, whatever effect they may have upon you, you will at least be able to perceive that they may excite profitable sympathies in many kind and good hearts, and may in some small degree enlarge our feelings of reverence for our species, and our knowledge of human nature, by shewing that our best qualities are possessed by men whom we are too apt to consider, not with reference to the points in which they resemble us, but to those in which they manifestly differ from us. I thought, at a time when these feelings are sapped in so many ways that the two poems might co-operate, however feebly, with the illustrious efforts which you have made to stem this and other evils with which the country is labouring, and it is on this account alone that I have taken the liberty of thus addressing you.

Wishing earnestly that the time may come when the country may perceive what it has lost by neglecting your advice, and hoping that your latter days may be attended with health and comfort.

I remain, With the highest respect and admiration,

Your most obedient and humble Servt

W Wordsworth

NOTES

1 Charles James Fox (1749–1806), M.P. for Midhurst, noted for his generally progressive attitudes towards the American colonies, revolutionary France, Roman Catholic emancipation, and other matters of national import current during Wordsworth's early manhood.

2 Quintilian, *De Institutione Oratoria*, x. vii. 15: 'For it is feeling and the force of the mind that makes men eloquent. Even the ignorant do not lack words if only they are stimulated by some feeling.' Wordsworth used this passage as a motto on the half-title of *Lyrical Ballads*, 1802.

6   Letter to John Wilson
1802

A reply by Wordsworth to a letter from John Wilson (then an under-graduate of seventeen), dated 24 May 1802, containing a thoughtful and reasoned criticism of *Lyrical Ballads*; for useful extracts see Elsie Smith, *An Estimate of William Wordsworth by his Contemporaries*, Oxford, 1932, 52–9. A draft manuscript of Wordsworth's letter survives in the Wordsworth Library, Grasmere, and is the basis of the following text, which is from *EY*, 352–8.

[Grasmere, 7 June 1802]

My dear Sir,[1]

Had it not been for a very amiable modesty you could not have imagined that your letter could give me any offence. It was on many accounts highly grateful to me. I was pleas'd to find that I had given so much pleasure to an ingenuous and able mind and I further considered the enjoyment which you had had from my poems as an earnest that others might be delighted with them in the same or a like manner. It is plain from your letter that the pleasure which I have given you has not been blind or unthinking you have studied the poems and prove that you have entered into the spirit of them. They have not given you a cheap or vulgar pleasure therefore I feel that you are entitled to my kindest thanks for having done some violence to your natural diffidence in the communication which you have made to me.

There is scarcely any part of your letter that does not deserve particular notice, but partly from a weakness in my stomach and digestion and partly from certain habits of mind I do not write any letters unless upon business not ev[en] to my dearest Friends. Except during absence from my own family I ha[ve] not written five letters of friendship during the last five years. I have mentioned this in order that I may retain your good opinion should my le[tter] be

103

less minute than you are entitled to expect. You seem to be desirous [of] my opinion on the influence of natural objects in forming the character of nati[ons]. This cannot be understood without first considering their influence upon men in [general?] first with reference to such subjects as are common to all countries: and [next?] such as belong exclusively to any particular country or in a greater d[egree] to it than to another. Now it is manifest that no human being can be so besotted and debased by oppression, penury or any other evil which unhum[anizes] man as to be utterly insensible to the colours, forms, or smell of flowers, the [voices?] and motions of birds and beasts, the appearances of the sky and heavenly bodies, the [genial?]² warmth of a fine day, the terror and uncomfortableness of a storm, &c &c. How dead soever many full-grown men may outwardly seem to these thi[ngs] they all are more or less affected by them, and in childhood, in the first practice and exercise of their senses, they must have been not the nourish[ers] merely, but often the fathers of their passions. There cannot be a doubt that in tracts of country where images of danger, melancholy, grandeur, or loveliness, softness, and ease prevail,³ that they will make themselves felt powerfully in forming the characters of the people, so as to produce a uniformity of national character, where the nation is small and is not made up of men who, inhabiting different soils, climates, &c by their civil usages, and relations materially interfere with each other. It was so formerly, no doubt, in the Highlands of Scotland but we cannot perhaps observe much of it in our own island at the present day, because, even in the most sequestered places, by manufactures, traffic, religion, Law, interchange of inhabitants &c distinctions are done away which would otherwise have been strong and obvious. This complex state of society does not, however, prevent the characters of individuals from frequently receiving a strong bias not merely from the impressions of general nature, but also from local objects and images. But it seems that to produce these effects in the degree in which we frequently find them to be produced there must be a peculiar sensibility of original organization combining with moral accidents, as is exhibited in *The Brothers* and in *Ruth*—I mean, to produce this in a marked degree not that I believe that any man was ever brought up in the country without loving it, especially in his better moments, or in a district of particular grandeur or beauty without feeling some stronger attachment to it on that account than he would otherwise have felt. I include, you will observe, in these considerations the influence of climate, changes in the atmosphere and elements and the labours and occupations which particular districts require.

You begin what you say upon the Idiot Boy with this observation, that nothing is a fit subject for poetry which does not please. But here follows a question, Does not please whom? Some have little knowledge of natural imagery of any kind, and, of course, little relish for it, some are disgusted with the very mention of the words pastoral poetry, sheep or shepherds, some cannot tolerate a poem with a ghost or any supernatural agency in it, others would shrink from an animated description of the pleasures of love, as from a thing carnal and libidinous some cannot bear to see delicate and refined feelings ascribed to men in low conditions of society, because their vanity and self-love tell them that these belong only to themselves and men like themselves in dress, station, and way of life: others are disgusted with the naked language of some of the most interesting passions of men, because either it is indelicate, or gross, or [vu]lgar, as many fine ladies could not bear certain expressions in The [Mad] Mother and the Thorn, and, as in the instance of Adam Smith, who, we [are] told, could not endure the Ballad of Clym of the Clough, because the [au]thor had not written like a gentleman;[4] then there are professional[, loca]l and national prejudices forevermore some take no interest in the [descri]ption of a particular passion or quality, as love of solitariness, we will say, [gen]ial activity of fancy, love of nature, religion, and so forth, because they have [little or?] nothing of it in themselves, and so on without end. I return then to [the] question, please whom? or what? I answer, human nature, as it has been [and eve]r will be. But where are we to find the best measure of this? I answer, [from with]in; by stripping our own hearts naked, and by looking out of ourselves to[wards me]n who lead the simplest lives most according to nature men who [ha]ve never known false refinements, wayward and artificial desires, false criti[ci]sms, effeminate habits of thinking and feeling, or who, having known these [t]hings, have outgrown them. This latter class is the most to be depended upon, but it is very small in number. People in our rank in life are perpetually falling into one sad mistake, namely, that of supposing that human nature and the persons they associate with are one and the same thing. Whom do we generally associate with? Gentlemen, persons of fortune, professional men, ladies persons who can afford to buy or can easily procure books of half a guinea price, hot-pressed, and printed upon superfine paper. These persons are, it is true, a part of human nature, but we err lamentably if we suppose them to be fair representatives of the vast mass of human existence. And yet few ever consider books but with reference to their power of pleasing these persons and men of a higher rank few descend lower among cottages and fields and among children. A man must have done this habitually before his judgment upon the Idiot Boy would be in any way decisive with me. I *know* I have done this myself habitually; I wrote the poem with exceeding delight and pleasure, and whenever I read it I read it with pleasure. You have given me praise for having reflected faithfully in my poems the feelings of human nature I would fain hope that I have done so. But a great Poet ought to do more than this he ought to a certain degree to rectify men's feelings, to give them new compositions of feeling, to render their feelings more sane pure and permanent, in short, more consonant to nature, that is, to eternal nature, and the great moving spirit of things. He ought to travel before men occasionally as well as at their sides.[5] I may illustrate this by a reference to natural objects. What false notions have prevailed from generation to generation as to the true character of the nightingale. As far as my Friend's Poem in the Lyrical Ballads, is read it will contribute greatly to rectify these. You will recollect a passage in Cowper where, speaking of rural sounds, he says—

> 'and *even* the boding Owl
> That hails the rising moon has charms for me.'

Cowper was passionately fond of natural objects yet you see he mentions it as a marvellous thing that he could connect pleasure with the cry of the owl. In the same poem he speaks in the same manner of that beautiful plant, the gorse; making in some degree an amiable boast of his loving it, '*unsightly* and unsmooth ['] as it is.[6] There are many aversions of this kind, which, though they have some foundation in nature, have yet so slight a one, that though they may have prevailed hundreds of years, a philosopher will look upon them as accidents. So with respect to many moral feelings, either of [lo]ve or dislike what excessive admiration was payed in former times to personal prowess and military success it is so with [the] latter even at the present day but surely not nearly so much as hereto[fore]. So with regard to birth, and innumerable other modes of sentiment, civil and religious. But you will be inclined to ask by this time how all this applies to the Idiot Boy. To this I can only say that the loathing and disgust which many people have at the sight of an Idiot, is a feeling which, though having som[e] foundation in human nature is not necessarily attached to it in any vi[rtuous?] degree, but is owing, in a great measure to a false delicacy, and, if I [may] say it without rudeness, a certain want of comprehensiveness of think[ing] and feeling. Persons in the lower classes of society have little or nothing [of] this: if an Idiot is born in a poor man's house, it must be taken car[e of] and cannot be boarded out, as it would be by gentlefolks, or sent [to a] public or private receptacle for such unfortunate beings. [Poor people] seeing frequently among their neighbours such objects, easily [forget what]ever there is of natural disgust about them, and have t[herefore] a sane state, so that without pain or suffering they [perform] their duties towards them. I could with pleasure pursue this subj[ect, but] I must now strictly adopt the plan which I proposed [to my]self when I began to write this letter, namely, that of setting down a few hints or memorandums, which you will think of for my sake.

I have often applied to Idiots, in my own mind, that sublime expression of scripture that, *'their life is hidden with God.'*[7] They are worshipped, probably from a feeling of this sort, in several parts of the East. Among the Alps where they are numerous, they are considered, I believe, as a blessing to the family to which they belong I have indeed often looked upon the conduct of fathers and mothers of the lower classes of society towards Idiots as the great triumph of the human heart. It is there that we see the strength, disinterestedness, and grandeur of love, nor have I ever been able to contemplate an object that calls out so many excellent and virtuous sentiments without finding it hallowed thereby and having something in me which bears down before it, like a deluge, every feeble sensation of disgust and aversion.

There are in my opinion, several important mistakes in the latter part of your letter which I could have wished to notice; but I find myself much fatigued. These refer both to the Boy and the Mother. I must content myself simply with observing that it is probable that the principle cause of your dislike to this particular poem lies in the *word* Idiot. If there had been any such word in our language, *to which we had attached passion*, as lack-wit, half-wit, witless &c I should have certainly employed it in preference but there is no such word. Observe, (this is entirely in reference to this particular poem) my Idiot is not one of those who cannot articulate and such as are usually disgusting in their persons—[8]

'Whether in cunning or in joy'
'And then his words were not a few' &c

and the last speech at the end of the poem. The Boy whom I had in my mind was, by no means disgusting in his appearance quite the contrary and I have known several with imperfect faculties who are handsome in their persons and features. There is one, at present, within a mile of my own house remarkably so, though there is something of a stare and vacancy in his countenance. A Friend of mine, knowing that some persons had a dislike to the poem such as you have expressed advised me to add a stanza describing the person of the Boy [so a]s entirely to separate him in the imaginations of my Readers from [that] class of idiots who are disgusting in their persons, but the narration [in] the poem is so rapid and impassioned that I could not find a place [in] which to insert the stanza without checking the progress of it, and [so lea]ving a deadness upon the feeling. This poem has, I know, frequently produced [the s]ame effect as it did upon you and your Friends but there are many [peo]ple also to whom it affords exquisite delight, and who indeed, prefer [it] to any other of my Poems. This proves that the feelings there delineated [are] such as all men *may* sympathize with. This is enough for my purpose. [It] is not enough for me as a poet, to delineate merely such feelings as all men *do* sympathize with but, it is also highly desirable to add to these others, such as all men *may* sympathize with, and such as there is reason to believe they would be better and more moral beings if they did sympathize with.[9]

I conclude with regret, because I have not said one half of [what I inten]ded to say: but I am sure you will deem my excuse suf[ficient when I] inform you that my head aches violently, and I am, in [other respect]s, unwell. I must, however, again give you my warmest [thanks] for your kind letter. I shall be happy to hear from you again [and] do not think it unreasonable that I should request a letter from you when I feel that the answer which I may make to it will not perhaps, be above three or four lines. This I mention to you with frankness, and you will not take it ill after what I have before said of my remissness in writing letters.

I am, dear Sir
With great Respect,
Yours sincerely W Wordsworth.

NOTES

1 John Wilson (1785–1854), later a resident in Elleray, Windermere, and in 1820 Professor of Moral Philosophy at the University of Edinburgh; with the support of Wordsworth (*MY*, ii. 594). Best known for his contributions to *Blackwood's* as 'Christopher North'.

2 The draft manuscript reads 'general'.

3 An early Wordsworthian statement of the Burkean distinction between the sublime and the beautiful; see also the penultimate sentence of this paragraph. On the effect of landscape on the mind, cf. especially *Prel*. vii. 716–40.

4 This observation is attributed to Adam Smith in the *European Magazine*, xx (August 1791), 135.

5 An anticipation of the stress on novelty as a desideratum in poetry which appears in the Essay, Supplementary (No. 12, pp. 211–12).

6 See Coleridge's 'The Nightingale', 12–49; Cowper, *The Task*, i. 205–6, 527–8.

7 Eph. 3:9; Col. 3:3.

8 'The Idiot Boy', lines 378 and 65 of the standard text. The 'last speech' is lines 450–1: ' "The cocks did crow to-whoo, to-whoo,/ And the sun did shine so cold!" '

9 See n. 5 above.

7   Letter to Lady Beaumont
1807

Evidently a reply to a report from Lady Beaumont, wife of Words-worth's friend and patron Sir George Beaumont, on the reception of Wordsworth's *Poems, in Two Volumes* (1807) by London society and by individuals. It anticipates several of the arguments of the Preface of 1815 and its Essay, Supplementary. The manuscript of this letter is in the Pierpont Morgan Library; my text is from *MY*, i. 145–51.

Coleorton,[1] Tuesday May 21st 1807.

Pray excuse this villainous paper, I cannot find any other
of the folio size.

My dear Lady Beaumont,

Though I am to see you so soon I cannot but write a word or two, to thank you for the interest you take in my Poems as evinced by your solicitude about their immediate reception. I write partly to thank you for this and to express the pleasure it has given me, and partly to remove any uneasiness from your mind which the dis-appointments you sometimes meet with in this labour of love may occasion. I see that you have many battles to fight for me; more than in the ardour and confidence of your pure and elevated mind you had ever thought of being summoned to; but be assured that this opposition is nothing more than what I distinctly foresaw that you and my other Friends would have to encounter. I say this, not to give myself credit for an eye of prophecy, but to allay any vexatious thoughts on my account which this opposition may have produced in you. It is impossible that any expectations can be lower than mine concerning the immediate effect of this little work upon what is called the Public.[2] I do not here take into consideration the envy and malevolence, and all the bad passions which always stand in the way of a work of any merit from a living Poet; but merely think of the

pure absolute honest ignorance, in which all worldlings of every rank
and situation must be enveloped, with respect to the thoughts, feelings, and images, on which the life of my Poems depends. The
things which I have taken, whether from within or without,—what
have they to do with routs, dinners, morning calls, hurry from door
to door, from street to street, on foot or in Carriage; with Mr. Pitt
or Mr. Fox, Mr. Paul or Sir Francis Burdett, the Westminster
Election or the Borough of Honiton;[3] in a word, for I cannot stop to
make my way through the hurry of images that present themselves
to me, what have they to do with endless talking about things nobody
cares anything for except as far as their own vanity is concerned, and
this with persons they care nothing for but as their vanity or *selfishness* is concerned; what have they to do (to say all at once) with a life
without love? in such a life there can be no thought; for we have no
thought (save thoughts of pain) but as far as we have love and
admiration.[4] It is an awful truth, that there neither is, nor can be,
any genuine enjoyment of Poetry among nineteen out of twenty of
those persons who live, or wish to live, in the broad light of the
world—among those who either are, or are striving to make themselves, people of consideration in society. This is a truth, and an
awful one, because to be incapable of a feeling of Poetry in my sense
of the word is to be without love of human nature and reverence
for God.

Upon this I shall insist elsewhere; at present let me confine myself to my object, which is to make you, my dear Friend, as easy-
hearted as myself with respect to these Poems. Trouble not yourself
upon their present reception; of what moment is that compared
with what I trust is their destiny, to console the afflicted, to add sun-
shine to daylight by making the happy happier, to teach the young
and the gracious of every age, to see, to think and feel, and therefore
to become more actively and securely virtuous; this is their office,
which I trust they will faithfully perform long after we (that is, all
that is mortal of us) are mouldered in our graves. I am well aware
how far it would seem to many I overrate my own exertions when I
speak in this way, in direct connection with the Volumes I have just
made public.

I am not, however, afraid of such censure, insignificant as
probably the majority of those poems would appear to very respectable persons; I do not mean London wits and witlings, for these have
too many bad passions about them to be respectable even if they had
more intellect than the benign laws of providence will allow to such

a heartless existence as theirs is; but grave, kindly-natured, worthy persons, who would be pleased if they could. I hope that these Volumes are not without some recommendations, even for Readers of this class, but their imagination has slept; and the voice which is the voice of my Poetry without Imagination cannot be heard.

Leaving these, I was going to say a word to such Readers as Mr. Rogers.[5] Such!—how would he be offended if he knew I considered him only as a representative of a class, and not as unique! 'Pity,' says Mr. R., 'that so many trifling things should be admitted to obstruct the view of those that have merit;' now, let this candid judge take, by way of example, the sonnets, which, probably, with the exception of two or three other Poems for which I will not contend appear to him the most trifling, as they are the shortest, I would say to him, omitting things of higher consideration, there is one thing which must strike you at once if you will only read these poems,—that those to Liberty,[6] at least, have a connection with, or a bearing upon, each other, and therefore, if individually they want weight, perhaps, as a Body, they may not be so deficient, at least this ought to induce you to suspend your judgement, and qualify it so far as to allow that the writer aims at least at comprehensiveness. But dropping this, I would boldly say at once, that these Sonnets, while they each fix the attention upon some important sentiment separately considered, do at the same time collectively make a Poem on the subject of civil Liberty and national independence, which, either for simplicity of style or grandeur of moral sentiment, is, alas! likely to have few parallels in the Poetry of the present day. Again, turn to the 'Moods of my own Mind'.[7] There is scarcely a Poem here of above thirty Lines, and very trifling these poems will appear to many; but, omitting to speak of them individually, do they not, taken collectively, fix the attention upon a subject eminently poetical, viz., the interest which objects in nature derive from the predominance of certain affections more or less permanent, more or less capable of salutary renewal in the mind of the being contemplating these objects? This is poetic, and essentially poetic, and why? because it is creative.

But I am wasting words, for it is nothing more than you know, and if said to those for whom it is intended, it would not be understood.

I see by your last Letter that Mrs. Fermor has entered into the spirit of these 'Moods of my own Mind.' Your transcript from her Letter gave me the greatest pleasure; but I must say that even she has something yet to receive from me. I say this with confidence, from her thinking that I have fallen below myself in the Sonnet beginning—'With ships the sea was sprinkled far and nigh.'[8] As to the other which she objects to, I will only observe that there is a misprint in the last line but two, 'And *though* this wilderness' for 'And *through* this wilderness'—that makes it unintelligible. This latter Sonnet for many reasons, though I do not abandon it, I will not now speak of; but upon the other, I could say something important in conversation, and will attempt now to illustrate it by a comment which I feel will be very inadequate to convey my meaning. There is scarcely one of my Poems which does not aim to direct the attention to some moral sentiment, or to some general principle, or law of thought, or of our intellectual constitution. For instance in the present case, who is there that has not felt that the mind can have no rest among a multitude of objects, of which it either cannot make one whole, or from which it cannot single out one individual, whereupon may be concentrated the attention divided among or distracted by a multitude? After a certain time we must either select one image or object, which must put out of view the rest wholly, or must subordinate them to itself while it stands forth as a Head:[9]

> Now glowed the firmament
> With living sapphires! Hesperus, that *led*
> The starry host, rode brightest; till the Moon,
> Rising in clouded majesty, at length,
> Apparent *Queen*, unveiled *her peerless* light,
> And o'er the dark her silver mantle threw.

Having laid this down as a general principle, take the case before us. I am represented in the Sonnet as casting my eyes over the sea, sprinkled with a multitude of Ships, like the heavens with stars, my mind may be supposed to float up and down among them in a kind of dreamy indifference with respect either to this or that one, only in a pleasurable state of feeling with respect to the whole prospect. 'Joyously it showed,' this continued till that feeling may be supposed to have passed away, and a kind of comparative listlessness or apathy to have succeeded, as at this line, 'Some veering up and down, one knew not why.' All at once, while I am in this state, comes forth an object, an individual, and my mind, sleepy and unfixed, is awakened and fastened in a moment. 'Hesperus, that *led* The starry host,' is a poetical object, because the glory of his own Nature gives him the pre-eminence the moment he appears; he calls forth the poetic faculty, receiving its exertions as a tribute: but this Ship in the Sonnet may, in a manner still more appropriate, be said to come upon a mission of the poetic Spirit, because in its own appearance and attributes it is barely sufficiently distinguish[ed] to rouse the creative faculty of the human mind; to exertions at all times welcome, but doubly so when they come upon us when in a state of remissness. The mind being once fixed and rouzed, all the rest comes from itself; it is merely a lordly Ship, nothing more:

> This ship was nought to me, nor I to her,
> Yet I pursued her with a lover's look.

My mind wantons with grateful joy in the exercise of its own powers, and, loving its own creation,

> This ship to all the rest I did prefer,

making her a sovereign or a regent, and thus giving body and life to all the rest; mingling up this idea with fondness and praise—

> where she comes the winds must stir;

and concluding the whole with

> On went She, and due north her journey took.

Thus taking up again the Reader with whom I began, letting him know how long I must have watched this favorite Vessel, and inviting him to rest his mind as mine is resting.

Having said so much upon a mere 14 lines, which Mrs. Fermor did not approve, I cannot but add a word or two upon my satisfaction in finding that my mind has so much in common with hers, and that we participate so many of each other's pleasures. I collect this from her having singled out the two little Poems, the Daffodils, and the Rock crowned with snowdrops.[10] I am sure that whoever is much pleased with either of these quiet and tender delineations must be fitted to walk through the recesses of my poetry with delight, and will there recognise, at every turn, something or other in which, and over which, it has that property and right which knowledge and love confer. The line, 'Come, blessed barrier, etc.,' in the sonnet upon Sleep,[11] which Mrs. F. points out, had before been mentioned to me by Coleridge, and indeed by almost everybody who had heard it, as eminently beautiful. My letter (as this 2nd sheet, which I am obliged to take, admonishes me) is growing to an enormous length; and yet, saving that I have expressed my calm confidence that these Poems will live, I have said nothing which has a particular application to the object of it, which was to remove all disquiet from your mind on account of the condemnation they may at present incur from that portion of my contemporaries who are called the Public. I am sure, my dear Lady Beaumont, if you attach any importance [to it] it can only be from an apprehension that it may affect me, upon which I have already set you at ease, or from a fear that this present blame is ominous of their future or final destiny. If this be the case, your tenderness for me betrays you; be assured that the decision of these persons has nothing to do with the Question; they are altogether incompetent judges. These people in the senseless hurry of their idle lives do not *read* books, they merely snatch a glance at them that they may talk about them. And even if this were not so, never forget what I believe was observed to you by Coleridge, that every great and original writer, in proportion as he is great or original, must himself create the taste by which he is to be relished;[12] he must teach the art by which he is to be seen; this, in a certain degree, even to all persons, however wise and pure may be their lives, and however unvitiated their taste; but for those who dip into books in order to give an opinion of them, or talk about them to take up an opinion—for this multitude of unhappy, and misguided, and misguiding beings, an entire regeneration must be produced; and if this be possible, it must be a work *of time*. To conclude, my ears are stone-dead to this idle buzz, and my flesh as insensible as iron to these petty stings; and after what I have said I am sure yours will be the same. I doubt not that you will share with me an invincible confidence that my writings (and among them these little Poems) will co-operate with the benign tendencies in human nature and society, wherever found; and that they will, in their degree, be efficacious in making men wiser, better, and happier. Farewell; I will not apologise for this Letter, though its length demands an apology. Believe me, eagerly wishing for the happy day when I shall see you and Sir George here, most affectionately yours,

Wm Wordsworth.

Do not hurry your coming hither on our account: my Sister regrets that she did not press this upon you, as you say in your Letter, 'we cannot *possibly* come before the first week in June'; from which we infer that your kindness will induce you to make sacrifices for our sakes. Whatever pleasure we may have in thinking of

Grasmere, we have no impatience to be gone, and think with full as much regret at leaving Coleorton. I had, for myself, indeed, a wish to be at Grasmere with as much of the summer before me as might be, but to this I attach no importance whatever, as far as the gratification of that wish interferes with any inclination or duty of yours. I could not be satisfied without seeing you here, and shall have great pleasure in waiting.

NOTES

1 The Wordsworths lived from October 1806 till June 1807 on the Beaumont estate at Coleorton, Leicestershire, while the Beaumonts were at their town residence in Grosvenor Square and, subsequently, in the Lake District, whither this letter was readdressed.

2 One member of Wordsworth's antithetical couple 'the public' and 'the people', which he seems to have invented about this time (see *MY*, i. 194) and was to use in the Essay, Supplementary (pp. 213–14).

3 William Pitt (1759–1806), Prime Minister during most of the early stages of the French war; Charles James Fox, see p. 102; James Paull (1770–1808) and Sir Francis Burdett (1770–1844), rival candidates for the Parliamentary seat of Westminster in 1807, fought a duel on 2 May 1807 in which both were wounded. Honiton had been held by Lord Cochrane, who abandoned it to contest the Westminster election, in which he and Burdett were returned.

4 Cf. *Exc.* iv. 763–5.

5 Samuel Rogers (1763–1855), poet, business man, and friend of Wordsworth.

6 The *Poems* of 1807 contain a section 'Sonnets dedicated to Liberty', the germ of the larger group 'Poems dedicated to National Independence and Liberty' in Wordsworth's standard text.

7 Another section in the *Poems* of 1807: its most notable poems are perhaps 'My heart leaps up', 'I wandered lonely', and 'To the Cuckoo'.

8 This elaborate discussion of a trivial poem anticipates the account of the 'creative' powers of the Imagination in the Preface of 1815 (pp. 183–4). Mrs Fermor, who called it forth, was Lady Beaumont's sister.

9 *Paradise Lost*, iv. 604–9.

10 'I wandered lonely' and 'Who fancied what a pretty sight' (*PW*, ii. 216–17, 148–9).

11 Wordsworth's third sonnet 'To Sleep', line 13 (*PW*, iii. 8–9).

12 Repeated in Essay, Supplementary (p. 210); the rest of the sentence anticipates the drift of the Essay.

8 Letter to S. T. Coleridge
1809

The first half of this letter is devoted to Peninsular affairs and to Wordsworth's pamphlet on *The Convention of Cintra*. The second half, which is printed here, contains the germ of Wordsworth's arrangement of his shorter poems into related groups which he made in the edition of 1815 and defended in the Preface to that edition (No. 11 below). The manuscript of this letter is in the Wordsworth Library, Grasmere; my text is from *MY*, i. 331, 334–6.

[May 5 1809]

My dear Coleridge . . .

I am half in mind to destroy this scrawl, and half in mind to scribble another sheet upon another subject, viz. my published Poems, and the arrangement which I mean to place them in if they are ever republished during my lifetime. I should begin thus, Poems relating to childhood,[1] and such feelings as rise in the mind in after life in direct contemplation of that state; to these I should prefix the motto 'the Child is father of the man—etc.' The class would begin with the simplest dawn of the affections or faculties, as the Foresight, or Children gathering flowers, the Pet Lamb, etc. and would ascend in a gradual scale of imagination to Hartley, 'there was a Boy', and it would conclude with the grand ode, 'There was a time', which perhaps might be preceded by We are Seven, if it were not advisable to place that earlier. This class would contain Gathering Flowers, Pet Lamb, Alice Fell, Lucy Gray, We are Seven, Anecdote for Fathers, Rural Architecture, Idle Shepherd Boys, To H. C. Six Years Old, There was a Boy, Ode. There may be others which I forget. (I am doubtful whether I should place the Butterfly and Sparrow's nest here or elsewhere.) The 2nd class would relate to the fraternal affections, to friendship and to love and to all those emotions, which follow after childhood, in youth and early manhood.[2] Here might come the Sparrow's Nest, etc., the Butterflies, those about Lucy, 'She was a phantom', Louisa, 'Dear child of nature', 'There is a change, and I am poor'. This class to ascend in a scale of imagination or interest through ' 'Tis said that some have died for love' Ellen Irwin—and to conclude with Ruth or The Brothers, printed with a separate Title as an adjunct, or this last might be placed elsewhere.—

Then 3d class Poems relating to natural objects and their influence on the mind either as growing or in an advanced state,[3] to begin with the simply human and conclude with the highly imaginative as the Tintern Abbey to be immediately preceded by the Cuckoo Poems, the Nutting, after having passed through all stages from objects as they affect the mere human being from properties with which they are endowed, and as they affect the mind by properties conferred; by the life found in them, or their life given. Here would come (I place them at Random) The daisies, the Celandines, The daffodils, the Nightingale and Stockdove, The green linnet, Waterfall and Eglantine, Oak and Broom, poor Susan perhaps, Poem on Rydale Island, on Grasmere, I heard a thousand blended notes, the Whirlblast from behind the hill, The Kitten and the falling leaves, Fidelity, those concerning Tom Hutchinson's dog; but with respect to the two or three last I am not sure that they may not be arranged better elsewhere.—The above class would be numerous, and conclude in the manner mentioned above with Tintern Abbey.

Next might come the Naming of Places,[4] as a Transition to the Poems relating to human life;[5] which might be prettily connected, harmoniously I may say, by Poor Susan mentioned before, and better perhaps placed here, Beggars, Simon Lee, last of Flock, Goody Blake, etc. to ascend through a regular scale of imagination to the Thorn, The Highland Girl, The Leech-gatherer, Hartleap Well. This class of poems I suppose to consist chiefly of objects most interesting to the mind not by its personal feelings or a strong appeal to the instincts or natural affections, but to be interesting to a meditative and imaginative mind either from the moral importance of the pictures or from the employment they give to the understanding affected through the imagination and to the higher faculties. Then might come, perhaps, those relating to the social and civic duties, and chiefly interesting to the imagination through the understanding, and not to the understanding through the imagination, as the political Sonnets,[6] Character of Happy Warrior, Rob Roy's

Grave, Personal talk, Poet's epitaph, Ode to Duty, To Burns'
Sons, etc. Then perhaps those relating to Maternal feeling,[7] con-
nubial or parental, Maternal to ascend from The Sailor's mother
through The Emigrant Mother, Affliction of M— of—, to The
Mad Mother, to conclude with the Idiot Boy.

Finally, the class of old age[8]—Animal tranquillity and decay,
The Childless Father, Though narrow be that old man's cares,
and near, The Two Thieves, The Matron of Jedborough, those
relating to Mathew, The Cumberland Beggar, to conclude perhaps
with Michael, which might conclude the whole. The Blind Highland Boy[9] ought to take its place among the Influences of Natural
Objects, (the sense of the eye being wanting) to produce an [?] of
imagination, and to throw the humblest [person] into sublime situations; feeling consecrating form, and form ennobling feeling.—This
may have sufficed to give you a notion of my views. The principle of
the arrangement is that there should be a scale in each class and in the
whole, and that each poem should be so placed as to direct the Reader's
attention by its position to its *primary* interest. I am writing illegibly.

Sara is, I think, full as well as usual.

Most affectionately your friend,

W. Wordsworth.

NOTES

1 'Poems referring to the Period of Childhood' in the edition of 1815,
   much as Wordsworth suggests here, but lacking 'There was a Boy' (in
   'Imagination') and 'the grand ode' (a section to itself).
2 'Poems founded on the Affections' in 1815. Most of 'those about Lucy',
   'She was a phantom', 'Dear child of nature', are lacking (most are in
   'Imagination'); and 'The Brothers' opens the group.
3 Most of these poems appear in 'Poems of the Fancy' and 'Poems of the
   Imagination' in 1815.
4 'Poems on the Naming of Places' in 1815.
5 'Simon Lee' is in 'Poems proceeding from Sentiment and Reflection'
   in 1815; 'The Last of the Flock' is in 'Affections'; all the other named
   poems are in 'Imagination'.
6 Presumably 'Sonnets dedicated to Liberty'. The following poems are
   in 'Sentiment and Reflection'.
7 These poems form the latter half of 'Affections' in 1815.
8 All but 'The Childless Father', 'those relating to Mathew', and
   'Michael' are in 'Poems referring to the Period of Old Age' in 1815.
9 In 'Childhood' in 1815.

9 *Essays upon Epitaphs*
1810?

The exact date of composition cannot be determined, but there is no
reason to suppose that it was much earlier than the date of publication of Essay I in Coleridge's *The Friend*, no. 25 (22 February 1810);
Wordsworth says, in the Fenwick note to his 'Epitaphs and Elegiac
Pieces' (*PW*, iv. 448), that it was 'written about [the] time' 'when
Mr. Coleridge was writing his "Friend"'. Essay I appeared here so that
an issue of *The Friend* could be filled at a time when Coleridge 'was
utterly unprovided'; though Wordsworth 'did not intend it to be
published now', it was 'ready' and therefore used as a stop-gap (*MY*,
i. 391). By 28 February Wordsworth had completed Essays II and
III and was willing to use them for a similar purpose (*MY*, i. 391):
but as *The Friend* failed after no. 27 (15 March 1810), they were not
so used. Coleridge wished to insert them in the reprint of *The Friend*
of 1812, but by accident or design this project failed (*CL*, iii. 392;
MY, ii. 13). Wordsworth used Essay I as the body of a note to *The
Excursion*, v. 978, and printed it in the first (1814) edition of that
poem, revising it in subsequent editions. The second and third
Essays appeared first, in an inaccurate text, in A. B. Grosart's edition
of Wordsworth's *Prose Works* (1876); Christopher Wordsworth had
made quotations from them, also inaccurate, in his *Memoirs of
William Wordsworth* (1851). My text of Essay I, with one necessary
correction, is Wordsworth's final version, in *Poetical Works* (1849–
50), vi. 287–300. This text lacks an introductory paragraph and a
second which makes clearer Wordsworth's disagreement with the
account of Pope's epitaphs in Johnson's *Life of Pope*; these paragraphs appear only in *The Friend*, but as *The Friend* in turn lacks
significant additions made during revision, I have preferred to print
Wordsworth's final version. My text of Essays II and III is based
on *Prose*, ii. 63–99, which is from the surviving manuscript, in the
hand of Mary Wordsworth, preserved in the Wordsworth Library,
Grasmere. The appended passage (pp. 165–6) is a proposed revision

of Essay II, to be inserted after the quotation of Lord Lyttleton's epitaph (p. 145) as a replacement for all or some of the following paragraph ('The prose part . . .', pp. 145–6). How much of this paragraph was to be excised cannot be determined from the manuscript, and the substitution cannot, therefore, be effectively made: see *Prose*, ii. 75, 97.

ESSAY UPON EPITAPHS, I

It need scarcely be said, that an Epitaph presupposes a Monument, upon which it is to be engraven. Almost all Nations have wished that certain external signs should point out the places where their dead are interred. Among savage tribes unacquainted with letters this has mostly been done either by rude stones placed near the graves, or by mounds of earth raised over them. This custom proceeded obviously from a twofold desire; first, to guard the remains of the deceased from irreverent approach or from savage violation: and, secondly, to preserve their memory. 'Never any,' says Camden, 'neglected burial but some savage nations; as the Bactrians, which cast their dead to the dogs; some varlet philosophers, as Diogenes, who desired to be devoured of fishes; some dissolute courtiers, as Mæcenas, who was wont to say, Non tumulum curo; sepelit natura relictos.

I'm careless of a grave:—Nature her dead will save.'[1]

As soon as nations had learned the use of letters, epitaphs were inscribed upon these monuments; in order that their intention might be more surely and adequately fulfilled. I have derived monuments and epitaphs from two sources of feeling: but these do in fact resolve themselves into one. The invention of epitaphs, Weever, in his Discourse of Funeral Monuments, says rightly, 'proceeded from the presage or fore-feeling of immortality, implanted in all men naturally, and is referred to the scholars of Linus the Theban poet, who flourished about the year of the world two thousand seven hundred; who first bewailed this Linus their Master, when he was slain, in doleful verses, then called of him Œlina, afterwards Epitaphia, for that they were first sung at burials, after engraved upon the sepulchres.'[2]

And, verily, without the consciousness of a principle of immortality in the human soul, Man could never have had awakened in him the desire to live in the remembrance of his fellows: mere love, or the yearning of kind towards kind, could not have produced it.

The dog or horse perishes in the field, or in the stall, by the side of his companions, and is incapable of anticipating the sorrow with which his surrounding associates shall bemoan his death, or pine for his loss; he cannot preconceive this regret, he can form no thought of it; and therefore cannot possibly have a desire to leave such regret or remembrance behind him. Add to the principle of love which exists in the inferior animals, the faculty of reason which exists in Man alone; will the conjunction of these account for the desire? Doubtless it is a necessary consequence of this conjunction; yet not I think as a direct result, but only to be come at through an intermediate thought, viz. that of an intimation or assurance within us, that some part of our nature is imperishable. At least the precedence, in order of birth, of one feeling to the other, is unquestionable. If we look back upon the days of childhood, we shall find that the time is not in remembrance when, with respect to our own individual Being, the mind was without this assurance; whereas, the wish to be remembered by our friends or kindred after death, or even in absence, is, as we shall discover, a sensation that does not form itself till the *social* feelings have been developed, and the Reason has connected itself with a wide range of objects. Forlorn, and cut off from communication with the best part of his nature, must that man be, who should derive the sense of immortality, as it exists in the mind of a child, from the same unthinking gaiety or liveliness of animal spirits with which the lamb in the meadow, or any other irrational creature is endowed; who should ascribe it, in short, to blank ignorance in the child; to an inability arising from the imperfect state of his faculties to come, in any point of his being, into contact with a notion of death; or to an unreflecting acquiescence in what had been instilled into him! Has such an unfolder of the mysteries of nature, though he may have forgotten his former self, ever noticed the early, obstinate, and unappeasable inquisitiveness of children upon the subject of origination? This single fact proves outwardly the monstrousness of those suppositions: for, if we had no direct external testimony that the minds of very young children meditate feelingly upon death and immortality, these inquiries, which we all know they are perpetually making concerning the *whence*, do necessarily include correspondent habits of interrogation concerning the *whither*. Origin and tendency are notions inseparably co-relative. Never did a child stand by the side of a running stream, pondering within himself what power was the feeder of the perpetual current, from what never-wearied sources the body of water was supplied, but he must have been inevitably propelled to follow this question by another: 'Towards what abyss is it in progress? what receptacle can contain the mighty influx?' And the spirit of the answer must have been, though the word might be sea or ocean, accompanied perhaps with an image gathered from a map, or from the real object in nature—these might have been the *letter*, but the *spirit* of the answer must have been *as* inevitably,—a receptacle without bounds or dimensions;—nothing less than infinity. We may, then, be justified in asserting, that the sense of immortality, if not a co-existent and twin birth with Reason, is among the earliest of her offspring: and we may further assert, that from these conjoined, and under their countenance, the human affections are gradually formed and opened out. This is not the place to enter into the recesses of these investigations; but the subject requires me here to make a plain avowal, that, for my own part, it is to me inconceivable, that the sympathies of love towards each other, which grow with our growth, could ever attain any new strength, or even preserve the old, after we had received from the outward senses the impression of death, and were in the habit of having that impression daily renewed and its accompanying feeling brought home to ourselves, and to those we love; if the same were not counteracted by those communications with our internal Being, which are anterior to all these experiences, and with which revelation coincides, and has through that coincidence alone (for otherwise it could not possess it) a power to affect us. I confess, with me the conviction is absolute, that, if the impression and sense of death were not thus counterbalanced, such a hollowness would pervade the whole system of things, such a want of correspondence and consistency, a disproportion so astounding betwixt means and ends, that there could be no repose, no joy. Were we to grow up unfostered by this genial warmth, a frost would chill the spirit, so penetrating and powerful, that there could be no motions of the life of love; and infinitely less could we have any wish to be remembered after we had passed away from a world in which each man had moved about like a shadow.—If, then, in a creature endowed with the faculties of foresight and reason, the social affections could not have unfolded themselves uncountenanced by the faith that Man is an immortal being; and if, consequently, neither could the individual dying have had a desire to survive in the remembrance of his fellows, nor on their side could they have felt a wish to preserve for future times vestiges of the departed; it follows, as a final inference, that without the belief in immortality, wherein these several desires originate, neither monuments nor epitaphs, in affectionate or laudatory commemoration of the deceased, could have existed in the world.

Simonides, it is related, upon landing in a strange country, found the corse of an unknown person lying by the sea-side; he buried it, and was honoured throughout Greece for the piety of that act.[3] Another ancient Philosopher, chancing to fix his eyes upon a dead body, regarded the same with slight, if not with contempt; saying, 'See the shell of the flown bird!' But it is not to be supposed that the moral and tender-hearted Simonides was incapable of the lofty movements of thought, to which that other Sage gave way at the moment while his soul was intent only upon the indestructible being; nor, on the other hand, that he, in whose sight a lifeless human body was of no more value than the worthless shell from which the living fowl had departed, would not, in a different mood of mind, have been affected by those earthly considerations which had incited the philosophic Poet to the performance of that pious duty. And with regard to this latter we may be assured that, if he had been destitute of the capability of communing with the more exalted thoughts that appertain to human nature, he would have cared no more for the corse of the stranger than for the dead body of a seal or porpoise which might have been cast up by the waves. We respect the corporeal frame of Man, not merely because it is the habitation of a rational, but of an immortal Soul. Each of these Sages was in sympathy with the best feelings of our nature; feelings which, though they seem opposite to each other, have another and a finer connection than that of contrast.—It is a connection formed through the subtle progress by which, both in the natural and the moral world, qualities pass insensibly into their contraries, and things revolve upon each other. As, in sailing upon the orb of this planet, a voyage towards the regions where the sun sets, conducts gradually to the quarter where we have been accustomed to behold it come forth at its rising; and, in like manner, a voyage towards the east, the birth-place in our imagination of the morning, leads finally to the quarter where the sun is last seen when he departs from our eyes; so the contemplative Soul, travelling in the direction of mortality, advances to the country of everlasting life; and, in like manner, may she continue to explore those cheerful tracts, till she is brought back, for her advantage and benefit, to the land of transitory things—of sorrow and of tears.

On a midway point, therefore, which commands the thoughts and feelings of the two Sages whom we have represented in contrast, does the Author of that species of composition, the laws of which it is our present purpose to explain, take his stand. Accordingly, recurring to the twofold desire of guarding the remains of the deceased and preserving their memory, it may be said that a sepulchral monument is a tribute to a man as a human being; and that an epitaph (in the ordinary meaning attached to the word) includes this general feeling and something more; and is a record to preserve the memory of the dead, as a tribute due to his individual worth, for a satisfaction to the sorrowing hearts of the survivors, and for the common benefit of the living: which record is to be accomplished, not in a general manner, but, where it can, in *close connection with the bodily remains of the deceased:* and these, it may be added, among the modern nations of Europe, are deposited within, or contiguous to, their places of worship. In ancient times, as is well known, it was the custom to bury the dead beyond the walls of towns and cities; and among the Greeks and Romans they were frequently interred by the way-sides.

I could here pause with pleasure, and invite the Reader to indulge with me in contemplation of the advantages which must have attended such a practice. We might ruminate upon the beauty which the monuments, thus placed, must have borrowed from the surrounding images of nature—from the trees, the wild flowers, from a stream running perhaps within sight or hearing, from the beaten road stretching its weary length hard by. Many tender similitudes must these objects have presented to the mind of the traveller leaning upon one of the tombs, or reposing in the coolness of its shade, whether he had halted from weariness or in compliance with the invitation, 'Pause, Traveller!' so often found upon the monuments. And to its epitaph also must have been supplied strong appeals to visible appearances or immediate impressions, lively and affecting analogies of life as a journey—death as a sleep overcoming the tired wayfarer—of misfortune as a storm that falls suddenly upon him—of beauty as a flower that passeth away, or of innocent pleasure as one that may be gathered—of virtue that standeth firm as a rock against the beating waves;—of hope 'undermined insensibly like the poplar by the side of the river that has fed it,'[4] or blasted in a moment like a pine-tree by the stroke of lightning upon the mountain-top—of admonitions and heart-stirring remembrances, like a refreshing breeze that comes without warning, or the taste of the waters of an unexpected fountain. These, and similar suggestions, must have given, formerly, to the language of the senseless stone a voice enforced and endeared by the benignity of that nature with which it was in unison.—We, in modern times, have lost much of these advantages; and they are but in a small degree counterbalanced to the inhabitants of large towns and cities, by the custom of depositing the dead within, or contiguous to, their places of worship; however splendid or imposing may be the appearance of those edifices, or however interesting or salutary the recollections associated with them. Even were it not true that tombs lose their monitory virtue when thus obtruded upon the notice of men occupied with the cares of the world, and too often sullied and defiled by those cares, yet still, when death is in our thoughts, nothing can make amends for the want of the soothing influences of nature, and for the absence of those types of renovation and decay, which the fields and woods offer to the notice of the serious and contemplative mind. To feel the force of this sentiment, let a man only compare in imagination the unsightly manner in which our monuments are crowded together in the busy, noisy, unclean, and almost grassless church-yard of a large town, with the still seclusion of a Turkish cemetery, in some remote place; and yet further sanctified by the grove of cypress in which it is embosomed. Thoughts in the same temper as these have already been expressed with true sensibility by an ingenuous Poet of the present day. The subject of his poem is 'All Saints' Church, Derby:' he has been deploring the forbidding and unseemly appearance of its burial-ground, and uttering a wish, that in past times the practice had been adopted of interring the inhabitants of large towns in the country:—5

> 'Then in some rural, calm, sequestered spot,
> Where healing Nature her benignant look
> Ne'er changes, save at that lorn season, when,
> With tresses drooping o'er her sable stole,
> She yearly mourns the mortal doom of man,
> Her noblest work, (so Israel's virgins erst,
> With annual moan upon the mountains wept
> Their fairest gone,) there in that rural scene,
> So placid, so congenial to the wish
> The Christian feels, of peaceful rest within
> The silent grave, I would have stray'd.

>   *   *   *   *

> —wandered forth, where the cold dew of heaven
> Lay on the humbler graves around, what time
> The pale moon gazed upon the turfy mounds,

Pensive, as though like me, in lonely muse,
'Twere brooding on the dead inhumed beneath.
There while with him, the holy man of Uz,
O'er human destiny I sympathised,
Counting the long, long periods prophecy
Decrees to roll, ere the great day arrives
Of resurrection, oft the blue-eyed Spring
Had met me with her blossoms, as the Dove,
Of old, returned with olive leaf, to cheer
The Patriarch mourning o'er a world destroyed:
And I would bless her visit; for to me
'Tis sweet to trace the consonance that links
As one, the works of Nature and the word
Of God.'—

JOHN EDWARDS.

A village church-yard, lying as it does in the lap of nature, may indeed be most favourably contrasted with that of a town of crowded population; and sepulture therein combines many of the best tendencies which belong to the mode practised by the Ancients, with others peculiar to itself. The sensations of pious cheerfulness, which attend the celebration of the sabbath-day in rural places, are profitably chastised by the sight of the graves of kindred and friends, gathered together in that general home towards which the thoughtful yet happy spectators themselves are journeying. Hence a parish-church, in the stillness of the country, is a visible centre of a community of the living and the dead; a point to which are habitually referred the nearest concerns of both.

As, then, both in cities and in villages, the dead are deposited in close connection with our places of worship, with us the composition of an epitaph naturally turns, still more than among the nations of antiquity, upon the most serious and solemn affections of the human mind; upon departed worth—upon personal or social sorrow and admiration—upon religion, individual and social—upon time, and upon eternity. Accordingly, it suffices, in ordinary cases, to secure a composition of this kind from censure, that it contain nothing that shall shock or be inconsistent with this spirit. But, to entitle an epitaph to praise, more than this is necessary. It ought to contain some thought or feeling belonging to the mortal or immortal part of our nature touchingly expressed; and if that be done, however general or even trite the sentiment may be, every man of pure mind will read the words with pleasure and gratitude. A husband bewails a wife; a parent breathes a sigh of disappointed hope over a lost child; a son utters a sentiment of filial reverence for a departed father or mother; a friend perhaps inscribes an encomium recording the companionable qualities, or the solid virtues, of the tenant of the grave, whose departure has left a sadness upon his memory. This and a pious admonition to the living, and a humble expression of Christian confidence in immortality, is the language of a thousand church-yards; and it does not often happen that anything, in a greater degree discriminate or appropriate to the dead or to the living, is to be found in them. This want of discrimination has been ascribed by Dr. Johnson, in his Essay upon the epitaphs of Pope, to two causes; first, the scantiness of the objects of human praise; and, secondly, the want of variety in the characters of men; or, to use his own words, 'to the fact, that the greater part of mankind have no character at all.'[6] Such language may be holden without blame among the generalities of common conversation; but does not become a critic and a moralist speaking seriously upon a serious subject. The objects of admiration in human-nature are not scanty, but abundant: and every man has a character of his own, to the eye that has skill to perceive it. The real cause of the acknowledged want of discrimination in sepulchral memorials is this: That to analyse the characters of others, especially of those whom we love, is not a common or natural employment of men at any time. We are not anxious unerringly to understand the constitution of the minds of those who have soothed, who have cheered, who have supported us: with whom we have been long and daily pleased or delighted. The affections are their own justification. The light of love in our hearts is a satisfactory evidence that there is a body of worth in the minds of our friends or kindred, whence that light has proceeded. We shrink from the thought of placing their merits and defects to be weighed against each other in the nice balance of pure intellect; nor do we find much temptation to detect the shades by which a good quality or virtue is discriminated in them from an excellence known by the same general name as it exists in the mind of another; and, least of all, do we incline to these refinements when under the pressure of sorrow, admiration, or regret, or when actuated by any of those feelings which incite men to prolong the memory of their friends and kindred, by records placed in the bosom of the all-uniting and equalising receptacle of the dead.

The first requisite, then, in an Epitaph is, that it should speak, in a tone which shall sink into the heart, the general language of humanity as connected with the subject of death—the source from which an epitaph proceeds—of death, and of life. To be born and to die are the two points in which all men feel themselves to be in absolute coincidence. This general language may be uttered so strikingly as to entitle an epitaph to high praise; yet it cannot lay claim to the highest unless other excellencies be superadded. Passing through all intermediate steps, we will attempt to determine at once what these excellencies are, and wherein consists the perfection of this species of composition.—It will be found to lie in a due proportion of the common or universal feeling of humanity to sensations excited by a distinct and clear conception, conveyed to the reader's mind, of the individual, whose death is deplored and whose memory is to be preserved; at least of his character as, after death, it appeared to those who loved him and lament his loss. The general sympathy ought to be quickened, provoked, and diversified, by particular thoughts, actions, images,—circumstances of age, occupation, manner of life, prosperity which the deceased had known, or adversity to which he had been subject; and these ought to be bound together and solemnised into one harmony by the general sympathy. The two powers should temper, restrain, and exalt each other. The reader ought to know who and what the man was whom he is called upon to think of with interest. A distinct conception should be given (implicitly where it can, rather than explicitly) of the individual lamented.—But the writer of an epitaph is not an anatomist, who dissects the internal frame of the mind; he is not even a painter, who executes a portrait at leisure and in entire tranquillity: his delineation, we must remember, is performed by the side of the grave; and, what is more, the grave of one whom he loves and admires. What purity and brightness is that virtue clothed in, the image of which must no longer bless our living eyes! The character of a deceased friend or beloved kinsman is not seen, no— nor ought to be seen, otherwise than as a tree through a tender haze or a luminous mist, that spiritualises and beautifies it; that takes away, indeed, but only to the end that the parts which are not abstracted may appear more dignified and lovely; may impress and affect the more. Shall we say, then, that this is not truth, not a faithful image; and that, accordingly, the purposes of commemoration cannot be answered?—It *is* truth, and of the highest order; for, though doubtless things are not apparent which did exist; yet, the object being looked at through this medium, parts and proportions are brought into distinct view which before had been only imperfectly or unconsciously seen: it is truth hallowed by love—the joint off-spring of the worth of the dead and the affections of the living! This may easily be brought to the test. Let one, whose eyes have been sharpened by personal hostility to discover what was amiss in the character of a good man, hear the tidings of his death, and what a change is wrought in a moment! Enmity melts away; and, as it disappears, unsightliness, disproportion, and deformity, vanish; and, through the influence of commiseration, a harmony of love and beauty succeeds. Bring such a man to the tombstone on which shall be inscribed an epitaph on his adversary, composed in the spirit which we have recommended. Would he turn from it as from an idle tale? No;—the thoughtful look, the sigh, and perhaps the in-voluntary tear, would testify that it had a sane, a generous, and good meaning; and that on the writer's mind had remained an impression which was a true abstract of the character of the deceased; that his gifts and graces were remembered in the simplicity in which they ought to be remembered. The composition and quality of the mind of a virtuous man, contemplated by the side of the grave where his body is mouldering, ought to appear, and be felt as something midway between what he was on earth walking about with his living frailties, and what he may be presumed to be as a Spirit in heaven.

It suffices, therefore, that the trunk and the main branches of the worth of the deceased be boldly and unaffectedly represented. Any further detail, minutely and scrupulously pursued, especially if this be done with laborious and antithetic discriminations, must in-evitably frustrate its own purpose; forcing the passing Spectator to this conclusion,—either that the dead did not possess the merits ascribed to him, or that they who have raised a monument to his memory, and must therefore be supposed to have been closely con-nected with him, were incapable of perceiving those merits; or at least during the act of composition had lost sight of them; for, the understanding having been so busy in its petty occupation, how could the heart of the mourner be other than cold? and in either of these cases, whether the fault be on the part of the buried person or the survivors, the memorial is unaffecting and profitless.

Much better is it to fall short in discrimination than to pursue it too far, or to labour it unfeelingly. For in no place are we so much disposed to dwell upon those points, of nature and condition, where-in all men resemble each other, as in the temple where the universal

Father is worshipped, or by the side of the grave which gathers all human Beings to itself, and 'equalises the lofty and the low.'[7] We suffer and we weep with the same heart; we love and are anxious for one another in one spirit; our hopes look to the same quarter; and the virtues by which we are all to be furthered and supported, as patience, meekness, good-will, justice, temperance, and temperate desires, are in an equal degree the concern of us all. Let an Epitaph, then, contain at least these acknowledgments to our common nature; nor let the sense of their importance be sacrificed to a balance of opposite qualities or minute distinctions in individual character; which if they do not, (as will for the most part be the case,) when examined, resolve themselves into a trick of words, will, even when they are true and just, for the most part be grievously out of place; for, as it is probable that few only have explored these intricacies of human nature, so can the tracing of them be interesting only to a few. But an epitaph is not a proud writing shut up for the studious: it is exposed to all—to the wise and the most ignorant; it is condescending, perspicuous, and lovingly solicits regard; its story and admonitions are brief, that the thoughtless, the busy, and indolent, may not be deterred, nor the impatient tired: the stooping old man cons the engraven record like a second horn-book;—the child is proud that he can read it;—and the stranger is introduced through its mediation to the company of a friend: it is concerning all, and for all:—in the church-yard it is open to the day; the sun looks down upon the stone, and the rains of heaven beat against it.

Yet, though the writer who would excite sympathy is bound in this case, more than in any other, to give proof that he himself has been moved, it is to be remembered, that to raise a monument is a sober and a reflective act; that the inscription which it bears is intended to be permanent, and for universal perusal; and that, for this reason, the thoughts and feelings expressed should be permanent also—liberated from that weakness and anguish of sorrow which is in nature transitory, and which with instinctive decency retires from notice. The passions should be subdued, the emotions controlled; strong, indeed, but nothing ungovernable or wholly involuntary. Seemliness requires this, and truth requires it also; for how can the narrator otherwise be trusted? Moreover, a grave is a tranquillising object: resignation in course of time springs up from it as naturally as the wild flowers, besprinkling the turf with which it may be covered, or gathering round the monument by which it is defended. The very form and substance of the monument which has received the inscription, and the appearance of the letters, testifying with what a slow and laborious hand they must have been engraven, might seem to reproach the author who had given way upon this occasion to transports of mind, or to quick turns of conflicting passion; though the same might constitute the life and beauty of a funeral oration or elegiac poem.

These sensations and judgments, acted upon perhaps unconsciously, have been one of the main causes why epitaphs so often personate the deceased, and represent him as speaking from his own tomb-stone. The departed Mortal is introduced telling you himself that his pains are gone; that a state of rest is come; and he conjures you to weep for him no longer. He admonishes with the voice of one experienced in the vanity of those affections which are confined to earthly objects, and gives a verdict like a superior Being, performing the office of a judge, who has no temptations to mislead him, and whose decision cannot but be dispassionate. Thus is death disarmed of its sting, and affliction unsubstantialised. By this tender fiction, the survivors bind themselves to a sedater sorrow, and employ the intervention of the imagination in order that the reason may speak her own language earlier than she would otherwise have been enabled to do. This shadowy interposition also harmoniously unites the two worlds of the living and the dead by their appropriate affections. And it may be observed, that here we have an additional proof of the propriety with which sepulchral inscriptions were referred to the consciousness of immortality as their primal source.

I do not speak with a wish to recommend that an epitaph should be cast in this mould preferably to the still more common one, in which what is said comes from the survivors directly; but rather to point out how natural those feelings are which have induced men, in all states and ranks of society, so frequently to adopt this mode. And this I have done chiefly in order that the laws, which ought to govern the composition of the other, may be better understood. This latter mode, namely, that in which the survivors speak in their own persons, seems to me upon the whole greatly preferable: as it admits a wider range of notices; and, above all, because, excluding the fiction which is the groundwork of the other, it rests upon a more solid basis.

Enough has been said to convey our notion of a perfect epitaph; but it must be borne in mind that one is meant which will best answer the *general* ends of that species of composition. According to the course pointed out, the worth of private life, through all varieties of situation and character, will be most honourably and profitably preserved in memory. Nor would the model recommended less suit public men, in all instances save of those persons who by the greatness of their services in the employments of peace or war, or by the surpassing excellence of their works in art, literature, or science, have made themselves not only universally known, but have filled the heart of their country with everlasting gratitude. Yet I must here pause to correct myself. In describing the general tenour of thought which epitaphs ought to hold, I have omitted to say, that if it be the *actions* of a man, or even some *one* conspicuous or beneficial act of local or general utility, which have distinguished him, and excited a desire that he should be remembered, then, of course, ought the attention to be directed chiefly to those actions or that act: and such sentiments dwelt upon as naturally arise out of them or it. Having made this necessary distinction, I proceed.—The mighty benefactors of mankind, as they are not only known by the immediate survivors, but will continue to be known familiarly to latest posterity, do not stand in need of biographic sketches, in such a place; nor of delineations of character to individualise them. This is already done by their Works, in the memories of men. Their naked names, and a grand comprehensive sentiment of civic gratitude, patriotic love, or human admiration—or the utterance of some elementary principle most essential in the constitution of true virtue;—or a declaration touching that pious humility and self-abasement, which are ever most profound as minds are most susceptible of genuine exaltation—or an intuition, communicated in adequate words, of the sublimity of intellectual power;—these are the only tribute which can here be paid—the only offering that upon such an altar would not be unworthy.[8]

> 'What needs my Shakspeare for his honoured bones
> The labour of an age in piled stones,
> Or that his hallowed reliques should be hid
> Under a star-ypointing pyramid?
> Dear Son of Memory, great Heir of Fame,
> What need'st thou such weak witness of thy name?
> Thou in our wonder and astonishment
> Hast built thyself a livelong monument,
> And so sepulchred, in such pomp dost lie,
> That kings for such a tomb would wish to die.'

ESSAY UPON EPITAPHS, II

Yet even these bones from insult to protect
Some frail memorial still erected nigh,
With uncouth rhymes and shapeless sculpture deck'd,
Implores the passing tribute of a sigh.

Their name, their years, spelt by the unletter'd Muse,
The place of fame and elegy supply,
And many a holy text around she strews,
That teach the rustic moralist to die.[1]

When a Stranger has walked round a Country Church-yard and
glanced his eye over so many brief Chronicles, as the tomb-stones
usually contain, of faithful Wives, tender Husbands, dutiful Children,
and good Men of all classes; he will be tempted to exclaim, in the
language of one of the Characters of a modern Tale[2] in a similar
situation, 'Where are all the *bad* People buried?' He may smile to
himself an answer to this question, and may regret that it has
intruded upon him so soon. For my own part such has been my lot.
And, indeed, a Man, who is in the habit of suffering his mind to be
carried passively towards truth as well as of going with conscious
effort in search of it, may be forgiven, if he has sometimes insensibly
yielded to the delusion of those flattering recitals, and found a
pleasure in believing that the prospect of real life had been as fair as
it was in that picture represented. And such a transitory oversight
will without difficulty be forgiven by those who have observed a
trivial fact in daily life, namely, how apt, in a series of calm weather,
we are to forget that rain and storms have been, and will return, to
interrupt any scheme of business or pleasure which our minds are
occupied in arranging. Amid the quiet of a Church-yard thus
decorated as it seemed by the hand of Memory, and shining, if I
may so say, in the light of love, I have been affected by sensations
akin to those which have risen in my mind while I have been standing by the side of a smooth Sea, on a Summer's day. It is such a
happiness to have, in an unkind World, one Enclosure where the
voice of detraction is not heard; where the traces of evil inclinations
are unknown; where contentment prevails, and there is no jarring
tone in the peaceful Concert of amity and gratitude. I have been
rouzed from this reverie by a consciousness, suddenly flashing upon
me, of the anxieties, the perturbations, and, in many instances, the

vices and rancorous dispositions, by which the hearts of those who lie under so smooth a surface and so fair an outside must have been agitated. The image of an unruffled Sea has still remained; but my fancy has penetrated into the depths of that Sea—with accompanying thoughts of Shipwreck, of the destruction of the Mariner's hopes, the bones of drowned Men heaped together, monsters of the deep, and all the hideous and confused sights which Clarence saw in his Dream![3]

Nevertheless, I have been able to return, (and who may not?) to a steady contemplation of the benign influence of such a favourable Register lying open to the eyes of all. Without being so far lulled as to imagine I saw in a Village Church-yard the eye or central point of a rural Arcadia, I have felt that with all the vague and general expressions of love, gratitude, and praise with which it is usually crowded, it is a far more faithful representation of homely life as existing among a Community in which circumstances have not been untoward, than any report which might be made by a rigorous observer deficient in that spirit of forbearance and those kindly prepossessions, without which human life can in no condition be profitably looked at or described. For we must remember that it is the nature of Vice to force itself upon notice, both in the act and by its consequences. Drunkenness, cruelty, brutal manners, sensuality, impiety, thoughtless prodigality, and idleness, are obstreperous while they are in the height and heyday of their enjoyment; and, when that is passed away, long and obtrusive is the train of misery which they draw after them. But, on the contrary, the virtues, especially those of humble life, are retired; and many of the highest must be sought for or they will be overlooked. Industry, œconomy, temperance, and cleanliness, are indeed made obvious by flourishing fields, rosy complexions, and smiling countenances; but how few know anything of the trials to which Men in a lowly condition are subject, or of the steady and triumphant manner in which those trials are often sustained, but they themselves! The afflictions which Peasants and rural Artizans have to struggle with are for the most part secret; the tears which they wipe away, and the sighs which they stifle,—this is all a labour of privacy. In fact their victories are to themselves known only imperfectly: for it is inseparable from virtue, in the pure sense of the word, to be unconscious of the might of her own prowess. This is true of minds the most enlightened by reflection; who have forecast what they may have to endure, and prepared themselves accordingly. It is true even of these, when they are called into action, that they necessarily lose sight of their own accomplishments, and support their conflicts in self-forgetfulness and humility. That species of happy ignorance, which is the consequence of these noble qualities, must exist still more frequently, and in a greater degree, in those persons to whom duty has never been matter of laborious specula-tion, and who have no intimations of the power to act and to resist which is in them, till they are summoned to put it forth. I could illustrate this by many examples, which are now before my eyes; but it would detain me too long from my principal subject which was to suggest reasons for believing that the encomiastic language of rural Tomb-stones does not so far exceed reality as might lightly be supposed. Doubtless, an inattentive or ill-disposed Observer, who should apply to the surrounding Cottages the knowledge which he may possess of any rural neighbourhood, would upon the first im-pulse confidently report that there was little in their living Inhabitants which reflected the concord and the virtue there dwelt upon so fondly. Much has been said, in a former paper[4] tending to correct this disposition; and which will naturally combine with the present considerations. Besides, to slight the uniform language of these memorials as on that account not trustworthy would obviously be unjustifiable. Enter a Church-yard by the Sea-coast, and you will be almost sure to find the Tomb-stones crowded with metaphors taken from the Sea and a Sea-faring life. These are uniformly in the same strain; but surely we ought not thence to infer that the words are used of course without any heart-felt sense of their propriety. Would not the contrary conclusion be right? But I will adduce a fact which more than a hundred analogical arguments will carry to the mind a conviction of the strength and sanctity of these feelings which persons in humble stations of society connect with their departed Friends & Kindred. We learn from the Statistical account of Scotland[5] that, in some districts, a general transfer of Inhabitants has taken place; and that a great majority of those who live, and labour, and attend public worship in one part of the Country, are buried in another. Strong and inconquerable still continues to be the desire of all, that their bones should rest by the side of their forefathers, and very poor Persons provide that their bodies should be conveyed if necessary to a great distance to obtain that last satisfaction. Nor can I refrain from saying that this natural interchange by which the living Inhabitants of a Parish have small knowledge of the dead who are buried in their Church-yards is grievously to be lamented where-soever it exists. For it cannot fail to preclude not merely much but the best part of the wholesome influence of that communion between living and dead which the conjunction in rural districts of the place of burial and place of worship tends so effectually to promote. Finally let us remember that if it be the nature of Man to be insensible to vexations and afflictions when they have passed away he is equally insensible to the height and depth of his blessings till they are removed from him.

An experienced and well-regulated mind will not, therefore, be insensible to this monotonous language of sorrow and affectionate admiration; but will find under that veil a substance of individual truth. Yet, upon all Men, and upon such a mind in particular, an Epitaph must strike with a gleam of pleasure, when the expression is of that kind which carries conviction to the heart at once that the Author was a sincere mourner, and that the Inhabitant of the Grave deserved to be so lamented. This may be done sometimes by a naked ejaculation; as in an instance which a friend of mine met with in a Church-yard in Germany;[6] thus literally translated. 'Ah! they have laid in the Grave a brave Man—he was to me more than many!'

> Ach! sie haben
> Einen Braven
> Mann begraben—
> Mir war er mehr als viele.

An effect as pleasing is often produced by the recital of an affliction endured with fortitude, or of a privation submitted to with contentment; or by a grateful display of the temporal blessings with which Providence had favoured the Deceased, and the happy course of life through which he had passed. And where these individualities are untouched upon it may still happen that the estate of man in his helplessness, in his dependence upon his Maker or some other inherent of his nature shall be movingly and profitably expressed. Every Reader will be able to supply from his own observation instances of all these kinds, and it will be more pleasing for him to refer to his memory than to have the page crowded with unnecessary Quotations. I will however give one or two from an old Book cited before. The following, of general application, was a great favourite with our Forefathers.[7]

> Farwel my Frendys, the tyd abidyth no man,
> I am departed hens, and so sal ye,

But in this passage the best song I can
Is *Requiem Eternam*, now Jesu grant it me.
When I have ended all myn adversity
Grant me in Paradys to have a mansion
That shedst thy bloud for my redemption.

This Epitaph might seem to be of the age of Chaucer, for it has the very tone and manner of his Prioress's Tale.

The next opens with a thought somewhat interrupting that complacency and gracious repose which the language and imagery of a Church-yard tend to diffuse; but the truth is weighty, and will not be less acceptable for the rudeness of the expression.[8]

When the bells be merrely roung
And the Masse devoutly soung
And the meate merrely eaten
Then sall Robert Trappis his Wyffs and his Chyldren
    be forgotten.

Wherfor Jesu that of Mary sproung
Set their soulys thy Saynts among
Though it be undeservyd on their syde
Yet good Lord let them evermor thy mercy abyde!

It is well known how fond our Ancestors were of a play upon the Name of the deceased when it admitted of a double sense. The following is an instance of this propensity not idly indulged. It brings home a general truth to the individual by the medium of a Pun, which will be readily pardoned, for the sake of the image suggested by it, for the happy mood of mind in which the Epitaph is composed, for the beauty of the language, and for the sweetness of the versification, which indeed, the date considered, is not a little curious—it is upon a man whose name was Palmer. I have modernized the spelling in order that its uncouthness may not interrupt the Reader's gratification.[9]

Palmers all our Fathers were
I a *Palmer* lived here
And travelled still till worn with age
I ended this world's pilgrimage,
On the blest Ascension-day
In the chearful month of May;
One thousand with four hundred seven,
And took my journey hence to heaven.

With this join the following, which was formerly to be seen upon a fair marble under the Portraiture of one of the Abbots of S͏ͭ Albans.[10]

> Hic quidem terra tegitur
> Peccati solvens debitum
> Cujus nomen non impositum
> In libro vitæ sit inscriptum.

The spirit of it may be thus given. 'Here lies, covered by the Earth, and paying his debt to sin, one whose Name is not set forth; may it be inscribed in the book of Life!'

But these instances, of the humility, the pious faith, and simplicity of our Forefathers have led me from the scene of our contemplations —a Country Church-yard! and from the memorials at this day commonly found in it. I began with noticing such as might be wholly uninteresting from the uniformity of the language which they exhibit; because, without previously participating the truths upon which these general attestations are founded, it is impossible to arrive at that state or disposition of mind necessary to make those Epitaphs thoroughly felt which have an especial recommendation. With the same view, I will venture to say a few words upon another characteristic of these Compositions almost equally striking; namely, the homeliness of some of the inscriptions, the strangeness of the illustrative images, the grotesque spelling, with the equivocal meaning often struck out by it, and the quaint jingle of the rhymes. These have often excited regret in serious minds, and provoked the unwilling to good-humoured laughter. Yet, for my own part, without affecting any superior sanctity, I must say that I have been better satisfied with myself, when in these evidences I have seen a proof how deeply the piety of the rude Forefathers of the hamlet is seated in their natures, I mean how habitual and constitutional it is, and how awful the feeling which they attach to the situation of their departed Friends—a proof of this rather than of their ignorance or of a deadness in their faculties to a sense of the ridiculous. And that this deduction may be just, is rendered probable by the frequent occurrence of passages, according to our present notion, full as ludicrous, in the Writings of the most wise and learned men of former ages, Divines or Poets, who in the earnestness of their souls have applied metaphors and illustrations, taken either from holy writ or from the usages of their own Country, in entire confidence that the sacredness of the theme they were discussing would sanctify the meanest object connected with it; or rather without ever conceiving it was possible that a ludicrous thought could spring up in any mind engaged in such meditations. And certainly, these odd and fantastic combinations are not confined to Epitaphs of the Peasantry, or of the lower orders of Society, but are perhaps still more commonly produced among the higher, in a degree equally or more striking. For instance, what shall we say to this upon Sir George Vane, the noted Secretary of State to King Charles Ist?[11]

> His Honour wonne i'th'field lies here in dust,
> His Honour got by grace shall never rust,
> The former fades, the latter shall fade never
> For why? He was Sr George once but S^t. George ever.

The date is 1679. When we reflect that the Father of this Personage must have had his taste formed in the punning Court of James Ist and that the Epitaph was composed at a time when our literature was stuffed with quaint or out-of-the-way thoughts, it will seem not unlikely that the Author prided himself upon what he might call a clever hit: I mean that his better affections were less occupied with the several associations belonging to the two ideas than his vanity delighted with that act of ingenuity by which they had been combined. But the first couplet consists of a just thought naturally expressed: and I should rather conclude the whole to be a work of honest simplicity; and that the sense of worldly dignity associated with the title, in a degree habitual to our Ancestors but which at this time we can but feebly sympathize with, and the imaginative feeling involved, viz, the saintly and chivalrous Name of the Champion of England, were unaffectedly linked together: and that both were united and consolidated in the Author's mind, and in the minds of his contemporaries whom no doubt he had pleased, by a devout contemplation of a happy immortality, the reward of the just.

At all events, leaving this particular case undecided, the general propriety of these notices cannot be doubted; and I gladly avail myself of this opportunity to place in a clear view the power and majesty of impassioned faith, whatever be its object: to shew how it subjugates the lighter motions of the mind, and sweeps away superficial difference in things. And this I have done, not to lower the witling and the worldling in their own esteem, but with a wish to bring the ingenuous into still closer communion with those primary sensations of the human heart, which are the vital springs of sublime and pathetic composition, in this and in every other kind. And, as from these primary sensations such composition speaks, so, unless correspondent ones listen promptly and submissively in the inner cell of the mind to whom it is addressed, the voice cannot be heard: its highest powers are wasted.

These suggestions may be further useful to establish a criterion of sincerity, by which a Writer may be judged; and this is of high import. For, when a Man is treating an interesting subject, or one which he ought not to treat at all unless he be interested, no faults have such a killing power as those which prove that he is not in earnest, that he is acting a part, has leisure for affectation, and feels that without it he could do nothing. This is one of the most odious of faults; because it shocks the moral sense: and is worse in a sepulchral inscription, precisely in the same degree as that mode of composition calls for sincerity more urgently than any other. And indeed, where the internal evidence proves that the Writer was moved, in other words where this charm of sincerity lurks in the language of a Tombstone and secretly pervades it, there are no errors in style or manner for which it will not be, in some degree, a recompence; but without habits of reflection a test of this inward simplicity cannot be come at: and, as I have said, I am now writing with a hope to assist the well-disposed to attain it.

Let us take an instance where no one can be at a loss. The following Lines are said to have been written by the illustrious Marquis of Montrose with the point of his Sword, upon being informed of the death of his Master Charles 1st.[12]

> Great, good, and just, could I but rate
> My griefs, and thy so rigid fate;
> I'd weep the world to such a strain,
> As it should deluge once again.
> But since thy loud-tongued blood demands supplies,
> More from Briareus hands than Argus eyes,
> I'll sing thy Obsequies with Trumpets sounds,
> And write thy Epitaph with blood and wounds.

These funereal verses would certainly be wholly out of their place upon a tombstone; but who can doubt that the Writer was transported to the height of the occasion?—that he was moved as it became an heroic Soldier, holding those Principles and opinions, to be moved? His soul labours;—the most tremendous event in the history of the Planet, namely, the Deluge, is brought before his imagination by the physical image of tears,—a connection awful from its very remoteness and from the slender bond that unites the ideas:—it passes into the region of Fable likewise; for all modes of existence that forward his purpose are to be pressed into the service. The whole is instinct with spirit, and every word has its separate life; like the Chariot of the Messiah, and the wheels of that Chariot, as they appeared to the imagination of Milton aided by that of the Prophet Ezekiel. It had power to move of itself but was conveyed by Cherubs.[13]

> as with stars their bodies all
> And wings were set with eyes, with eyes the wheels
> Of Beryl, and careering fires between.

Compare with the above Verses of Montrose the following Epitaph upon Sir Philip Sidney, which was formerly placed over his Grave in S.t Paul's Church.[14]

> England, Netherland, the Heavens, and the Arts,
> The Soldiers, and the World, have made six parts
> Of noble Sidney: for who will suppose
> That a small heap of Stones can Sidney enclose?

> England hath his Body, for she it fed,
> Netherland his Blood, in her defence shed:
> The Heavens have his Soul, the Arts have his Fame,
> The Soldiers the grief, the World his good Name.

There were many points in which the case of Sidney resembled that of Charles I.st: He was a Sovereign but of a nobler kind—a Sovereign in the hearts of Men: and after his premature death he was truly, as he hath been styled, 'the world-mourned Sidney'.[15] So fondly did the admiration of his Contemporaries settle upon him, that the sudden removal of a man so good, great, and thoroughly accomplished, wrought upon many even to repining, and to the questioning the dispensations of Providence. Yet he, whom Spenser and all the Men of Genius of his Age had tenderly bemoaned, is thus commemorated upon his Tombstone; and to add to the indignity, the memorial is nothing more than the second-hand Coat of a French Commander! It is a servile translation from a French Epitaph, which, says Weever, 'was by some English Wit happily imitated and ingeniously applied to the honour of our worthy Chieftain'.[16] Yet Weever, in a foregoing Paragraph thus expresses himself upon the same Subject; giving without his own knowledge, in my opinion, an example of the manner in which such an Epitaph ought to have been composed.—[17]

'But here I cannot pass over in silence Sir Philip Sidney the elder brother, being (to use Camden's words) the glorious star of this family, a lively pattern of virtue, and the lovely joy of all the learned sort; who fighting valiantly with the enemy before Zutphen in Gelderland, dyed manfully. This is that Sidney, whom, as God's will was, he should therefore be born into the world even to shew unto our age a sample of ancient virtues: so his good pleasure was, before any man looked for it, to call for him again, and take him out of the world, as being more worthy of heaven than earth. Thus we may see perfect virtue suddenly vanisheth out of sight, and the best men continue not long.'

There can be no need to analyse this simple effusion of the moment in order to contrast it with the laboured composition before given: the difference will flash upon the Reader at once. But I may say, it is not likely that such a frigid composition as the former would have ever been applied to a Man whose death had so stirred up the hearts of his Contemporaries, if it had not been felt that something different from that nature which each Man carried in his own breast was in this case requisite; and that a certain *straining* of mind was inseparable from the Subject. Accordingly, an Epitaph is adopted in which the Writer had turned from the genuine affections and their self-forgetting inspirations, to the end that his Understanding, or the faculty designated by the word *head* as opposed to *heart*, might curiously construct a fabric to be wondered at. Hyperbole in the language of Montrose is a mean instrument made mighty because wielded by an afflicted Soul, and strangeness is here the order of Nature. Montrose stretched after remote things but was at the same time propelled towards them; the French Writer goes deliberately in search of them; no wonder then if what he brings home does not prove worth the carriage!

Let us return to an instance of common life. I quote it with reluctance, not so much for its absurdity as that the expression in one place will strike at first sight as little less than impious; and it is indeed, though unintentionally so, most irreverent. But I know no other example that will so forcibly illustrate the important truth I wish to establish. The following Epitaph is to be found in a Church-yard in Westmorland which the present Writer has reason to think of with interest as it contains the remains of some of his Ancestors and Kindred. The date is 1673.[18]

Under this Stone, Reader, inter'd doth lye,
   Beauty and virtue's true epitomy.
At her appearance the noone-son
   Blush'd and shrunk in 'cause quite outdon.
In her concenter'd did all graces dwell:
   God pluck'd my rose that he might take a smel.
I'll say no more: But weeping wish I may
   Soone with thy dear chaste ashes com to lay.
                              Sic efflevit Maritus

Can any thing go beyond this in extravagance? Yet, if the funda-
mental thoughts be translated into a natural style, they will be found
reasonable and affecting—

'The Woman who lies here interred, was in my eyes a perfect
image of beauty and virtue; she was to me a brighter object than
the Sun in heaven: God took her, who was my delight, from this
earth to bring her nearer to himself. Nothing further is worthy to
be said than that weeping I wish soon to lie by thy dear chaste
ashes—Thus did the Husband pour out his tears.'

These verses are preceeded by a brief account of the Lady, in
Latin prose; in which the little that is said is the uncorrupted
language of affection. But, without this introductory communication, I should myself have had no doubt, after recovering from the
first shock of surprize and disapprobation, that this man, notwithstanding his extravagant expressions was a sincere mourner; and
that his heart, during the very act of composition, was moved. These
fantastic images, though they stain the writing, stained not his soul.
—They did not even touch it; but hung like globules of rain sus-
pended above a green leaf, along which they may roll and leave no
trace that they have passed over it. This simple-hearted Man must
have been betrayed by a common notion that what was natural in
prose would be out of place in verse;—that it is not the Muse which
puts on the Garb but the Garb which makes the Muse. And, having
adopted this notion at a time when vicious writings of this kind
accorded with the public taste, it is probable that, in the excess of
his modesty, the blankness of his inexperience, and the intensity of
his affection, he thought that the further he wandered from nature[19]
in his language the more would he honour his departed Consort,
who now appeared to him to have surpassed humanity in the
excellence of her endowments. The quality of his fault and its very
excess are both in favour of this conclusion.

Let us contrast this Epitaph with one taken from a celebrated Writer of the last Century.[20]

> '*To the memory of* LUCY LYTTLETON, *Daughter &c*
> *who departed this life &c aged 29. Having employed*
> *the short time assigned to her here in the uniform*
> *practice of religion and virtue.*
>
> Made to engage all hearts, and charm all eyes;
> Though meek, magnanimous; though witty, wise;
> Polite, as all her life in courts had been;
> Yet good, as she the world had never seen;
> The noble fire of an exalted mind,
> With gentle female tenderness combined.
> Her speech was the melodious voice of love,
> Her song the warbling of the vernal grove;
> Her eloquence was sweeter than her song,
> Soft as her heart, and as her reason strong;
> Her form each beauty of the mind express'd,
> Her mind was Virtue by the Graces drest.'

The prose part of this inscription has the appearance of being intended for a Tomb-stone; but there is nothing in the verse that would suggest such a thought. The composition is in the style of those laboured portraits in words which we sometimes see placed at the bottom of a print, to fill up lines of expression which the bungling Artist had left imperfect. We know from other evidence that Lord Lyttleton dearly loved his wife: he has indeed composed a monody to her memory which proves this, and that she was an amiable Woman; neither of which facts could have been gathered from these inscriptive Verses. This Epitaph would derive little advantage from being translated into another style as the former was; for there is no under current, no skeleton or stamina, of thought and feeling. The Reader will perceive at once that nothing in the heart of the Writer had determined either the choice, the order, or the expression, of the ideas—that there is no interchange of action from within and from without—that the connections are mechanical and arbitrary, and the lowest kind of these—Heart and Eyes—petty alliterations, as meek and magnanimous, witty and wise, combined with oppositions in thoughts where there is no necessary or natural opposition. These defects run through the whole; the only tolerable verse is,

'Her speech was the melodious voice of love.'

Observe, the question is not which of these Epitaphs is better or worse; but which faults are of a worse *kind*. In the former case we have a Mourner whose soul is occupied by grief and urged forward by his admiration. He deems in his simplicity that no hyperbole can transcend the perfections of her whom he has lost: for the version which I have given fairly demonstrates that, in spite of his outrageous expressions, the under current of his thoughts was natural and pure. We have therefore in him the example of a mind misled during the act of composition by false taste—to the highest possible degree; and, in that of Lord Lyttleton, we have one of a feeling heart, not merely misled, but wholly laid asleep by the same power. Lord Lyttleton could not have written in this way upon such a subject, if he had not been seduced by the example of Pope, whose sparkling and tuneful manner had bewitched the men of letters his Contemporaries, and corrupted the judgment of the Nation through all ranks of society.[21]

The course which we have taken having brought us to the name of this distinguished Writer, I will in this place give a few observations upon his Epitaphs, the largest collection we have in our language, from the pen of any Writer of eminence. As the Epitaphs of Pope, and also those of Chiabrera,[22] which occasioned this disquisition, are in metre, it may be proper here to enquire how far the notion of a perfect Epitaph, as given in a former Paper, may be modified by the choice of metre for the vehicle in preference to prose. If our opinions be just, it is manifest that the basis must remain the same in either case; and that the difference can only lie in the superstructure; and it is equally plain, that a judicious Man will be less disposed in this case than in any other to avail himself of the liberty given by metre to adopt phrases of fancy, or to enter into the more remote regions of illustrative imagery. For the occasion of writing an Epitaph is matter of fact in its intensity, and forbids more authoritatively than any other species of composition all modes of fiction, except those which the very strength of passion has created; which have been acknowledged by the human heart, and have become so familiar that they are converted into substantial realities. When I come to the Epitaphs of Chiabrera, I shall perhaps give instances in which I think he has not written under the impression of this truth: where the poetic imagery does not elevate, deepen, or refine the human passion, which it ought always to do or not to act at all, but excludes it. In a far greater degree are Pope's Epitaphs debased by faults into which he could not I think have fallen if he had written in prose as a plain Man, and not as a metrical Wit. I will transcribe from Pope's Epitaphs the one upon M:ˢ Corbet (who died of a Cancer); D: Johnson having extolled it highly and pronounced it the best of the collection.[23]

> Here rests a Woman, good without pretence,
> Blest with plain reason and with sober sense;
> No conquest she but o'er herself desir'd;
> No arts essayed, but not to be admir'd.
> Passion and pride were to her soul unknown,
> Convinc'd that virtue only is our own.
> So unaffected, so compos'd a mind,
> So firm, yet soft, so strong, yet so refin'd
> Heaven as it's purest gold by tortures tried
> The Saint sustain'd it, but the Woman died.

This *may* be the best of Pope's Epitaphs; but if the standard which we have fixed be a just one it cannot be approved of. First, it must be observed, that in the Epitaphs of this Writer the true impulse is always wanting, and that his motions must of necessity be feeble. For he has no other aim than to give a favourable *Portrait* of the Character of the Deceased. Now mark the process by which this is performed. Nothing is represented implicitly, that is, with its accompaniment of circumstances, or conveyed by its effects. The Author forgets that it is a living creature that must interest us and not an intellectual Existence, which a mere character is. Insensible to this distinction the brain of the Writer is set at work to report as flatteringly as he may of the mind of his subject; the good qualities are separately abstracted (can it be otherwise than coldly and un-feelingly?) and put together again as coldly and unfeelingly. The Epitaph now before us owes what exemption it may have from these defects in its general plan to the excruciating disease of which the Lady died; but it too is liable to the same censure; and is, like the rest, further objectionable in this: namely, that the thoughts have their nature changed and moulded by the vicious expression in which they are entangled, to an excess rendering them wholly unfit for the place which they occupy.

> 'Here rests a Woman good without pretence
> Blest with plain reason'

—from which, *sober sense* is not sufficiently distinguishable. This verse and a half, and the one, *so unaffected, so composed a mind*, are characteristic,[24] and the expression is true to nature; but they are, if I may take the liberty of saying it, the only parts of the Epitaph which have this merit. Minute criticism is in its nature irksome; and, as commonly practised in books and conversation, is both irksome and injurious. Yet every mind must occasionally be exercised in this discipline, else it cannot learn the art of bringing words rigorously to the test of thoughts; and these again to a comparison with things, their archetypes; contemplated first in themselves, and secondly in relation to each other; in all which processes the mind must be skilful, otherwise it will be perpetually imposed upon. In the next couplet the word, *conquest*, is applied in a manner that would have been displeasing even from its triteness in a copy of complimentary Verses to a fashionable Beauty; but to talk of making conquests in an Epitaph is not to be endured. *No arts essayed, but not to be admired* —are words expressing that she had recourse to artifices to conceal her amiable and admirable qualities; and the context implies that there was a merit in this; which surely no sane mind would allow. But the meaning of the Author, simply and honestly given, was nothing more than that she shunned admiration, probably with a more apprehensive modesty than was common; and more than this would have been inconsistent with the praise bestowed upon her— that she had an unaffected mind. This couplet is further objection- able, because the sense of love and peaceful admiration, which such a character naturally inspires, is disturbed by an oblique and ill- timed stroke of satire. She is not praised so much as others are blamed—and is degraded by the Author in thus being made a covert or stalking-horse for gratifying a propensity the most abhorrent from her own nature. '*Passion and pride were to her soul unknown*'— It cannot be meant that she had no Passions, but that they were moderate and kept in subordination to her reason; but the thought is not here expressed; nor is it clear that a conviction in the under- standing that *virtue only is our own*, though it might suppress her pride, would be itself competent to govern or abate many other affec- tions and passions to which our frail nature is, and ought, in various degrees, to be subject.—In fact, the Author appears to have had no precise notion of his own meaning. If she was '*good without pretence*' it seems unnecessary to say that she was not proud. D[r]. Johnson, making an exception of the verse, *Convinced that virtue only is our own*, praises this Epitaph for 'containing nothing taken from common places.'[25] Now in fact, as may be deduced from the principles of this discourse, it is not only no fault but a primary requisite in an Epitaph that it shall contain thoughts and feelings which are in their substance common-place, and even trite. It is grounded upon the universal intellectual property of man;—sensations which all men have felt and feel in some degree daily and hourly;—truths whose very interest and importance have caused them to be unattended to, as things which could take care of themselves. But it is required that these truths should be instinctively ejaculated, or should rise irresistibly from circumstances; in a word that they should be uttered in such connection as shall make it felt that they are not adopted—not spoken by rote, but perceived in their whole compass with the freshness and clearness of an original intuition. The Writer must introduce the truth with such accompaniment as shall imply that he has mounted to the sources of things—penetrated the dark cavern from which the River that murmurs in every one's ear has flowed from generation to generation. The line *'Virtue only is our own'*—is objectionable, not from the commonplaceness of the Truth, but from the vapid manner in which it is conveyed. A similar sentiment is expressed with appropriate dignity in an Epitaph by Chiabrera, where he makes the Archbishop of Urbino say of himself, that he was[26]

> —'smitten by the great Ones of the world,
> But did not fall; for Virtue braves all shocks,
> Upon herself resting immoveably.'

'So firm yet soft, so strong yet so refined'—these intellectual operations (while they can be conceived of as operations of intellect at all, for in fact one half of the process is mechanical, words doing their own work, and one half of the line manufacturing the rest) remind me of the motions of a Posture-Master, or of a Man balancing a Sword upon his finger, which must be kept from falling at all hazards. *'The Saint sustained it but the Woman died'*—Let us look steadily at this antithesis—the *Saint*, that is her soul strengthened by Religion supported the anguish of her disease with patience and resignation;—but the *Woman*, that is her *body*, (for if any thing else be meant by the word, woman, it contradicts the former part of the proposition and the passage is nonsense) was overcome. Why was not this simply expressed; without playing with the Reader's fancy to the delusion and dishonour of his Understanding, by a trifling epigrammatic point? But alas! ages must pass away before men will have their eyes open to the beauty and majesty of Truth, and will be taught to venerate Poetry no further than as She is a Handmaid pure as her Mistress—the noblest Handmaid in her train!

ESSAY UPON EPITAPHS, III

I vindicate the rights and dignity of Nature,[1] and, as long as I condemn nothing without assigning reasons not lightly given, I cannot suffer any Individual, however highly and deservedly honoured by my Countrymen, to stand in my way. If my notions are right, the Epitaphs of Pope cannot well be too severely condemned: for not only are they almost wholly destitute of those universal feelings and simple movements of mind which we have called for as indispensible, but they are little better than a tissue of false thoughts, languid and vague expression, unmeaning antithesis, and laborious attempts at discrimination. Pope's mind had been employed chiefly in observation upon the vices and follies of men. Now, vice and folly are in contradiction with the moral principle which can never be extinguished in the mind: and, therefore, wanting this controul, are irregular, capricious, and inconsistent with themselves. If a man has once said, (see FRIEND No. 6) 'Evil be thou my Good!'[2] and has acted accordingly, however strenuous may have been his adherence to this principle, it will be well known by those who have had an opportunity of observing him narrowly that there have been perpetual obliquities in his course; evil passions thwarting each other in various ways; and, now and then, revivals of his better nature, which check him for a short time or lead him to remeasure his steps: —not to speak of the various necessities of counterfeiting virtue which the furtherance of his schemes will impose upon him, and the division which will be consequently introduced into his nature.

It is reasonable, then, that Cicero, when holding up Catiline to detestation; and, (without going to such an extreme case) that Dryden and Pope, when they are describing Characters like Buckingham, Shaftsbury, Wharton, and the Duchess of Marlborough,[3] should represent qualities and actions at war with each other and with themselves: and that the page should be suitably crowded with antithetical expressions. But all this argues an obtuse moral sensibility and a consequent want of knowledge, if applied where virtue ought to be described in the language of affectionate admiration. In the mind of the truly great and good every thing that is of importance is at peace with itself; all is stillness, sweetness, and stable grandeur. Accordingly the contemplation of virtue is attended with repose. A lovely quality, if its loveliness be clearly perceived, fastens the mind with absolute sovereignty upon itself; permitting or inciting it to pass, by smooth gradation or gentle transition, to some other kindred quality. Thus a perfect image of meekness, (I refer to an instance before given)[4] when looked at by a tender mind in its happiest mood, might easily lead on to the thought of magnanimity: for assuredly there is nothing incongruous in those virtues. But the mind would not then be separated from the Person who is the object of its thoughts: it would still be confined to that Person, or to others of the same general character; that is, would be kept within the circle of qualities which range themselves quietly by each other's sides. Whereas, when meekness and magnanimity are represented antithetically, the mind is not only carried from the main object, but is compelled to turn to a subject in which the quality exists divided from some other as noble, its natural ally:—a painful feeling! that checks the course of love, and repels the sweet thoughts that might be settling round the Person whom it was the Author's wish to endear to us; but for whom, after this interruption, we no longer care. If then a Man, whose duty it is to praise departed excellence not without some sense of regret or sadness, to do this or to be silent, should upon all occasions exhibit that mode of connecting thoughts which is only natural while we are delineating vice under certain relations, we may be assured that the nobler sympathies are not alive in him; that he has no clear insight into the internal constitution of virtue; nor has himself been soothed, cheared, harmonized, by those outward effects which follow every where her goings,—declaring the presence of the invisible deity. And though it be true that the most admirable of Men must fall far short of perfection, and that the majority of those whose worth is commemorated upon their Tombstones must have been Persons in whom good and evil were intermixed in various proportions, and stood in various degrees of opposition to each other, yet the reader will remember what has been said before upon that medium of love, sorrow, and admiration through which a departed friend is viewed: how it softens down or removes these harshnesses and contradictions; which, moreover, must be supposed never to have been grievous: for there can be no true love but between the good; and no Epitaph ought to be written upon a bad Man, except for a warning.

The purpose of the remarks given in the last Essay was chiefly to assist the reader in separating truth and sincerity from falsehood and affectation; presuming that if the unction of a devout heart be wanting every thing else is of no avail. It was shewn that a current of just thought and feeling may flow under a surface of illustrative imagery so impure as to produce an effect the opposite of that which was intended. Yet, though this fault may be carried to an intolerable *degree*, the reader will have gathered that in our estimation it is not *in kind* the most offensive and injurious. We have contrasted it in its excess with instances where the genuine current or vein was wholly wanting; where the thoughts and feelings had no vital union; but were artificially connected, or formally accumulated, in a manner that would imply discontinuity and feebleness of mind upon any occasion; but still more reprehensible here! I will proceed to give milder examples, not of this last kind but of the former; namely of failure from various causes where the groundwork is good.[5]

> Take, holy earth! all that my soul holds dear:
> Take that best gift which Heaven so lately gave:
> To Bristol's fount I bore with trembling care,
> Her faded form. She bow'd to taste the wave—
> And died. Does youth, does beauty read the line?
> Does sympathetic fear their breasts alarm?
> Speak, dead Maria! breathe a strain divine;
> Even from the grave thou shalt have power to charm.
> Bid them be chaste, be innocent, like thee:
> Bid them in duty's sphere as meekly move:
> And if so fair, from vanity as free,
> As firm in friendship, and as fond in love;
> Tell them, tho tis an awful thing to die,
> ('Twas e'en to thee) yet, the dread path once trod;
> Heaven lifts its everlasting portals high,
> And bids 'the pure in heart behold their God.'

This Epitaph has much of what we have demanded: but it is debased in some instances by weakness of expression, in others by false prettiness. '*She bow'd to taste the wave and died.*' The plain truth was, she drank the Bristol waters which failed to restore her, and her death soon followed; but the expression involves a multitude of petty occupations for the fancy: '*She bowed*'—was there any truth in this?—'*to taste the wave,*' the water of a mineral spring which must have been drunk out of a Goblet. Strange application of the word *Wave*! '*and died.*' This would have been a just expression if the water had killed her; but, as it is, the tender thought involved in the disappointment of a hope however faint is left unexpressed; and a shock of surprize is given, entertaining perhaps to a light fancy, but to a steady mind unsatisfactory—because false. '*Speak! dead*

Maria breathe a strain divine!' This verse flows nobly from the heart
and the imagination; but perhaps it is not one of those impassioned
thoughts which should be fixed in language upon a sepulchral stone.
It is in its nature too poignant and transitory. A Husband meditating
by his Wife's grave would throw off such a feeling, and would give
voice to it; and it would be in its place in a Monody to her Memory
but, if I am not mistaken, ought to have been suppressed here, or
uttered after a different manner. The implied impersonation of the
Deceased (according to the tenor of what has before been said) ought
to have been more general and shadowy. '*And if so fair, from vanity
as free—As firm in friendship and as fond in love—Tell them*', these
are two sweet verses, but the long suspension of the sense excites the
expectation of a thought less common than the concluding one; and
is an instance of a failure in doing what is most needful and most
difficult in an Epitaph to do; namely, to give to universally received
truths a pathos and spirit which shall re-admit them into the soul
like revelations of the moment.

I have said that this excellence is difficult to attain; and why? is
it because nature is weak?—no! Where the soul has been thoroughly
stricken, (and Heaven knows, the course of life has placed all men, at
some time or other, in that condition) there is never a want of
positive strength; but because the adversary of nature, (call that
adversary Art or by what name you will) is *comparatively* strong. The
far-searching influence of the power, which, for want of a better
name, we will denominate, Taste, is in nothing more evinced than in
the changeful character and complexion of that species of composition which we have been reviewing. Upon a call so urgent, it might
be expected that the affections, the memory, and the imagination
would be *constrained* to speak their genuine language. Yet if the few
specimens which have been given in the course of this enquiry do
not demonstrate the fact, the Reader need only look into any collection of Epitaphs to be convinced that the faults predominant in the
literature of every age will be as strongly reflected in the sepulchral
inscriptions as any where; nay perhaps more so, from the anxiety of
the Author to do justice to the occasion: and especially if the composition be in verse; for then it comes more avowedly in the shape
of a work of art; and, of course, is more likely to be coloured by the
works of art holden in most esteem at the time. In a bulky Volume
of Poetry entitled, ELEGANT EXTRACTS in Verse,[6] which must be known
to most of my Readers, as it is circulated every where and in fact
constitutes at this day the poetical library of our Schools, I find a

number of Epitaphs, in verse, of the last century; and there is
scarcely one which is not thoroughly tainted by the artifices which
have overrun our writings in metre since the days of Dryden and
Pope. Energy, stillness, grandeur, tenderness, those feelings which
are the pure emanations of nature, those thoughts which have the
infinitude of truth, and those expressions which are not what the
garb is to the body[7] but what the body is to the soul, themselves a
constituent part and power or function in the thought—all these are
abandoned for their opposites,—as if our Countrymen, through
successive generations, had lost the sense of solemnity and pensive-
ness (not to speak of deeper emotions) and resorted to the Tombs of
their Forefathers and Contemporaries only to be tickled and sur-
prized. Would we not recoil from such gratifications, in such a place,
if the general literature of the Country had not co-operated with
other causes insidiously to weaken our sensibilities and deprave our
judgements? Doubtless, there are shocks of event and circumstance,
public and private, by which for all minds the truths of Nature will
be elicited; but sorrow for that Individual or people to whom these
special interferences are necessary, to bring them into communion
with the inner spirit of things! for such intercourse must be profitless
in proportion as it is unfrequent, irregular, and transient. Words are
too awful an instrument for good and evil to be trifled with: they
hold above all other external powers a dominion over thoughts. If
words be not (recurring to a metaphor before used) an incarnation
of the thought but only a clothing for it, then surely will they prove
an ill gift; such a one as those poisoned vestments,[8] read of in the
stories of superstitious times, which had power to consume and to
alienate from his right mind the victim who put them on. Language,
if it do not uphold, and feed, and leave in quiet, like the power of
gravitation or the air we breathe, is a counter-spirit, unremittingly
and noiselessly at work to derange, to subvert, to lay waste, to vitiate,
and to dissolve. From a deep conviction then that the excellence of
writing, whether in prose or verse, consists in a conjunction of
Reason and Passion, a conjunction which must be of necessity
benign; and that it might be deduced from what has been said that
the taste, intellectual Power, and morals of a Country are inseparably
linked in mutual dependence, I have dwelt thus long upon this argument. And the occasion justifies me: for how could the tyranny of
bad taste be brought home to the mind more aptly than by shewing
in what degree the feelings of nature yield to it when we are rendering to our friends this solemn testimony of our love? more forcibly

than by giving proof that thoughts cannot, even upon this impulse, assume an outward life without a transmutation and a fall?

'Epitaph on Miss Drummond in the Church of
Brodsworth, Yorkshire
Mason[9]

Here sleeps what once was beauty, once was grace;
Grace, that with tenderness and sense combin'd
To form that harmony of soul and face,
Where beauty shines the mirror of the mind,
Such was the maid, that in the morn of youth,
In virgin innocence, in nature's pride,
Blest with each art, that owes its charms to truth,
Sunk in her Father's fond embrace, and died.
He weeps: O venerate the holy tear!
Faith lends her aid to ease affliction's load;
The parent mourns his Child upon the bier,
The christian yields an angel to his God.'

The following is a translation from the Latin, communicated to a Lady in her Childhood and by her preserved in memory. I regret that I have not seen the original.

She is gone—my beloved Daughter Eliza is gone,
Fair, chearful, benign, my child is gone.
Thee long to be regretted a Father mourns,
Regretted—but thanks to the most perfect God! not lost
For a happier age approaches
When again my child I shall behold
And live with thee for ever.

Mathew Dobson to his dear, engaging, happy Eliza.

Who in the 18th year of her Age
Passed peaceably into heaven.[10]

The former of these Epitaphs is very far from being the worst of its kind, and on that account I have placed the two in contrast. Unquestionably, as the Father in the latter speaks in his own Person, the situation is much more pathetic; but, making due allowance for this advantage, who does not here feel a superior truth and sanctity, which is not dependent upon this circumstance, but merely the result of the expression and the connection of the thoughts? I am not so fortunate as to have any knowledge of the Author of this affecting Composition, but I much fear, if he had called in the assistance of English verse the better to convey his thoughts, such sacrifices would, from various influences, have been made *even by him*, that, though he might have excited admiration in thousands, he would have truly moved no one. The latter part of the following by Gray is almost the only instance, among the metrical Epitaphs in our language of the last Century, which I remember, of affecting thoughts rising naturally and keeping themselves pure from vicious diction.

Epitaph on Mrs Clark.[11]

> Lo! where the silent marble weeps,
> A friend, a wife, a mother, sleeps;
> A heart, within whose sacred cell
> The peaceful virtues lov'd to dwell.
> Affection warm, and love sincere,
> And soft humanity were there.
> In agony, in death resigned,
> She felt the wound she left behind.
> Her infant image, here below,
> Sits smiling on a father's woe:
> Whom what awaits, while yet he strays
> Along the lonely vale of days?
> A pang to secret sorrow dear;
> A sigh, an unavailing tear,
> Till time shall every grief remove,
> With life, with memory, and with love.

I have been speaking of faults which are aggravated by temptations thrown in the way of modern Writers when they compose in metre. The first six lines of this Epitaph are vague and languid, more so than I think would have been possible had it been written in prose. Yet Gray, who was so happy in the remaining part, especially the last four lines, has grievously failed *in prose*, upon a subject which it might have been expected would have bound him indissolubly to the propriety of Nature and comprehensive reason. I allude to the conclusion of the Epitaph upon his Mother, where he says, 'she was the careful tender Mother of many Children, one of whom alone had the misfortune to survive her.'[12] This is a searching thought, but wholly out of place. Had it been said of an ideot, of a palsied child, or of an adult from any cause dependent upon his Mother to a degree of helplessness which nothing but maternal tenderness and watchfulness could answer, that he had the misfortune to survive his Mother, the thought would have been just. The same might also have been wrung from any Man (thinking of himself) when his soul was smitten with compunction or remorse, through the consciousness of a misdeed, from which he might have been preserved (as he hopes or believes) by his Mother's prudence, by her anxious care if longer continued or by the reverential fear of offending or distressing her. But even then (unless accompanied with a detail of extraordinary circumstances) if transferred to her monument, it would have been mis-placed, as being too peculiar; and for reasons which have been before alledged, namely, as too transitory and poignant. But in an ordinary case, for a Man permanently and conspicuously to record that this was his fixed feeling; what is it but to run counter to the course of nature, which has made it matter of expectation and congratulation that Parents should die before their Children? what is it, if searched to the bottom, but lurking and sickly selfishness? Does not the regret include a wish that the Mother should have survived all her offspring, have witnessed that bitter desolation, where the order of things is disturbed and inverted? And finally does it not withdraw the attention of the Reader from the Subject to the Author of the Memorial, as one to be commiserated for his strangely unhappy condition, or to be condemned for the morbid constitution of his feelings, or for his deficiency in judgment? A fault of the same kind, though less in degree, is found in the Epitaph of Pope upon Harcourt; of whom it is said that 'he never gave his father grief but when he died.'[13] I need not point out how many situations there are in which such an expression of feeling would be natural and becoming; but in a permanent Inscription things only should be admitted that have an enduring place in the mind: and a nice selection is required even among these. The Duke of Ormond said of his Son Ossory, 'that he preferred his dead Son to any living Son in Christendom,'—a thought which (to adopt an expression used before) has the infinitude of truth! But, though in this there is no momentary illusion, nothing fugitive, it would still have been unbecoming, had it been placed in open view over the Son's grave; inasmuch as such expression of it would have had an ostentatious air, and would have implied a disparagement of others. The sublimity of the sentiment consists in its being the secret possession of the Father.[14]

Having been engaged so long in the ungracious office of sitting in judgement where I have found so much more to censure than to approve, though wherever it was in my power, I have placed good by the side of evil, that the Reader might intuitively receive the truths which I wished to communicate, I now turn back with pleasure to Chiabrera; of whose productions in this department the Reader of THE FRIEND may be enabled to form a judgment who has attentively perused the few specimens only which have been given.[15] 'An Epitaph' says Weever 'is a superscription (either in verse or prose) or an astrict pithie Diagram, writ, carved, or engraven, upon the tomb, grave, or sepulchre of the defunct, briefly declaring (*and that with a kind of commiseration*) the name, the age, the deserts, the dignities, the state, *the praises both of body and minde*, the good and bad fortunes in the life and the manner and time of the death of the person therein interred.'[16] This account of an Epitaph, which as far as it goes is just, was no doubt taken by Weever from the Monuments of our own Country, and it shews that in his conception an Epitaph was not to be an abstract character of the deceased but an epitomized biography blended with description by which an impression of the character was to be conveyed. Bring forward the one incidental expression, a kind of commiseration, unite with it a concern on the part of the dead for the well-being of the living made known by exhortation and admonition, and let this commiseration and concern pervade and brood over the whole so that what was peculiar to the individual shall still be subordinate to a sense of what he had in common with the species—our notion of a perfect Epitaph would then be realized, and it pleases me to say that this is the very model upon which those of Chiabrera are for the most part framed. Observe how exquisitely this is exemplified in the one beginning 'Pause courteous Stranger! Baldi supplicates' given in THE FRIEND some weeks ago.[17] The Subject of the Epitaph is introduced intreating, not directly in his own Person but through the mouth of the Author, that according to the religious belief of his Country a Prayer for his soul might be preferred to the Redeemer of the World. Placed in counterpoize with this right which he has in common with all the dead, his individual earthly accomplishments appear light to his funereal Biographer, as they did to the person of whom he speaks when alive, nor could Chiabrera have ventured to touch upon them but under the sanction of this previous acknowledgement. He then goes on to say how various and profound was his learning and how deep a hold it took upon his affections, but that he weaned himself

from these things as vanities and was devoted in later life exclusively
to the divine truths of the Gospel as the only knowledge in which he
could find perfect rest. Here we are thrown back upon the introductory supplication and made to feel its especial propriety in this
case: his life was long and every part of it bore appropriate fruits;
Urbino his birth-place might be proud of him, and the Passenger
who was entreated to pray for his soul has a wish breathed for his
welfare.—This composition is a perfect whole; there is nothing
arbitrary or mechanical, but it is an organized body of which the
members are bound together by a common life and are all justly pro-
portioned. If I had not gone so much into detail, I should have
given further instances of Chiabrera's Epitaphs, but I must content
myself with saying that if he had abstained from the introduction of
heathen mythology of which he is lavish—an inexcusable fault for
an Inhabitant of a Christian country, yet admitting of some palliation
in an Italian who treads classic soil and has before his eyes the ruins
of the temples which were dedicated to those ficticious beings as
objects of worship by the majestic People, his Ancestors—had
omitted also some uncharacteristic particulars and had not on some
occasions forgotten that truth is the soul of passion, he would have
left his readers little to regret. I do not mean to say that higher and
nobler thoughts may not be found in sepulchral Inscriptions than
his contain, but he understood his work; the principles upon which
he composed are just. The Reader of THE FRIEND has had proofs of
this; one shall be given of his mixed manner, exemplifying some of
the points in which he has erred.[18]

> O Lelius, beauteous flower of gentleness,
> The fair Aglaia's friend above all friends,
> O darling of the fascinating Loves,
> By what dire envy moved did Death uproot
> Thy days ere yet full blown, and what ill chance
> Hath robbed Savona of her noblest grace?
> She weeps for thee, and shall for ever weep,
> And if the fountain of her tears should fail,
> She would implore Sebeto to supply
> Her need; Sebeto sympathizing stream,
> Who on his margin saw thee close thine eyes
> On the chaste bosom of thy Lady dear.
> Ah what do riches, what does youth avail?
> Dust are our hopes; I weeping did inscribe

> In bitterness thy Monument, and pray
> Of every gentle Spirit bitterly
> To read the record with as copious tears.

This Epitaph is not without some tender thoughts, but a comparison of it with the one upon the youthful Pozzobonelli (see FRIEND No. 20)[19] will more clearly shew that Chiabrera has here neglected to ascertain whether the passions expressed were in kind and degree a dispensation of reason or at least commodities issued under her licence and authority.

The Epitaphs of Chiabrera are twenty-nine in number, all of them save two upon Men probably little known at this day in their own Country and scarcely at all beyond the limits of it, and the reader is generally made acquainted with the moral and intellectual excellence which distinguished them by a brief history of the course of their lives or a selection of events and circumstances, and thus they are individualized; but in the two other instances—namely, those of Tasso and Raphael—he enters into no particulars, but contents himself with four lines expressing one sentiment, upon the principle laid down in the former part of this discourse[20] where the Subject of an Epitaph is a Man of prime note.[21]

> Torquato Tasso rests within this Tomb:
> This Figure, weeping from her inmost heart,
> Is Poesy: from such impassioned grief
> Let every one conclude what this Man was.

The Epitaph which Chiabrera composed for himself has also an appropriate brevity and is distinguished for its grandeur, the sentiment being the same as that which the Reader has before seen so happily enlarged upon.[22]

As I am brought back to Men of first rate distinction and public Benefactors, I cannot resist the pleasure of transcribing the metrical part of an Epitaph which formerly was inscribed in the Church of St. Paul's to that Bishop of London who prevailed with William the Conqueror to secure to the inhabitants of the City all the liberties and privileges which they had enjoyed in the time of Edward the Confessor.[23]

> These marble Monuments to thee thy Citizens assigne,
> Rewards (O Father) farre unfit to those deserts of thine,
> Thee unto them a faithful friend, thy London people found,

And to this towne of no small weight a stay both sure and sound.
Their liberties restorde to them, by meanes of thee have beene,
Their publicke weale by meanes of thee, large gifts have felt
   and seene,
Thy riches, stocke, and beauty brave, one hour hath them
   supprest,
Yet these thy virtues, and good deeds with us for ever rest.

Thus have I attempted to determine what a sepulchral Inscription
ought to be, and taken at the same time a survey of what Epitaphs
are good and bad, and have shewn to what deficiencies in sensibility
and to what errors in taste and judgement most commonly are to be
ascribed.[24]—It was my intention to have given a few specimens from
those of the Ancients but I have already I fear taken up too much of
the Reader's time. I have not animadverted upon such—alas! far too
numerous—as are reprehensible from the want of moral rectitude in
those who have composed them or given it to be understood that
they should be so composed: boastful and haughty panegyrics,
ludicrously contradicting the solid remembrance of those who knew
the deceased, shocking the common sense of mankind by their
extravagance and affronting the very altar with their impious falsehood. These I leave to general scorn, not however without a general
recommendation that they who have offended or may be disposed to
offend in this manner would take into serious thought the heinous-
ness of their transgression.

   Upon reviewing what has been written, I think it better here to
add a few favourable specimens such as are ordinarily found in our
Country Church-Yards at this day. If those primary sensations upon
which I have dwelt so much be not stifled in the heart of the Reader,
they will be read with pleasure; otherwise neither these nor more
exalted strains can by him be truly interpreted.[25]

> *Aged 87 and 83*
> Not more with silver hairs than virtue crown'd
> The good old Pair take up this spot of ground:
> Tread in their steps and you will surely find
> Their Rest above, below their peace of mind.

> At the Last day I'm sure I shall appear
> To meet with Jesus Christ my Saviour dear,
> Where I do hope to live with him in bliss;
> Oh, what a joy in my last hour was this!

Aged 3 Month
What Christ said once he said to all:
Come unto me, ye Children small;
None shall do you any wrong,
For to my kingdom you belong.

Aged 10 Weeks
The Babe was sucking at the breast
When God did call him to his rest.[25]

In an obscure corner of a Country Church-yard I once espied, half-overgrown with Hemlock and Nettles, a very small Stone laid upon the ground, bearing nothing more than the name of the Deceased with the date of birth and death, importing that it was an Infant which had been born one day and died the following. I know not how far the Reader may be in sympathy with me, but more awful thoughts of rights conferred, of hopes awakened, of remembrances stealing away or vanishing were imparted to my mind by that Inscription there before my eyes than by any other that it has ever been my lot to meet with upon a Tomb-stone.[26]

The most numerous class of sepulchral Inscriptions do indeed record nothing else but the name of the buried Person, but that he was born upon one day and died upon another. Addison in the Spectator making this observation says, 'that he cannot look upon those registers of existence whether of brass or marble but as a kind of satire upon the departed persons who had left no other memorial of them than that they were born and that they died.'[27] In certain moods of mind this is a natural reflection, yet not perhaps the most salutary which the appearance might give birth to. As in these registers the name is mostly associated with others of the same family, this is a prolonged companionship, however shadowy; even a Tomb like this is a shrine to which the fancies of a scattered family may repair in pilgrimage; the thoughts of the individuals, without any communication with each other, must oftentimes meet here.— Such a frail memorial then is not without its tendency to keep families together; it feeds also local attachment, which is the tap-root of the tree of Patriotism.

I know not how I can withdraw more satisfactorily from this long disquisition than by offering to the Reader as a farewell memorial the following Verses, suggested to me by a concise Epitaph which I met with some time ago in one of the most retired vales among the

Mountains of Westmorland. There is nothing in the detail of the
Poem which is not either founded upon the Epitaph or gathered from
enquiries concerning the Deceased made in the neighbourhood.[28]

Beneath that Pine which rears its dusky head
Aloft, and covered by a plain blue stone
Briefly inscribed, a gentle Dalesman lies,
From whom in early childhood was withdrawn
The precious gift of hearing. He grew up
From year to year in loneliness of soul;
And this deep mountain valley was to him
Soundless, with all its streams. The bird of dawn
Did never rouze this Cottager from sleep
With startling summons: not for his delight
The vernal cuckoo shouted; not for him
Murmured the labouring bee. When stormy winds
Were working the broad bosom of the lake
Into a thousand, thousand sparkling waves,
Rocking the trees, or driving cloud on cloud
Along the sharp edge of yon lofty crags,
The agitated scene before his eye
Was silent as a picture: evermore
Were all things silent, wheresoe'er he moved.
Yet, by the solace of his own calm thoughts
Upheld, he duteously pursued the round
Of rural labours: the steep mountain side
Ascended with his staff and faithful dog.
The plough he guided, and the scythe he swayed;
And the ripe corn before his sickle fell
Among the jocund reapers. For himself,
All watchful and industrious as he was,
He wrought not; neither field nor flock he owned:
No wish for wealth had place within his mind;
Nor husband's love, nor father's hope or care.
Though born a younger Brother, need was none
That from the floor of his paternal home
He should depart to plant himself anew.
And when, mature in manhood, he beheld
His Parents laid in earth, no loss ensued
Of rights to him, but he remained well pleased,
By the pure bond of independent love

An inmate of a second family,
The fellow-labourer and friend of him
To whom the small inheritance had fallen.
Nor deem that his mild presence was a weight
That pressed upon his Brother's house, for books
Were ready comrades whom he could not tire,—
Of whose society the blameless Man
Was never satiate. Their familiar voice,
Even to old age, with unabated charm
Beguiled his leisure hours; refreshed his thoughts;
Beyond its natural elevation raised
His introverted spirit; and bestowed
Upon his life an outward dignity
Which all acknowledged. The dark winter night,
The stormy day, had each its own resource;
Song of the muses, sage historic tale,
Science severe, or word of holy writ
Announcing immortality and joy
To the assembled spirits of the just,
From imperfection and decay secure.
Thus soothed at home, thus busy in the field,
To no perverse suspicion he gave way,
No languor, peevishness, nor vain complaint:
And they who were about him did not fail
In reverence or in courtesy; they prized
His gentle manners: and his peaceful smiles,
The gleams of his slow-varying countenance,
Were met with answering sympathy and love.
—At length, when sixty years and five were told,
A slow disease insensibly consumed
The powers of nature; and a few short steps
Of friends and kindred bore him from his home
(Yon Cottage shaded by the woody crags)
To the profounder stillness of the grave.
Nor was his funeral denied the grace
Of many tears, virtuous and thoughtful grief;
Heart-sorrow rendered sweet by gratitude.
And now that monumental Stone preserves
His name, and unambitiously relates
How long, and by what kindly outward aids,
And in what pure contentedness of mind,

The sad privation was by him endured.
And yon tall Pine-tree, whose composing sound
Was wasted on the good Man's living ear,
Hath now its own peculiar sanctity;
And at the touch of every wandering breeze
Murmurs not idly o'er his peaceful grave.

APPENDIX

I am anxious not to be misunderstood. It has already been stated that in this species of composition, above every other, our sensations and judgment depend upon our opinion or feeling of the Author's state of mind. Literature is here so far identified with morals, the quality of the act so far determined by our notion of the aim and purpose of the agent, that nothing can please us—however well executed in its kind—if we are persuaded that the primary virtues of sincerity, earnestness, and a real interest in the main object are wanting. Insensibility here shocks us and still more so if manifested by a Writer's going wholly out of his way in search of supposed beauties, which if he were truly moved, he could set no value upon—could not even think of. We are struck in this case not merely with a sense of disproportion and unfitness, but we cannot refrain from attributing no small part of his intellectual to a moral demerit. And here the difficulties of the question begin: namely, in ascertaining what errors in the choice of, or the mode of expressing, the thoughts most surely indicate the want of that which is most indispensable. Bad taste, whatever shape it may put on, is injurious to the heart and the understanding. If a man attaches much interest to the faculty of taste as it exists in himself and employs much time in those studies of which this faculty (I use the word *taste* in its comprehensive, though most unjustifiable, sense) is reckoned the arbiter, certain it is his moral notions and dispositions must either be purified and strengthened, or corrupted and impaired. How can it be otherwise when his ability to enter in the spirit of works in literature must depend upon his feeling, his imagination, and his understanding—that is, upon his recipient, upon his creative or active and upon his judging powers, and upon the accuracy and compass of his knowledge—in fine, upon all that makes up the moral and intellectual Man? What is true of individuals is equally true of nations. Nevertheless, a man called to a task in which he is not practised may have his expression thoroughly defiled and clogged by the style prevalent in his age; yet still through the force of circumstances that have roused him, his under feeling may remain strong and pure. Yet this may be wholly concealed from common view. Indeed, the favourite style of different ages is so different and wanders so far from propriety that if it were not that first rate writers in all nations and tongues are governed by common principles, we might suppose that truth and nature were things not to be looked for in books. Hence, to an unpractised reader the productions of every age will present obstacles in various degrees hard to surmount. A deformity of style, not the worst in itself but of that kind with which he is least familiar, will, on the one hand, be most likely to render him insensible to a pith and power which may be within; and, on the other hand, he will be the least able to see through that sort of falsehood which is most prevalent in the works of his own time. Many of my readers—to apply these general observations to the present case—must have derived much pleasure from the Epitaph of Lord Lyttleton, and no doubt will be startled at the comparison I have made. But bring it to the test recommended; it will then be found that its faults, though not in degree so intolerable, are in kind more radical and deadly than those of the strange composition with which it has been compared. It can derive no advantage from being translated into another style; it would not even admit of the process, for there is here no under-current, no skeleton, or stamina of appropriate feeling. The attentive Reader will perceive that nothing in the *heart* of the Writer had determined either the choice, the order, or the expression of the ideas; that there is no interchange of action from within or from without—no f[?], no stream. In the absence of a constituent vital power, the connections are mechanical and arbitrary, and the lowest kind of these: petty alliterations, as *meek* and *magnanimous*, combined with opposition in thoughts where there is no necessary or natural opposition. Then follow *voice, song, eloquence, form, mind*, each enumerated by a separate act as if the Author had been making a Catalogue Raisonné. Lord Lyttleton was a Man of real sensibility and could not have written in this way

NOTES

Essay upon Epitaphs, [*I*]

1 Wordsworth quotes Camden's *Remaines concerning Britain* as quoted, emended, and supplemented in John Weever, *Ancient Funerall Monuments*, London, 1631, 23. Weever is the source of many of Wordsworth's examples and of several passages of exposition. See *Prose*, ii. 100–19, *passim*.
2 Weever, op. cit. 9.
3 From Valerius Maximus, *Facta et Dicta Memorabilia*, I. vii, or Cicero, *De Divinatione*, I. xxvii. Cf. the sonnet 'I find it written', *PW*, iii. 408. The other 'ancient Philosopher' has not been identified.
4 Unidentified.
5 *All Saints' Church, Derby: A Poem*, Derby, 1805, 40–1. Just before the marked omission, Wordsworth's later texts read, wrongly, 'stayed'. Edwards was an admirer of Wordsworth's poems and Coleridge's *Friend*.
6 *Lives*, iii. 264. Johnson adapts Pope, *Moral Essays*, II. 2: 'Most women have no characters at all'.
7 'Epitaphs translated from Chiabrera', IV. 24 (*PW*, iv. 250).
8 Milton, 'On Shakespear', omitting six lines after 'monument'.

Essay upon Epitaphs, II

1 Gray, *Elegy written in a Country Churchyard*, 77–84.
2 Charles Lamb's *Rosamund Gray* (1798).
3 Shakespeare, *Richard III*, I. iii. 24–33. The phrase 'monsters of the deep' just before is from *King Lear*, IV. ii. 50, suggested by 'the slimy bottom of the deep' in the lines from *Richard III*.
4 See pp. 129–30 above.
5 *A Statistical Account of Scotland, drawn from the Communications of the Ministers of the Different Parishes. By Sir John Sinclair, Bart.*, 21 vols, Edinburgh, 1791–9. Various parishes report the kind of information Wordsworth is using: see *Prose*, ii. 106.
6 Reported and translated by Coleridge in a letter of 1799 (*CL*, i. 515).
7 Weever, op. cit. 545.
8 Ibid. 392.
9 Ibid. 331–2.
10 Ibid. 556.
11 Probably from William Hutchinson, *History and Antiquities of the County Palatine of Durham*, Carlisle, 1794, iii. 168. The epitaph is at Long Newton. Sir George Vane was not 'the noted Secretary of State' (Sir Henry Vane), but his son.

12 Probably from William Winstanley, *England's Worthies*, London, 1684, 532–3.

13 *Paradise Lost*, vi. 754–6; Ezek. 1 *passim*.

14 Weever, op. cit. 321.

15 In Joshua Sylvester's translation of Du Bartas; Wordsworth probably had the phrase from Winstanley, op. cit. 220.

16 Weever, op. cit. 320. The poem is an adaptation of Du Bellay's 'Epitaphe du Seigneur Bonivet'.

17 Weever, op. cit. 320. He is not 'expressing himself', but quoting Philemon Holland's translation (London, 1637, 329) of Camden's *Britannia*.

18 The memorial plate of Francisca Dawes, in Barton parish church, near Penrith. Wordsworth may have seen it himself, or taken it from Joseph Nicolson and Richard Burn, *History and Antiquities of the Counties of Westmorland and Cumberland*, London, 1777, i. 405. Richard Wordsworth of Sockburn, Wordsworth's grandfather, is buried there.

19 Natural expression.

20 Probably from Robert Anderson's *Poets of Great Britain*, London, 1795, x. 265. The 'monody' mentioned just below is in ibid. 262.

21 For a variant version see my headnote (pp. 120–1) and the Appendix (p. 165).

22 Gabriello Chiabrera (1552–1638). Six of his epitaphs in Wordsworth's translation appeared in *The Friend*, nos 19, 20, 25 (28 December 1809, 4 January, 22 February 1810); others are in Wordsworth's collected poems in the section 'Epitaphs and Elegiac Pieces'.

23 *Lives*, iii. 262. For the epitaph see Pope, *Poems*, ed. J. Butt, London, 1963, 809–10.

24 Not 'characteristic of Pope', but 'revealing the character of the deceased'.

25 Op. cit. iii. 262.

26 Wordsworth's 'Epitaphs from Chiabrera', iii. 10–12; Chiabrera's 'Per Monsignor Giuseppe Ferreri, Arcivescovo di Urbino'.

Essay upon Epitaphs, III

1 Natural feelings or natural expression.

2 *The Friend*, no. 6 (21 September 1809): 'to him [*read* he] who has once said with his whole heart, Evil be thou my Good! [*Paradise Lost*, iv. 110] has removed a world of Obstacles by the very decision, that he will have no Obstacles but those of force and brute matter. . . . Happily for Mankind, however, the obstacles which a consistent evil mind no longer finds in itself, it finds in its own unsuitableness to Human nature.'

3 Dryden, *Absalom and Achitophel*, 150–99, 544–68 (Shaftesbury, Buckingham); Pope, *Moral Essays*, i. 174–209 (Wharton); ii. 115–50 (Duchess of Marlborough, as commonly interpreted).

4 The epitaph on Lucy Lyttleton (p. 145).

5 William Mason, 'Epitaph on Mrs. Mason, in the Cathedral at Bristol'. Wordsworth probably took this, Mason's epitaph on Miss Drummond (p. 155), and Gray's on Mrs Clark (p. 156) from Vicesimus Knox's anthology *Elegant Extracts* (1789 etc.; see p. 153), where they occur in the order used by Wordsworth and in succession.

6 See n. 5.

7 Commonplace in the critical utterances of Dryden, Pope, and Johnson; see *Prose*, ii. 114. Wordsworth's alternative nomenclature is expounded by De Quincey in his fourth essay on Style, in *Collected Writings*, ed. D. Masson, Edinburgh, 1890, x. 220–30.

8 E.g. the shirt of Nessus in the story of Hercules.

9 See n. 5.

10 Source not identified.

11 See n. 5.

12 Gray, *Works*, ed. Mason, 4th ed., London, 1807, ii. 82.

13 Pope, *Poems*, ed. Butt, London, 1963, 473.

14 Probably from Scott's notes to Dryden's *Absalom and Achitophel*, in *Works*, London, 1808, ix. 300. Other versions exist.

15 See Essay II, n. 22 (p. 168).

16 Weever, op. cit. 8.

17 'Epitaphs from Chiabrera', ix; in *The Friend*, no. 20 (4 January 1810).

18 'Epitaphs from Chiabrera', vii.

19. 'Epitaphs from Chiabrera', viii; in *The Friend*, no. 20.

20 See p. 133.

21 Unpublished by Wordsworth. The epitaph on Raphael: 'To make painted images more beautiful, he took such care in painting living ones that Nature, to make her real ones beautiful, is these days willing to imitate his feigned ones.'

22 'Friend, I while I lived sought comfort on Mount Parnassus. You, better advised, seek it on Mount Calvary.'

23 Weever, op. cit. 361–2.

24 The text is just intelligible, but probably some such phrase as 'the faults of bad epitaphs' has dropped out of the manuscript after 'judgement'.

25 Coleridge noted these four epitaphs in his notebooks (ed. Coburn, London, 1957–   ), ii. 2982 (the first and fourth, from Ashby church-yard, Leics.) and i. 1267 (the second and third, from Laugharne, Carms.).

26 Source not identified.

27 *Spectator*, no. 26.

28 Wordsworth saw the epitaph in Mardale churchyard, which is now submerged by the Haweswater reservoir. The stone, however, is now in Shap churchyard: it belongs to Thomas Holme (see *Prose*, ii. 118–19). The lines following are a version of *Exc.* vii. 395–481.

10 Preface to *The Excursion*
1814

Written probably in spring or summer 1814; first published in *The Excursion* (1814), and, with revisions, in all subsequent editions of the poem. The date of the appended extract from *The Recluse* is considerably earlier, probably 1806: see John Alban Finch, 'On the Dating of *Home at Grasmere*', in *Bicentenary Wordsworth Studies*, ed. J. Wordsworth, Ithaca and London, 1970, 14–28. My text is Wordsworth's final version, in *Poetical Works* (1849–50), vi. 3–8.

PREFACE TO THE EDITION OF 1814.

The Title-page announces that this is only a portion of a poem;[1] and the Reader must be here apprised that it belongs to the second part of a long and laborious Work, which is to consist of three parts.— The Author will candidly acknowledge that, if the first[2] of these had been completed, and in such a manner as to satisfy his own mind, he should have preferred the natural order of publication, and have given that to the world first; but, as the second division of the Work was designed to refer more to passing events,[3] and to an existing state of things, than the others were meant to do, more continuous exertion was naturally bestowed upon it, and greater progress made here than in the rest of the poem; and as this part does not depend upon the preceding, to a degree which will materially injure its own peculiar interest, the Author, complying with the earnest entreaties of some valued Friends, presents the following pages to the Public.

It may be proper to state whence the poem, of which The Excursion is a part, derives its Title of THE RECLUSE.—Several years ago, when the Author retired to his native mountains,[4] with the hope of being enabled to construct a literary Work that might live, it was a reasonable thing that he should take a review of his own mind, and examine how far Nature and Education had qualified him for such employment. As subsidiary to this preparation, he undertook to record, in verse, the origin and progress of his own powers, as far as

he was acquainted with them. That Work,[5] addressed to a dear
Friend, most distinguished for his knowledge and genius, and to
whom the Author's Intellect is deeply indebted, has been long
finished; and the result of the investigation which gave rise to it was
a determination to compose a philosophical poem, containing views
of Man, Nature, and Society; and to be entitled, The Recluse; as
having for its principal subject the sensations and opinions of a poet
living in retirement.—The preparatory poem is biographical, and
conducts the history of the Author's mind to the point when he was
emboldened to hope that his faculties were sufficiently mature for
entering upon the arduous labour which he had proposed to himself; and the two Works have the same kind of relation to each other,
if he may so express himself, as the ante-chapel has to the body of a
gothic church. Continuing this allusion, he may be permitted to add,
that his minor Pieces, which have been long before the Public, when
they shall be properly arranged,[6] will be found by the attentive
Reader to have such connection with the main Work as may give
them claim to be likened to the little cells, oratories, and sepulchral
recesses, ordinarily included in those edifices.

The Author would not have deemed himself justified in saying,
upon this occasion, so much of performances either unfinished, or
unpublished, if he had not thought that the labour bestowed by him
upon what he has heretofore and now laid before the Public, entitled
him to candid attention for such a statement as he thinks necessary
to throw light upon his endeavours to please and, he would hope, to
benefit his countrymen.—Nothing further need be added, than that
the first and third parts of The Recluse will consist chiefly of meditations in the Author's own person; and that in the intermediate part
(The Excursion) the intervention of characters speaking is employed,
and something of a dramatic form adopted.

It is not the Author's intention formally to announce a system:
it was more animating to him to proceed in a different course; and
if he shall succeed in conveying to the mind clear thoughts, lively
images, and strong feelings, the Reader will have no difficulty in
extracting the system for himself. And in the meantime the following passage,[7] taken from the conclusion of the first book of The
Recluse, may be acceptable as a kind of *Prospectus* of the design and
scope of the whole Poem.[8]

'On Man, on Nature, and on Human Life,
Musing in solitude, I oft perceive

Fair trains of imagery before me rise,
Accompanied by feelings of delight
Pure, or with no unpleasing sadness mixed;
And I am conscious of affecting thoughts
And dear remembrances, whose presence soothes
Or elevates the Mind, intent to weigh
The good and evil of our mortal state.
—To these emotions, whencesoe'er they come,
Whether from breath of outward circumstance,
Or from the Soul—an impulse to herself—
I would give utterance in numerous verse.
Of Truth, of Grandeur, Beauty, Love, and Hope,
And melancholy Fear subdued by Faith;
Of blessed consolations in distress;
Of moral strength, and intellectual Power;
Of joy in widest commonalty spread;
Of the individual Mind that keeps her own
Inviolate retirement, subject there
To Conscience only, and the law supreme
Of that Intelligence which governs all—
I sing:—'fit audience let me find though few!'

So prayed, more gaining than he asked, the Bard—
In holiest mood. Urania, I shall need
Thy guidance, or a greater Muse, if such
Descend to earth or dwell in highest heaven!
For I must tread on shadowy ground, must sink
Deep—and, aloft ascending, breathe in worlds
To which the heaven of heavens is but a veil.
All strength—all terror, single or in bands,
That ever was put forth in personal form—
Jehovah—with his thunder, and the choir
Of shouting Angels, and the empyreal thrones—
I pass them unalarmed. Not Chaos, not
The darkest pit of lowest Erebus,
Nor aught of blinder vacancy, scooped out
By help of dreams—can breed such fear and awe
As fall upon us often when we look
Into our Minds, into the Mind of Man—
My haunt, and the main region of my song.
—Beauty—a living Presence of the earth,

Surpassing the most fair ideal Forms
Which craft of delicate Spirits hath composed
From earth's materials—waits upon my steps;
Pitches her tents before me as I move,
An hourly neighbour. Paradise, and groves
Elysian, Fortunate Fields—like those of old
Sought in the Atlantic Main—why should they be
A history only of departed things,
Or a mere fiction of what never was?
For the discerning intellect of Man,
When wedded to this goodly universe
In love and holy passion, shall find these
A simple produce of the common day.
—I, long before the blissful hour arrives,
Would chant, in lonely peace, the spousal verse
Of this great consummation:—and, by words
Which speak of nothing more than what we are,
Would I arouse the sensual from their sleep
Of Death, and win the vacant and the vain
To noble raptures; while my voice proclaims
How exquisitely the individual Mind
(And the progressive powers perhaps no less
Of the whole species) to the external World
Is fitted:—and how exquisitely, too—
Theme this but little heard of among men—
The external World is fitted to the Mind;
And the creation (by no lower name
Can it be called) which they with blended might
Accomplish:—this is our high argument.
—Such grateful haunts foregoing, if I oft
Must turn elsewhere—to travel near the tribes
And fellowships of men, and see ill sights
Of madding passions mutually inflamed;
Must hear Humanity in fields and groves
Pipe solitary anguish; or must hang
Brooding above the fierce confederate storm
Of sorrow, barricadoed evermore
Within the walls of cities—may these sounds
Have their authentic comment; that even these
Hearing, I be not downcast or forlorn!—
Descend, prophetic Spirit! that inspir'st

The human Soul of universal earth,
Dreaming on things to come; and dost possess
A metropolitan temple in the hearts
Of mighty Poets: upon me bestow
A gift of genuine insight; that my Song
With star-like virtue in its place may shine,
Shedding benignant influence, and secure,
Itself, from all malevolent effect
Of those mutations that extend their sway
Throughout the nether sphere!—And if with this
I mix more lowly matter; with the thing
Contemplated, describe the Mind and Man
Contemplating; and who, and what he was—
The transitory Being that beheld
This Vision; when and where, and how he lived;—
Be not this labour useless. If such theme
May sort with highest objects, then—dread Power!
Whose gracious favour is the primal source
Of all illumination—may my Life
Express the image of a better time,
More wise desires, and simpler manners:—nurse
My Heart in genuine freedom:—all pure thoughts
Be with me;—so shall thy unfailing love
Guide, and support, and cheer me to the end!'

NOTES

1 The title-page has the sub-title: 'Being a Portion of THE RECLUSE'.
2 *The Recluse*, of which a fragment exists and of which a smaller fragment appears below.
3 E.g. the French Revolution.
4 Wordsworth 'retired' to Grasmere in December 1799.
5 *The Prelude*, completed May 1805; addressed to Coleridge. The poem arose from the preliminary stages of *The Recluse*, rather than led to it.
6 As in the edition of 1815.
7 *The Recluse*, I. i. 754 ff.
8 *Paradise Lost*, vii. 31. For several other reminiscences of *Paradise Lost*, meant to indicate that Wordsworth's theme of the human mind is more heroic than Milton's, see *Prose*, iii. 11–12.

11 Preface of 1815

1815

This document and the Essay, Supplementary (No. 12) were written in January 1815; on 22 December 1814 Wordsworth told R. P. Gillies that he would not write a new preface to the new edition of his poems (1815), but he was writing to De Quincey on 8 February 1815 about '*rough* Copies of the Preface' and 'the after draught', and on 14 February to Gillies about 'an additional preface and a supplementary Essay' on which he had been engaged 'for some weeks past' (*MY*, ii. 180, 195, 196). They first appeared in Wordsworth's *Poems* (1815), and were reprinted, with revisions, in all subsequent collected editions of Wordsworth's poems. My text of both is based on Wordsworth's final version, in *Poetical Works* (1849–50), v. 233–50 (Preface), and v. 196–230 (Essay); with certain corrections, from earlier texts, of obvious errors introduced by Wordsworth during revision. The illogical order in which the works appeared in 1849–50 was first used in Wordsworth's *Poems* (1845), and emerged from the *Poetical Works* of 1836–7, where, for some inexplicable reason, Wordsworth indicated that the Essay was supplementary to the Preface to *Lyrical Ballads*. In all earlier texts (1815, 1820, 1827, 1832) it was rightly referred to the Preface of 1815; see *Prose*, iii. 55. Early texts of the Preface (1815–36) contain somewhat more material than is given here. The more important omitted passages are recorded in my notes; for the others see the apparatus in *Prose*, iii. 26–39. The final text of the Essay is on the whole the fullest, except that it omits, as do all Wordsworth's texts after the first (1815), an opening paragraph of cool insult aimed at Jeffrey.

PREFACE TO THE EDITION OF 1815.

The powers requisite for the production of poetry are:[1] first, those of Observation and Description,—*i.e.*, the ability to observe with accuracy things as they are in themselves, and with fidelity to describe them, unmodified by any passion or feeling existing in the mind of the describer; whether the things depicted be actually present to the senses, or have a place only in the memory. This power, though indispensable to a Poet, is one which he employs only in submission to necessity, and never for a continuance of time: as its exercise supposes all the higher qualities of the mind to be passive, and in a state of subjection to external objects, much in the same way as a translator or engraver ought to be to his original. 2ndly, Sensibility,—which, the more exquisite it is, the wider will be the range of a poet's perceptions; and the more will he be incited to observe objects, both as they exist in themselves and as re-acted upon by his own mind. (The distinction between poetic and human sensibility has been marked in the character of the Poet delineated in the original preface).[2] 3dly, Reflection,—which makes the Poet acquainted with the value of actions, images, thoughts, and feelings; and assists the sensibility in perceiving their connection with each other. 4thly, Imagination and Fancy,—to modify, to create, and to associate. 5thly, Invention,—by which characters are composed out of materials supplied by observation; whether of the Poet's own heart and mind, or of external life and nature; and such incidents and situations produced as are most impressive to the imagination, and most fitted to do justice to the characters, sentiments, and passions, which the Poet undertakes to illustrate. And, lastly, Judgment,—to decide how and where, and in what degree, each of these faculties ought to be exerted; so that the less shall not be sacrificed to the greater; nor the greater, slighting the less, arrogate, to its own injury, more than its due. By judgment, also, is determined what are the laws and appropriate graces of every species of composition.[3]

The materials of Poetry, by these powers collected and produced, are cast, by means of various moulds, into divers forms. The moulds may be enumerated, and the forms specified, in the following order. 1st, The Narrative,—including the Epopœia, the Historic Poem, the Tale, the Romance, the Mock-heroic, and, if the spirit of Homer will tolerate such neighbourhood, that dear production of our days, the metrical Novel.[4] Of this Class, the distinguishing mark is, that the Narrator, however liberally his speaking agents be introduced, is himself the source from which every thing primarily flows. Epic Poets, in order that their mode of composition may accord with the elevation of their subject, represent themselves as *singing* from the inspiration of the Muse, 'Arma virumque *cano;*'[5] but this is a fiction, in modern times, of slight value: the Iliad or the Paradise Lost would gain little in our estimation by being chanted. The other poets who belong to this class are commonly content to *tell* their tale;—so that of the whole it may be affirmed that they neither require nor reject the accompaniment of music.

2ndly, The Dramatic,—consisting of Tragedy, Historic Drama, Comedy, and Masque, in which the Poet does not appear at all in his own person, and where the whole action is carried on by speech and dialogue of the agents; music being admitted only incidentally and rarely. The Opera may be placed here, inasmuch as it proceeds by dialogue; though depending, to the degree that it does, upon music, it has a strong claim to be ranked with the lyrical. The characteristic[6] and impassioned Epistle, of which Ovid and Pope have given examples, considered as a species of monodrama, may, without impropriety, be placed in this class.

3rdly, The Lyrical,—containing the Hymn, the Ode, the Elegy, the Song, and the Ballad; in all which, for the production of their *full* effect, an accompaniment of music is indispensable.

4thly, The Idyllium,—descriptive chiefly either of the processes and appearances of external nature, as the Seasons of Thomson; or of characters, manners, and sentiments, as are Shenstone's School-mistress. The Cotter's Saturday Night of Burns, The Twa Dogs of the same Author; or of these in conjunction with the appearances of Nature, as most of the pieces of Theocritus, the Allegro and Penseroso of Milton, Beattie's Minstrel, Goldsmith's Deserted Village. The Epitaph, the Inscription, the Sonnet, most of the epistles of poets writing in their own persons, and all loco-descriptive poetry, belong to this class.

5thly, Didactic,—the principal object of which is direct instruction; as the Poem[7] of Lucretius, the Georgics of Virgil, The Fleece of Dyer, Mason's English Garden, &c.

And, lastly, philosophical Satire, like that of Horace and Juvenal; personal and occasional Satire rarely comprehending sufficient of the general in the individual to be dignified with the name of poetry.

Out of the three last has been constructed a composite order, of which Young's Night Thoughts, and Cowper's Task, are excellent examples.

It is deducible from the above, that poems, apparently miscellaneous, may with propriety be arranged either with reference to the powers of mind *predominant* in the production of them; or to the mould in which they are cast; or, lastly, to the subjects to which they relate. From each of these considerations, the following Poems have been divided into classes; which, that the work may more obviously correspond with the course of human life, and for the sake of exhibiting in it the three requisites of a legitimate whole, a beginning, a middle, and an end,[8] have been also arranged, as far as it was possible, according to an order of time, commencing with Childhood, and terminating with Old Age, Death, and Immortality. My guiding wish was, that the small pieces of which these volumes consist, thus discriminated, might be regarded under a two-fold view; as composing an entire work within themselves, and as adjuncts to the philosophical Poem, 'The Recluse.' This arrangement has long presented itself habitually to my own mind. Nevertheless, I should have preferred to scatter the contents of these volumes at random, if I had been persuaded that, by the plan adopted, any thing material would be taken from the natural effect of the pieces, individually, on the mind of the unreflecting Reader. I trust there is a sufficient variety in each class to prevent this; while, for him who reads with reflection, the arrangement will serve as a commentary unostentatiously directing his attention to my purposes, both particular and general. But, as I wish to guard against the possibility of misleading by this classification, it is proper first to remind the Reader, that certain poems are placed according to the powers of mind, in the Author's conception, predominant in the production of them; *predominant*, which implies the exertion of other faculties in less degree. Where there is more imagination than fancy in a poem, it is placed under the head of imagination, and *vice versâ*. Both the above classes might without impropriety have been enlarged from that consisting of 'Poems founded on the Affections;' as might this latter from those, and from the class 'proceeding from Sentiment and Reflection.'[9] The most striking characteristics of each piece, mutual illustration, variety, and proportion, have governed me throughout.[10]

None of the other Classes, except those of Fancy and Imagination, require any particular notice. But a remark of general application may be made. All Poets, except the dramatic, have been in the practice of feigning that their works were composed to the music of the harp or lyre: with what degree of affectation this has been done in modern times, I leave to the judicious to determine. For my own part, I have not been disposed to violate probability so far, or to make such a large demand upon the Reader's charity. Some of these pieces are essentially lyrical; and, therefore, cannot have their due force without a supposed musical accompaniment; but, in much the greatest part, as a substitute for the classic lyre or romantic harp, I require nothing more than an animated or impassioned recitation, adapted to the subject. Poems, however humble in their kind, if they be good in that kind, cannot read themselves; the law of long syllable and short must not be so inflexible,—the letter of metre must not be so impassive to the spirit of versification,—as to deprive the Reader of all voluntary power to modulate, in subordination to the sense, the music of the poem;—in the same manner as his mind is left at liberty, and even summoned, to act upon its thoughts and images. But, though the accompaniment of a musical instrument be frequently dispensed with, the true Poet does not therefore abandon his privilege distinct from that of the mere Proseman;

> 'He murmurs near the running brooks
> A music sweeter than their own.'[11]

Let us come now to the consideration of the words Fancy and Imagination, as employed in the classification of the following Poems. 'A man,' says an intelligent author,

'has imagination in proportion as he can distinctly copy in idea the impressions of sense: it is the faculty which *images* within the mind the phenomena of sensation. A man has fancy in proportion as he can call up, connect, or associate, at pleasure, those internal images (φαντάζειν is to cause to appear) so as to complete ideal representations of absent objects. Imagination is the power of depicting, and fancy of evoking and combining. The imagination is formed by patient observation; the fancy by a voluntary activity in shifting the scenery of the mind. The more accurate the imagination, the more safely may a painter, or a poet, undertake a delineation, or a description, without the presence of the objects to be characterised. The more versatile the fancy, the more original and striking will be the decorations produced.'— *British Synonyms discriminated, by W. Taylor.*[12]

Is not this as if a man should undertake to supply an account of a building, and be so intent upon what he had discovered of the foundation, as to conclude his task without once looking up at the superstructure? Here, as in other instances throughout the volume, the judicious Author's mind is enthralled by Etymology; he takes up the original word as his guide and escort, and too often does not perceive how soon he becomes its prisoner, without liberty to tread in any path but that to which it confines him. It is not easy to find out how imagination, thus explained, differs from distinct remembrance of images; or fancy from quick and vivid recollection of them: each is nothing more than a mode of memory. If the two words bear the above meaning, and no other, what term is left to designate that faculty of which the Poet is 'all compact;'[13] he whose eye glances from earth to heaven, whose spiritual attributes body forth what his pen is prompt in turning to shape; or what is left to characterise Fancy, as insinuating herself into the heart of objects with creative activity?—Imagination, in the sense of the word as giving title to a class of the following Poems, has no reference to images that are merely a faithful copy, existing in the mind, of absent external objects; but is a word of higher import, denoting operations of the mind upon those objects, and processes of creation or of composition, governed by certain fixed laws. I proceed to illustrate my meaning by instances. A parrot *hangs* from the wires of his cage by his beak or by his claws; or a monkey from the bough of a tree by his paws or his tail. Each creature does so literally and actually. In the first Eclogue of Virgil, the shepherd, thinking of the time when he is to take leave of his farm, thus addresses his goats:—[14]

'Non ego vos posthac viridi projectus in antro
Dumosa *pendere* procul de rupe videbo.'

——'half way down
Hangs one who gathers samphire,'[15]

is the well-known expression of Shakspeare, delineating an ordinary image upon the cliffs of Dover. In these two instances is a slight exertion of the faculty which I denominate imagination, in the use of one word: neither the goats nor the samphire-gatherer do literally hang, as does the parrot or the monkey; but, presenting to the senses something of such an appearance, the mind in its activity, for its own gratification, contemplates them as hanging.[16]

'As when far off at sea a fleet descried
Hangs in the clouds, by equinoctial winds
Close sailing from Bengala, or the isles
Of Ternate or Tidore, whence merchants bring
Their spicy drugs; they on the trading flood
Through the wide Ethiopian to the Cape
Ply, stemming nightly toward the Pole: so seemed
Far off the flying Fiend.'

Here is the full strength of the imagination involved in the word *hangs*, and exerted upon the whole image: First, the fleet, an aggregate of many ships, is represented as one mighty person, whose track, we know and feel, is upon the waters; but, taking advantage of its appearance to the senses, the Poet dares to represent it as *hanging in the clouds*, both for the gratification of the mind in contemplating the image itself, and in reference to the motion and appearance of the sublime object[17] to which it is compared.

From impressions of sight we will pass to those of sound; which, as they must necessarily be of a less definite character, shall be selected from these volumes:[18]

'Over his own sweet voice the Stock-dove *broods;*'

of the same bird,[19]

'His voice was *buried* among trees,
Yet to be come at by the breeze;'

'O, Cuckoo! shall I call thee *Bird*,
Or but a wandering *Voice?*'[20]

The stock-dove is said to *coo*,[21] a sound well imitating the note of the bird; but, by the intervention of the metaphor *broods*, the affections are called in by the imagination to assist in marking the manner in which the bird reiterates and prolongs her soft note, as if herself delighting to listen to it, and participating of a still and quiet satisfaction, like that which may be supposed inseparable from the continuous process of incubation. 'His voice was buried among trees,' a metaphor expressing the love of *seclusion* by which this Bird is marked; and characterising its note as not partaking of the shrill and the piercing, and therefore more easily deadened by the intervening shade; yet a note so peculiar and withal so pleasing, that the breeze, gifted with that love of the sound which the Poet feels, penetrates the shades in which it is entombed, and conveys it to the ear of the listener.

'Shall I call thee Bird,
Or but a wandering Voice?'

This concise interrogation characterises the seeming ubiquity of the voice of the cuckoo, and dispossesses the creature almost of a corporeal existence; the Imagination being tempted to this exertion of her power by a consciousness in the memory that the cuckoo is almost perpetually heard throughout the season of spring, but seldom becomes an object of sight.

Thus far of images independent of each other, and immediately endowed by the mind with properties that do not inhere in them, upon an incitement from properties and qualities the existence of which is inherent and obvious. These processes of imagination are carried on either by conferring additional properties upon an object, or abstracting from it some of those which it actually possesses, and thus enabling it to re-act upon the mind which hath performed the process, like a new existence.

I pass from the Imagination acting upon an individual image to a consideration of the same faculty employed upon images in a conjunction by which they modify each other. The Reader has already had a fine instance before him in the passage quoted from Virgil, where the apparently perilous situation of the goat, hanging upon the shaggy precipice, is contrasted with that of the shepherd contemplating it from the seclusion of the cavern in which he lies stretched at ease and in security. Take these images separately, and how unaffecting the picture compared with that produced by their being thus connected with, and opposed to, each other![22]

> 'As a huge stone is sometimes seen to lie
> Couched on the bald top of an eminence,
> Wonder to all who do the same espy
> By what means it could thither come, and whence,
> So that it seems a thing endued with sense,
> Like a sea-beast crawled forth, which on a shelf
> Of rock or sand reposeth, there to sun himself.
>
> Such seemed this Man; not all alive or dead
> Nor all asleep, in his extreme old age.
>
>   *   *   *   *
>
> Motionless as a cloud the old Man stood,
> That heareth not the loud winds when they call,
> And moveth altogether if it move at all.'

In these images, the conferring, the abstracting, and the modifying powers of the Imagination, immediately and mediately acting, are all brought into conjunction. The stone is endowed with something of the power of life to approximate it to the sea-beast; and the sea-beast stripped of some of its vital qualities to assimilate it to the stone; which intermediate image is thus treated for the purpose of bringing the original image, that of the stone, to a nearer resemblance to the figure and condition of the aged Man; who is divested of so much of the indications of life and motion as to bring him to the point where the two objects unite and coalesce in just comparison. After what has been said, the image of the cloud need not be commented upon.

Thus far of an endowing or modifying power: but the Imagination also shapes and *creates;* and how?[23] By innumerable processes; and in none does it more delight than in that of consolidating numbers into unity, and dissolving and separating unity into number,—alternations proceeding from, and governed by, a sublime consciousness of the soul in her own mighty and almost divine powers. Recur to the passage already cited from Milton. When the compact Fleet, as one Person, has been introduced 'Sailing from Bengala,' 'They,' *i.e.* the 'merchants,' representing the fleet resolved into a multitude of ships, 'ply' their voyage towards the extremities of the earth: 'So,' (referring to the word 'As' in the commencement) 'seemed the flying Fiend;' the image of his Person acting to re-combine the multitude of ships into one body,—the point from which the comparison set out. 'So seemed,' and to whom seemed? To the heavenly Muse who dictates the poem, to the eye of the Poet's mind, and to that of the Reader, present at one moment in the wide Ethiopian, and the next in the solitudes, then first broken in upon, of the infernal regions![24]

'Modo me Thebis, modo ponit Athenis.'

Hear again this mighty Poet,—speaking of the Messiah going forth to expel from heaven the rebellious angels,[25]

'Attended by ten thousand thousand Saints
He onward came: far off his coming shone,'—

the retinue of Saints, and the Person of the Messiah himself, lost almost and merged in the splendour of that indefinite abstraction 'His coming!'

As I do not mean here to treat this subject further than to throw some light upon the present Volumes, and especially upon one division of them, I shall spare myself and the Reader the trouble of considering the Imagination as it deals with thoughts and sentiments, as it regulates the composition of characters, and determines the course of actions: I will not consider it (more than I have already done by implication) as that power which, in the language of one of my most esteemed Friends, 'draws all things to one; which makes things animate or inanimate, beings with their attributes, subjects with their accessaries, take one colour and serve to one effect.'[26] The grand store-houses of enthusiastic and meditative Imagination, of poetical, as contradistinguished from human and dramatic Imagination,[27] are the prophetic and lyrical parts of the Holy Scriptures, and the works of Milton; to which I cannot forbear to add those of Spenser. I select these writers in preference to those of ancient Greece and Rome, because the anthropomorphitism of the Pagan religion subjected the minds of the greatest poets in those countries too much to the bondage of definite form; from which the Hebrews were preserved by their abhorrence of idolatry. This abhorrence was almost as strong in our great epic Poet, both from circumstances of his life, and from the constitution of his mind. However imbued the surface might be with classical literature, he was a Hebrew in soul; and all things tended in him towards the sublime. Spenser, of a gentler nature, maintained his freedom by aid of his allegorical spirit, at one time inciting him to create persons out of abstractions; and, at another, by a superior effort of genius, to give the universality and permanence of abstractions to his human beings, by means of attributes and emblems that belong to the highest moral truths and the purest sensations,—of which his character of Una is a glorious example. Of the human and dramatic Imagination the works of Shakspeare are an inexhaustible source.[28]

> 'I tax not you, ye Elements, with unkindness,
> I never gave you kingdoms, call'd you Daughters!'

And if, bearing in mind the many Poets distinguished by this prime quality, whose names I omit to mention; yet justified by recollection of the insults which the ignorant, the incapable, and the presumptuous, have heaped upon these and my other writings, I may be permitted to anticipate the judgment of posterity upon myself, I shall declare (censurable, I grant, if the notoriety of the fact above stated does not justify me) that I have given in these unfavourable times, evidence of exertions of this faculty upon its worthiest objects, the external universe, the moral and religious sentiments of Man, his natural affections, and his acquired passions; which have the same ennobling tendency as the productions of men, in this kind, worthy to be holden in undying remembrance.[29]

To the mode in which Fancy has already been characterised as the power of evoking and combining, or, as my friend Mr. Coleridge has styled it, 'the aggregative and associative power,'[30] my objection is only that the definition is too general. To aggregate and to associate, to evoke and to combine, belong as well to the Imagination as to the Fancy; but either the materials evoked and combined are different; or they are brought together under a different law, and for a different purpose. Fancy does not require that the materials which she makes use of should be susceptible of change in their constitution, from her touch; and, where they admit of modification, it is enough for her purpose if it be slight, limited, and evanescent. Directly the reverse of these, are the desires and demands of the Imagination. She recoils from every thing but the plastic, the pliant, and the indefinite. She leaves it to Fancy to describe Queen Mab as coming,[31]

> 'In shape no bigger than an agate-stone
> On the fore-finger of an alderman.'

Having to speak of stature, she does not tell you that her gigantic Angel was as tall as Pompey's Pillar; much less that he was twelve cubits, or twelve hundred cubits high; or that his dimensions equalled those of Teneriffe or Atlas;—because these, and if they were a million times as high it would be the same, are bounded: The expression is, 'His stature reached the sky!'[32] the illimitable firmament!—When the Imagination frames a comparison, if it does not strike on the first presentation, a sense of the truth of the likeness, from the moment that it is perceived, grows—and continues to grow —upon the mind; the resemblance depending less upon outline of form and feature, than upon expression and effect; less upon casual and outstanding, than upon inherent and internal, properties: moreover, the images invariably modify each other.—The law under which the processes of Fancy are carried on is as capricious as the accidents of things, and the effects are surprising, playful, ludicrous, amusing, tender, or pathetic, as the objects happen to be appositely produced or fortunately combined. Fancy depends upon the rapidity and profusion with which she scatters her thoughts and images; trusting that their number, and the felicity with which they are linked together, will make amends for the want of individual value: or she prides herself upon the curious subtilty and the successful elaboration with which she can detect their lurking affinities.[33] If she can win you over to her purpose, and impart to you her feelings, she cares not how unstable or transitory may be her influence, knowing that it will not be out of her power to resume it upon an apt occasion. But the Imagination is conscious of an indestructible dominion;—the Soul may fall away from it, not being able to sustain its grandeur; but, if once felt and acknowledged, by no act of any other faculty of the mind can it be relaxed, impaired, or diminished. —Fancy is given to quicken and to beguile the temporal part of our nature, Imagination to incite and to support the eternal.—Yet is it not the less true that Fancy, as she is an active, is also, under her own laws and in her own spirit, a creative faculty. In what manner Fancy ambitiously aims at a rivalship with Imagination, and Imagination stoops to work with the materials of Fancy, might be illustrated from the compositions of all eloquent writers, whether in prose or verse; and chiefly from those of our own Country. Scarcely a page of the impassioned parts of Bishop Taylor's Works can be opened that shall not afford examples.—Referring the Reader to those inestimable volumes, I will content myself with placing a conceit (ascribed to Lord Chesterfield) in contrast with a passage from the Paradise Lost:—[34]

> 'The dews of the evening most carefully shun,
> They are the tears of the sky for the loss of the sun.'

After the transgression of Adam, Milton, with other appearances of sympathising Nature, thus marks the immediate consequence,[35]

> 'Sky lowered, and, muttering thunder, some sad drops
> Wept at completion of the mortal sin.'

The associating link is the same in each instance: Dew and rain, not distinguishable from the liquid substance of tears, are employed as indications of sorrow. A flash of surprise is the effect in the former case; a flash of surprise, and nothing more; for the nature of things does not sustain the combination. In the latter, the effects from the act, of which there is this immediate consequence and visible sign, are so momentous, that the mind acknowledges the justice and reasonableness of the sympathy in nature so manifested; and the sky weeps drops of water as if with human eyes, as 'Earth had before trembled from her entrails, and Nature given a second groan.'[36]

Finally, I will refer to Cotton's 'Ode upon Winter,' an admirable composition, though stained with some peculiarities of the age in which he lived, for a general illustration of the characteristics of Fancy. The middle part of this ode contains a most lively description of the entrance of Winter, with his retinue, as 'A palsied king,' and yet a military monarch,—advancing for conquest with his army; the several bodies of which, and their arms and equipments, are described with a rapidity of detail, and a profusion of *fanciful* comparisons, which indicate on the part of the poet extreme activity of intellect, and a correspondent hurry of delightful feeling. He[37] retires from the foe into his fortress, where[38]

> ——'a magazine
> Of sovereign juice is cellared in;
> Liquor that will the siege maintain
> Should Phœbus ne'er return again.'

Though myself a water-drinker, I cannot resist the pleasure of transcribing what follows, as an instance still more happy of Fancy employed in the treatment of feeling than, in its preceding passages, the Poem supplies of her management of forms.

> ''Tis that, that gives the poet rage,
> And thaws the gelly'd blood of age;
> Matures the young, restores the old,
> And makes the fainting coward bold.
>
> It lays the careful head to rest,
> Calms palpitations in the breast,
> Renders our lives' misfortune sweet;
>
>   *   *   *   *
>
> Then let the chill Sirocco blow,
> And gird us round with hills of snow,
> Or else go whistle to the shore,
> And make the hollow mountains roar,
>
> Whilst we together jovial sit
> Careless, and crowned with mirth and wit,
> Where, though bleak winds confine us home
> Our fancies round the world shall roam.
>
> We'll think of all the Friends we know,
> And drink to all worth drinking to;
> When having drunk all thine and mine,
> We rather shall want healths than wine.
>
> But where Friends fail us, we'll supply
> Our friendships with our charity;
> Men that remote in sorrows live,
> Shall by our lusty brimmers thrive.
>
> We'll drink the wanting into wealth,
> And those that languish into health,
> The afflicted into joy; th' opprest
> Into security and rest.

The worthy in disgrace shall find
Favour return again more kind,
And in restraint who stifled lie,
Shall taste the air of liberty.

The brave shall triumph in success,
The lover shall have mistresses,
Poor unregarded Virtue, praise,
And the neglected Poet, bays.

Thus shall our healths do others good,
Whilst we ourselves do all we would;
For, freed from envy and from care,
What would we be but what we are?'[39]

When I sate down to write this Preface, it was my intention to have made it more comprehensive; but, thinking that I ought rather to apologise for detaining the reader so long, I will here conclude.

NOTES

1 The text of 1815 begins with two introductory paragraphs, which are retained, with small variants, until the edition of 1845:

> The observations prefixed to that portion of these Volumes, which was published many years ago, under the title of 'Lyrical Ballads,' have so little of a special application to the greater part, perhaps, of this collection, as subsequently enlarged and diversified, that they could not with any propriety stand as an Introduction to it. Not deeming it, however, expedient to suppress that exposition, slight and imperfect as it is, of the feelings which had determined the choice of the subjects, and the principles which had regulated the composition of those Pieces, I have transferred it to the end of the second Volume, to be attended to, or not, at the pleasure of the Reader.
>
> In the Preface to that part of 'The Recluse,' lately published under the title of 'The Excursion,' I have alluded to a meditated arrangement of my minor Poems, which should assist the attentive Reader in perceiving their connection with each other, and also their subordination to that Work. I shall here say a few words explanatory of this arrangement, as carried into effect in the present Volumes.

2 Preface to *Lyrical Ballads* (pp. 77–83).
3 As sensibility to harmony of numbers, and the power of producing it,

are invariably attendants upon the faculties above specified, nothing has been said upon those requisites. [Wordsworth's note.]

4 Crabbe's *Tales*? Scott's narrative poems?

5 Virgil, *Aeneid*, 1.1: 'I sing of arms and the man'.

6 I.e. revealing character. Examples are Ovid's *Heroides* and Pope's *Eloisa to Abelard*.

7 *De Rerum Natura* (*On the nature of things*).

8 Aristotle's criterion for 'a complete thing': *Poetics*, 1450. b. 28-9.

9 See the letter to Coleridge (No. 8) and notes.

10 Here the text of 1815 inserts a paragraph, retained with variants until 1845:

> It may be proper in this place to state, that the Extracts in the 2nd Class entitled 'Juvenile Pieces,' are in many places altered from the printed copy, chiefly by omission and compression. The slight alterations of another kind were for the most part made not long after the publication of the Poems from which the Extracts are taken. These Extracts seem to have a title to be placed here as they were the productions of youth, and represent implicitly some of the features of a youthful mind, at a time when images of nature supplied to it the place of thought, sentiment, and almost of action; or, as it will be found expressed, of a state of mind when
>
> > 'the sounding cataract
> > Haunted me like a passion: the tall rock,
> > The mountain, and the deep and gloomy wood,
> > Their colours and their forms were then to me
> > An appetite, a feeling and a love,
> > That had no need of a remoter charm,
> > By thought supplied, or any interest
> > Unborrowed from the eye'—
>
> I will own that I was much at a loss what to select of these descriptions, and perhaps it would have been better either to have reprinted the whole, or suppressed what I have given.

The 'extracts' are from *An Evening Walk*, *Descriptive Sketches*, and *Guilt and Sorrow*. The verse quoted is 'Tintern Abbey', 76-83.

11 'A Poet's Epitaph', 39-40.

12 William Taylor, Jr, of Norwich, *English Synonyms Discriminated*, London, 1813, 242.

13 Shakespeare, *Midsummer Night's Dream*, v. i. 7 ff.

14 Virgil, *Eclogues*, i. 75-6: 'I shall not, as I lie in this green cavern, see you again hanging from the bushy rock.'

15 *King Lear*, IV. vi. 15-16.

16 *Paradise Lost*, ii. 636-43.

17 Late texts read 'objects', wrongly.

18 'Resolution and Independence', 5.

19 'O Nightingale', 13–14.

20 'To the Cuckoo', 3–4.

21 As in 'O Nightingale', 15.

22 'Resolution and Independence', 57–65, 75–7.

23 Cf. the discussion of 'With ships the sea was scattered' in No. 7, pp. 113–14.

24 Horace, *Epistles*, II. i. 213: 'He [the poet] puts me at one time in Thebes, at another in Athens.'

25 *Paradise Lost*, vi. 767–8.

26 Charles Lamb upon the genius of Hogarth. [Wordsworth's note.] The passage is quoted from 'On the Genius and Character of Hogarth', in the *Reflector*, iii (April–September 1811). See Lamb's *Works*, ed. T. Hutchinson, London, 1908, i. 95–6. Lamb is describing Hogarth's 'Gin Lane'.

27 A version of John Dennis's 'ordinary' and 'enthusiastic' passion; see p. 49, and *Prose*, iii. 47.

28 *King Lear*, III. ii. 16–17.

29 Here 1815 inserts a paragraph, retained with variants until 1845:

> I dismiss this subject with observing—that, in the series of Poems placed under the head of Imagination, I have begun with one of the earliest processes of Nature in the development of this faculty. Guided by one of my own primary consciousnesses, I have represented a commutation and transfer of internal feelings, co-operating with external accidents, to plant, for immortality, images of sound and sight, in the celestial soil of the Imagination. The Boy, there introduced, is listening, with something of a feverish and restless anxiety, for the recurrence of the riotous sounds which he had previously excited; and, at the moment when the intenseness of his mind is beginning to remit, he is surprised into a perception of the solemn and tranquillizing images which the Poem describes.—The Poems next in succession exhibit the faculty exerting itself upon various objects of the external universe; then follow others, where it is employed upon feelings, characters, and actions; and the Class is concluded with imaginative pictures of moral, political, and religious sentiments.

The poem discussed is 'There was a Boy'.

30 In Southey's *Omniana, or Horæ Otiosores*, London, 1812, ii. 12–14; repeated in *Biog. Lit.* i. 193–4.

31 *Romeo and Juliet*, I. iv. 56–7.

32 *Paradise Lost*, iv. 985–8.

33 Cf. the definition in the Note to 'The Thorn' (p. 96).

34 'Advice to a Lady in Autumn', in *The Life of the late Earl of Chester-field*, London, 1774, ii. 248–9.
35 *Paradise Lost*, ix. 1002–3.
36 Ibid. 1000–1. Here 1815 inserts a paragraph, retained until 1845:

> Awe-stricken as I am by contemplating the operations of the mind of this truly divine Poet, I scarcely dare venture to add that 'An address to an Infant,' which the Reader will find under the Class of Fancy in the present Volumes, exhibits something of this communion and interchange of instruments and functions between the two powers; and is, accordingly, placed last in the class, as a preparation for that of Imagination which follows.

The poem mentioned is 'Address to my Infant Daughter'.

37 Late texts read 'Winter', wrongly.
38 Stanza 39 of Cotton's poem; the remainder of Wordsworth's quotation follows to the end of stanza 49. The line omitted from stanza 41 is 'And Venus frolic in the sheet'. The passage summarized before the quotation begins at about stanza 24.
39 At the end of this quotation 1815 inserts a paragraph explaining the omission of Coleridge's poems and the inclusion of three by Dorothy Wordsworth.

For the history of this Essay and details of the text used see the head-note to No. 11 (p. 175).

ESSAY, SUPPLEMENTARY TO THE PREFACE.

With the young of both sexes, Poetry is, like love, a passion;[1] but, for much the greater part of those who have been proud of its power over their minds, a necessity soon arises of breaking the pleasing bondage; or it relaxes of itself;—the thoughts being occupied in domestic cares, or the time engrossed by business. Poetry then becomes only an occasional recreation; while to those whose existence passes away in a course of fashionable pleasure, it is a species of luxurious amusement. In middle and declining age, a scattered number of serious persons resort to poetry, as to religion, for a protection against the pressure of trivial employments, and as a consolation for the afflictions of life. And, lastly, there are many, who, having been enamoured of this art in their youth, have found leisure, after youth was spent, to cultivate general literature; in which poetry has continued to be comprehended *as a study*.

Into the above classes the Readers of poetry may be divided; Critics abound in them all; but from the last only can opinions be collected of absolute value, and worthy to be depended upon, as prophetic of the destiny of a new work. The young, who in nothing can escape delusion, are especially subject to it in their intercourse with Poetry. The cause, not so obvious as the fact is unquestionable, is the same as that from which erroneous judgments in this art, in the minds of men of all ages, chiefly proceed; but upon Youth it operates with peculiar force. The appropriate business of poetry, (which, nevertheless, if genuine, is as permanent as pure science,) her appropriate employment, her privilege and her *duty*, is to treat of things not as they *are*, but as they *appear;* not as they exist in themselves, but as they *seem* to exist to the *senses*, and to the *passions*.

What a world of delusion does this acknowledged obligation prepare for the inexperienced! what temptations to go astray are here held forth for them whose thoughts have been little disciplined by the understanding, and whose feelings revolt from the sway of reason!— When a juvenile Reader is in the height of his rapture with some vicious passage, should experience throw in doubts, or common-sense suggest suspicions, a lurking consciousness that the realities of the Muse are but shows, and that her liveliest excitements are raised by transient shocks of conflicting feeling and successive assemblages of contradictory thoughts—is ever at hand to justify extravagance, and to sanction absurdity. But, it may be asked, as these illusions are unavoidable, and, no doubt, eminently useful to the mind as a pro-cess, what good can be gained by making observations, the tendency of which is to diminish the confidence of youth in its feelings, and thus to abridge its innocent and even profitable pleasures? The reproach implied in the question could not be warded off, if Youth were incapable of being delighted with what is truly excellent; or, if these errors always terminated of themselves in due season. But, with the majority, though their force be abated, they continue through life. Moreover, the fire of youth is too vivacious an element to be extinguished or damped by a philosophical remark; and, while there is no danger that what has been said will be injurious or painful to the ardent and the confident, it may prove beneficial to those who, being enthusiastic, are, at the same time, modest and ingenuous. The intimation may unite with their own misgivings to regulate their sensibility, and to bring in, sooner than it would otherwise have arrived, a more discreet and sound judgment.

If it should excite wonder that men of ability, in later life, whose understandings have been rendered acute by practice in affairs, should be so easily and so far imposed upon when they happen to take up a new work in verse, this appears to be the cause;—that, having discontinued their attention to poetry, whatever progress may have been made in other departments of knowledge, they have not, as to this art, advanced in true discernment beyond the age of youth. If, then, a new poem fall in their way, whose attractions are of that kind which would have enraptured them during the heat of youth, the judgment not being improved to a degree that they shall be disgusted, they are dazzled; and prize and cherish the faults for having had power to make the present time vanish before them, and to throw the mind back, as by enchantment, into the happiest season of life. As they read, powers seem to be revived, passions are regenerated, and pleasures restored. The Book was probably taken up after an escape from the burden of business, and with a wish to forget the world, and all its vexations and anxieties. Having obtained this wish, and so much more, it is natural that they should make report as they have felt.

If Men of mature age, through want of practice, be thus easily beguiled into admiration of absurdities, extravagances, and misplaced ornaments, thinking it proper that their understandings should enjoy a holiday, while they are unbending their minds with verse, it may be expected that such Readers will resemble their former selves also in strength of prejudice, and an inaptitude to be moved by the un-ostentatious beauties of a pure style. In the higher poetry, an enlightened Critic chiefly looks for a reflection of the wisdom of the heart and the grandeur of the imagination. Wherever these appear, simplicity accompanies them; Magnificence herself, when legitimate, depending upon a simplicity of her own, to regulate her ornaments. But it is a well-known property of human nature, that our estimates are ever governed by comparisons, of which we are conscious with various degrees of distinctness. Is it not, then, inevitable (confining these observations to the effects of style merely) that an eye, accustomed to the glaring hues of diction by which such Readers are caught and excited, will for the most part be rather repelled than attracted by an original Work, the colouring of which is disposed according to a pure and refined scheme of harmony? It is in the fine arts as in the affairs of life, no man can *serve* (i.e. obey with zeal and fidelity) two Masters.[2]

As Poetry is most just to its own divine origin when it administers the comforts and breathes the spirit of religion, they who have learned to perceive this truth, and who betake themselves to reading verse for sacred purposes, must be preserved from numerous illusions to which the two Classes of Readers, whom we have been considering, are liable. But, as the mind grows serious from the weight of life, the range of its passions is contracted accordingly; and its sympathies become so exclusive, that many species of high excellence wholly escape, or but languidly excite, its notice. Besides, men who read from religious or moral inclinations, even when the subject is of that kind which they approve, are beset with misconceptions and mistakes peculiar to themselves. Attaching so much importance to the truths which interest them, they are prone to over-rate the Authors by whom those truths are expressed and enforced. They come prepared to impart so much passion to the

Poet's language, that they remain unconscious how little, in fact, they receive from it. And, on the other hand, religious faith is to him who holds it so momentous a thing, and error appears to be attended with such tremendous consequences, that, if opinions touching upon religion occur which the Reader condemns, he not only cannot sympathise with them, however animated the expression, but there is, for the most part, an end put to all satisfaction and enjoyment. Love, if it before existed, is converted into dislike; and the heart of the Reader is set against the Author and his book.—To these excesses, they, who from their professions ought to be the most guarded against them, are perhaps the most liable; I mean those sects whose religion, being from the calculating understanding, is cold and formal. For when Christianity, the religion of humility, is founded upon the proudest faculty of our nature, what can be expected but contradictions? Accordingly, believers of this cast are at one time contemptuous; at another, being troubled, as they are and must be, with inward misgivings, they are jealous and suspicious;—and at all seasons, they are under temptation to supply by the heat with which they defend their tenets, the animation which is wanting to the constitution of the religion itself.[3]

Faith was given to man that his affections, detached from the treasures of time, might be inclined to settle upon those of eternity;—the elevation of his nature, which this habit produces on earth, being to him a presumptive evidence of a future state of existence; and giving him a title to partake of its holiness. The religious man values what he sees chiefly as an 'imperfect shadowing forth'[4] of what he is incapable of seeing. The concerns of religion refer to indefinite objects, and are too weighty for the mind to support them without relieving itself by resting a great part of the burthen upon words and symbols. The commerce between Man and his Maker cannot be carried on but by a process where much is represented in little, and the Infinite Being accommodates himself to a finite capacity. In all this may be perceived the affinity between religion and poetry; between religion—making up the deficiencies of reason by faith; and poetry—passionate for the instruction of reason; between religion—whose element is infinitude, and whose ultimate trust is the supreme of things, submitting herself to circumscription, and reconciled to substitutions; and poetry—ethereal and transcendent, yet incapable to sustain her existence without sensuous incarnation. In this community of nature may be perceived also the lurking incitements of kindred error;—so that we shall find that no poetry has been more subject to distortion, than that species, the argument and scope of which is religious; and no lovers of the art have gone farther astray than the pious and the devout.

Whither then shall we turn for that union of qualifications which must necessarily exist before the decisions of a critic can be of absolute value? For a mind at once poetical and philosophical; for a critic whose affections are as free and kindly as the spirit of society, and whose understanding is severe as that of dispassionate government? Where are we to look for that initiatory composure of mind which no selfishness can disturb? For a natural sensibility that has been tutored into correctness without losing anything of its quickness; and for active faculties, capable of answering the demands which an Author of original imagination shall make upon them, associated with a judgment that cannot be duped into admiration by aught that is unworthy of it?—among those and those only, who, never having suffered their youthful love of poetry to remit much of its force, have applied to the consideration of the laws of this art the best power of their understandings. At the same time it must be observed—that, as this Class comprehends the only judgments which are trust-worthy, so does it include the most erroneous and perverse. For to be mistaught is worse than to be untaught; and no perverseness equals that which is supported by system, no errors are so difficult to root out as those which the understanding has pledged its credit to uphold. In this Class are contained censors, who, if they be pleased with what is good, are pleased with it only by imperfect glimpses, and upon false principles; who, should they generalise rightly, to a certain point, are sure to suffer for it in the end; who, if they stumble upon a sound rule, are fettered by misapplying it, or by straining it too far; being incapable of perceiving when it ought to yield to one of higher order. In it are found critics too petulant to be passive to a genuine poet, and too feeble to grapple with him; men, who take upon them to report of the course which *he* holds whom they are utterly unable to accompany,—confounded if he turn quick upon the wing, dismayed if he soar steadily 'into the region;'⁵— men of palsied imaginations and indurated hearts; in whose minds all healthy action is languid, who therefore feed as the many direct them, or, with the many, are greedy after vicious provocatives;— judges, whose censure is auspicious, and whose praise ominous! In this class meet together the two extremes of best and worst.

The observations presented in the foregoing series are of too ungracious a nature to have been made without reluctance; and, were it only on this account, I would invite the reader to try them by the test of comprehensive experience. If the number of judges who can be confidently relied upon be in reality so small, it ought to follow that partial notice only, or neglect, perhaps long continued, or attention wholly inadequate to their merits—must have been the fate of most works in the higher departments of poetry; and that, on the other hand, numerous productions have blazed into popularity, and have passed away, leaving scarcely a trace behind them: it will be further found, that when Authors shall have at length raised themselves into general admiration and maintained their ground, errors and prejudices have prevailed concerning their genius and their works, which the few who are conscious of those errors and prejudices would deplore; if they were not recompensed by perceiving that there are select Spirits for whom it is ordained that their fame shall be in the world an existence like that of Virtue, which owes its being to the struggles it makes, and its vigour to the enemies whom it provokes;—a vivacious quality, ever doomed to meet with opposition, and still triumphing over it; and, from the nature of its dominion, incapable of being brought to the sad conclusion of Alexander, when he wept that there were no more worlds for him to conquer.[6]

Let us take a hasty retrospect of the poetical literature of this Country for the greater part of the last two centuries, and see if the facts support these inferences.

Who is there that now reads the 'Creation' of Dubartas?[7] Yet all Europe once resounded with his praise; he was caressed by kings; and, when his Poem was translated into our language, the Faery Queen faded before it. The name of Spenser, whose genius is of a higher order than even that of Ariosto, is at this day scarcely known beyond the limits of the British Isles. And if the value of his works is to be estimated from the attention now paid to them by his countrymen, compared with that which they bestow on those of some other writers, it must be pronounced small indeed.[8]

> 'The laurel, meed of mighty conquerors
> And poets *sage*'—

are his own words; but his wisdom has, in this particular, been his worst enemy: while its opposite, whether in the shape of folly or madness, has been *their* best friend. But he was a great power, and bears a high name: the laurel has been awarded to him.

A dramatic Author, if he write for the stage, must adapt himself to the taste of the audience, or they will not endure him; accordingly the mighty genius of Shakspeare was listened to. The people were delighted: but I am not sufficiently versed in stage antiquities to determine whether they did not flock as eagerly to the representation of many pieces of contemporary Authors, wholly undeserving to appear upon the same boards. Had there been a formal contest for superiority among dramatic writers, that Shakspeare, like his predecessors Sophocles and Euripides, would have often been subject to the mortification of seeing the prize adjudged to sorry competitors, becomes too probable, when we reflect that the admirers of Settle and Shadwell were, in a later age, as numerous, and reckoned as respectable in point of talent, as those of Dryden. At all events, that Shakspeare stooped to accommodate himself to the People, is sufficiently apparent; and one of the most striking proofs of his almost omnipotent genius, is, that he could turn to such glorious purpose those materials which the prepossessions of the age compelled him to make use of. Yet even this marvellous skill appears not to have been enough to prevent his rivals from having some advantage over him in public estimation; else how can we account for passages and scenes that exist in his works, unless upon a supposition that some of the grossest of them, a fact which in my own mind I have no doubt of, were foisted in by the Players, for the gratification of the many?

But that his Works, whatever might be their reception upon the stage, made but little impression upon the ruling Intellects of the time, may be inferred from the fact that Lord Bacon, in his multifarious writings, nowhere either quotes or alludes to him.[9] His dramatic excellence enabled him to resume possession of the stage after the Restoration; but Dryden tells us that in his time two of the plays of Beaumont and Fletcher were acted for one of Shakspeare's.[10] And so faint and limited was the perception of the poetic beauties of his dramas in the time of Pope, that, in his Edition of the Plays, with a view to rendering to the general reader a necessary service, he printed between inverted commas those passages which he thought most worthy of notice.[11]

At this day, the French Critics have abated nothing of their aversion to this darling of our Nation: 'the English, with their bouffon de Shakspeare,' is as familiar an expression among them as in the time of Voltaire.[12] Baron Grimm[13] is the only French writer who seems to have perceived his infinite superiority to the first names of the French Theatre; an advantage which the Parisian Critic owed to his German blood and German education. The most enlightened Italians, though well acquainted with our language, are wholly incompetent to measure the proportions of Shakspeare. The Germans only, of foreign nations, are approaching towards a knowledge and feeling of what he is. In some respects they have acquired a superiority over the fellow-countrymen of the Poet: for among us it is a current, I might say, an established opinion, that Shakspeare is justly praised when he is pronounced to be 'a wild irregular genius, in whom great faults are compensated by great beauties.'[14] How long may it be before this misconception passes away, and it becomes universally acknowledged that the judgment of Shakspeare in the selection of his materials, and in the manner in which he has made them, heterogeneous as they often are, constitute a unity of their own, and contribute all to one great end, is not less admirable than his imagination, his invention, and his intuitive knowledge of human Nature?

There is extant a small Volume of miscellaneous poems, in which Shakspeare expresses his own feelings in his own person.[15] It is not difficult to conceive that the Editor, George Steevens, should have been insensible to the beauties of one portion of that Volume, the Sonnets; though in no part of the writings of this Poet is found, in an equal compass, a greater number of exquisite feelings felicitously expressed. But, from regard to the Critic's own credit, he would not have ventured to talk of an[16] act of parliament not being strong enough to compel the perusal of those little pieces, if he had not known that the people of England were ignorant of the treasures contained in them: and if he had not, moreover, shared the too common propensity of human nature to exult over a supposed fall into the mire of a genius whom he had been compelled to regard with admiration, as an inmate of the celestial regions—'there sitting where he durst not soar.'[17]

Nine years before the death of Shakspeare, Milton was born; and early in life he published several small poems,[18] which, though on their first appearance they were praised by a few of the judicious, were afterwards neglected to that degree, that Pope in his youth could borrow from them without risk of its being known. Whether these poems are at this day justly appreciated, I will not undertake to decide: nor would it imply a severe reflection upon the mass of readers to suppose the contrary; seeing that a man of the acknowledged genius of Voss, the German poet, could suffer their spirit to

evaporate; and could change their character, as is done in the translation made by him of the most popular of those pieces.[19] At all
events, it is certain that these Poems of Milton are now much read,
and loudly praised; yet were they little heard of till more than 150
years after their publication; and of the Sonnets, Dr. Johnson, as
appears from Boswell's Life of him, was in the habit of thinking and
speaking as contemptuously as Steevens wrote upon those of Shakspeare.[20]

About the time when the Pindaric odes of Cowley and his imitators, and the productions of that class of curious thinkers whom
Dr. Johnson has strangely styled metaphysical Poets,[21] were beginning to lose something of that extravagant admiration which they
had excited, the Paradise Lost made its appearance.[22] 'Fit audience
find though few,'[23] was the petition addressed by the Poet to his
inspiring Muse. I have said elsewhere that he gained more than he
asked; this I believe to be true; but Dr. Johnson has fallen into a
gross mistake when he attempts to prove, by the sale of the work,
that Milton's Countrymen were '*just* to it' upon its first appearance.[24]
Thirteen hundred Copies were sold in two years; an uncommon
example, he asserts, of the prevalence of genius in opposition to so
much recent enmity as Milton's public conduct had excited. But, be
it remembered that, if Milton's political and religious opinions, and
the manner in which he announced them, had raised him many
enemies, they had procured him numerous friends; who, as all
personal danger was passed away at the time of publication, would
be eager to procure the master-work of a man whom they revered,
and whom they would be proud of praising. Take, from the number
of purchasers, persons of this class, and also those who wished to
possess the Poem as a religious work, and but few I fear would be
left who sought for it on account of its poetical merits. The demand
did not immediately increase; 'for,' says Dr. Johnson, 'many more
readers' (he means persons in the habit of reading poetry) 'than were
supplied at first the Nation did not afford.' How careless must a
writer be who can make this assertion in the face of so many existing
title-pages to belie it! Turning to my own shelves, I find the folio of
Cowley, seventh edition, 1681. A book near it is Flatman's Poems,
fourth edition, 1686; Waller, fifth edition, same date. The Poems of
Norris of Bemerton not long after went, I believe, through nine
editions. What further demand there might be for these works I do
not know; but I well remember, that, twenty-five years ago, the
booksellers' stalls in London swarmed with the folios of Cowley.

This is not mentioned in disparagement of that able writer and amiable man; but merely to show—that, if Milton's work were not more read, it was not because readers did not exist at the time. The early editions of the Paradise Lost were printed in a shape which allowed them to be sold at a low price, yet only three thousand copies of the Work were sold in eleven years; and the Nation, says Dr. Johnson, had been satisfied from 1623 to 1664, that is, forty-one years, with only two editions of the Works of Shakspeare; which probably did not together make one-thousand Copies; facts adduced by the critic to prove the 'paucity of Readers.'—There were readers in multitudes; but their money went for other purposes, as their admiration was fixed elsewhere. We are authorised, then, to affirm, that the reception of the Paradise Lost, and the slow progress of its fame, are proofs as striking as can be desired that the positions which I am attempting to establish are not erroneous.[25]—How amusing to shape to one's self such a critique as a Wit of Charles's days, or a Lord of the Miscellanies or trading Journalist of King William's time, would have brought forth, if he had set his faculties industriously to work upon this Poem, everywhere impregnated with *originat* excellence.

So strange indeed are the obliquities of admiration, that they whose opinions are much influenced by authority will often be tempted to think that there are no fixed principles[26] in human nature for this art to rest upon. I have been honoured by being permitted to peruse in MS. a tract composed between the period of the Revolution and the close of that century.[27] It is the Work of an English Peer of high accomplishments, its object to form the character and direct the studies of his son. Perhaps nowhere does a more beautiful treatise of the kind exist. The good sense and wisdom of the thoughts, the delicacy of the feelings, and the charm of the style, are, throughout, equally conspicuous. Yet the Author, selecting among the Poets of his own country those whom he deems most worthy of his son's perusal, particularises only Lord Rochester, Sir John Denham, and Cowley. Writing about the same time, Shaftesbury, an author at present unjustly depreciated, describes the English Muses as only yet lisping in their cradles.[28]

The arts by which Pope, soon afterwards, contrived to procure to himself a more general and a higher reputation than perhaps any English Poet ever attained during his life-time, are known to the judicious. And as well known is it to them, that the undue exertion of those arts is the cause why Pope has for some time held a rank in literature, to which, if he had not been seduced by an over-love of immediate popularity, and had confided more in his native genius, he never could have descended. He bewitched the nation by his melody, and dazzled it by his polished style, and was himself blinded by his own success. Having wandered from humanity in his Eclogues with boyish inexperience, the praise, which these compositions obtained, tempted him into a belief that Nature was not to be trusted, at least in pastoral Poetry. To prove this by example, he put his friend Gay upon writing those Eclogues which their author intended to be burlesque.[29] The instigator of the work, and his admirers, could perceive in them nothing but what was ridiculous. Nevertheless, though these Poems contain some detestable passages, the effect, as Dr. Johnson well observes, 'of reality and truth became conspicuous even when the intention was to show them grovelling and degraded.' The Pastorals, ludicrous to such as prided themselves upon their refinement, in spite of those disgusting passages, 'became popular, and were read with delight, as just representations of rural manners and occupations.'

Something less than sixty years after the publication of the Paradise Lost appeared Thomson's Winter; which was speedily followed by his other Seasons.[30] It is a work of inspiration; much of it is written from himself, and nobly from himself. How was it received?

'It was no sooner read,' says one of his contemporary biographers,[31] 'than universally admired: those only excepted who had not been used to feel, or to look for anything in poetry, beyond a *point* of satirical or epigrammatic wit, a smart *antithesis* richly trimmed with rhyme, or the softness of an *elegiac* complaint. To such his manly classical spirit could not readily commend itself; till, after a more attentive perusal, they had got the better of their prejudices, and either acquired or affected a truer taste. A few others stood aloof, merely because they had long before fixed the articles of their poetical creed, and resigned themselves to an absolute despair of ever seeing any thing new and original. These were somewhat mortified to find their notions disturbed by the appearance of a poet, who seemed to owe nothing but to nature and his own genius. But, in a short time, the applause became unanimous; every one wondering how so many pictures, and pictures so familiar, should have moved them but faintly to what they felt in his descriptions. His digressions too, the overflowings of a tender benevolent heart, charmed the reader no less; leaving him in doubt, whether he should more admire the Poet or love the Man.'

This case appears to bear strongly against us:—but we must distinguish between wonder and legitimate admiration. The subject of the work is the changes produced in the appearances of nature by the revolution of the year: and, by undertaking to write in verse, Thomson pledged himself to treat his subject as became a Poet. Now it is remarkable that, excepting the nocturnal Reverie of Lady Winchilsea, and a passage or two in the Windsor Forest of Pope, the poetry of the period intervening between the publication of the Paradise Lost and the Seasons does not contain a single new image of external nature; and scarcely presents a familiar one from which it can be inferred that the eye of the Poet had been steadily fixed upon his object, much less that his feelings had urged him to work upon it in the spirit of genuine imagination. To what a low state knowledge of the most obvious and important phenomena had sunk, is evident from the style in which Dryden has executed a description of Night in one of his Tragedies, and Pope his translation of the celebrated moonlight scene in the Iliad.[32] A blind man, in the habit of attending accurately to descriptions casually dropped from the lips of those around him, might easily depict these appearances with more truth. Dryden's lines are vague, bombastic, and senseless;[33] those of Pope, though he had Homer to guide him, are throughout false and contradictory. The verses of Dryden, once highly celebrated, are forgotten; those of Pope still retain their hold upon public estimation,— nay, there is not a passage of descriptive poetry, which at this day finds so many and such ardent admirers. Strange to think of an enthusiast, as may have been the case with thousands, reciting those verses under the cope of a moonlight sky, without having his raptures in the least disturbed by a suspicion of their absurdity!—If these two distinguished writers could habitually think that the visible universe was of so little consequence to a poet, that it was scarcely necessary for him to cast his eyes upon it, we may be assured that those passages of the elder poets which faithfully and poetically describe the phenomena of nature, were not at that time holden in much estimation, and that there was little accurate attention paid to those appearances.

Wonder is the natural product of Ignorance; and as the soil was *in such good condition* at the time of the publication of the Seasons the crop was doubtless abundant. Neither individuals nor nations become corrupt all at once, nor are they enlightened in a moment. Thomson was an inspired poet, but he could not work miracles; in cases where the art of seeing had in some degree been learned, the teacher would further the proficiency of his pupils, but he could do little *more;* though so far does vanity assist men in acts of self-deception, that many would often fancy they recognised a likeness when they knew nothing of the original. Having shown that much of what his biographer deemed genuine admiration must in fact have been blind wonderment—how is the rest to be accounted for?—Thomson was fortunate in the very title of his poem, which seemed to bring it home to the prepared sympathies of every one: in the next place, notwithstanding his high powers, he writes a vicious style; and his false ornaments are exactly of that kind which would be most likely to strike the undiscerning. He likewise abounds with sentimental common-places, that, from the manner in which they were brought forward, bore an imposing air of novelty. In any well-used copy of the Seasons the book generally opens of itself with the rhapsody on love, or with one of the stories (perhaps Damon and Musidora);[34] these also are prominent in our collections of Extracts, and are the parts of his Work, which, after all, were probably most efficient in first recommending the author to general notice. Pope, repaying praises which he had received, and wishing to extol him to the highest, only styles him 'an elegant and philosophical Poet;'[35] nor are we able to collect any unquestionable proofs that the true characteristics of Thomson's genius as an imaginative poet[36] were perceived, till the elder Warton, almost forty years after the publication of the Seasons, pointed them out by a note in his Essay on the Life and Writings of Pope.[37] In the Castle of Indolence (of which Gray speaks so coldly)[38] these characteristics were almost as conspicuously displayed, and in verse more harmonious, and diction more pure. Yet that fine poem was neglected on its appearance, and is at this day the delight only of a few!

When Thomson died, Collins breathed forth his regrets in an Elegiac Poem, in which he pronounces a poetical curse upon *him* who should regard with insensibility the place where the Poet's remains were deposited.[39] The Poems of the mourner himself have now passed through innumerable editions, and are universally known; but if, when Collins died, the same kind of imprecation had been pronounced by a surviving admirer, small is the number whom it would not have comprehended. The notice which his poems attained during his lifetime was so small, and of course the sale so insignificant, that not long before his death he deemed it right to repay to the bookseller the sum which he had advanced for them, and threw the edition into the fire.[40]

Next in importance to the Seasons of Thomson, though at considerable distance from that work in order of time, come the Reliques of Ancient English Poetry; collected, new-modelled, and in many instances (if such a contradiction in terms may be used) composed by the Editor, Dr. Percy.[41] This work did not steal silently into the world, as is evident from the number of legendary tales, that appeared not long after its publication; and had been modelled, as the authors persuaded themselves, after the old Ballad. The Compilation was however ill suited to the then existing taste of city society; and Dr. Johnson, 'mid the little senate to which he gave laws, was not sparing in his exertions to make it an object of contempt. The critic triumphed, the legendary imitators were deservedly disregarded, and, as undeservedly, their ill-imitated models sank, in this country, into temporary neglect; while Bürger, and other able writers of Germany, were translating, or imitating these Reliques, and composing, with the aid of inspiration thence derived, poems which are the delight of the German nation. Dr. Percy was so abashed by the ridicule flung upon his labours from the ignorance and insensibility of the persons with whom he lived, that, though while he was writing under a mask he had not wanted resolution to follow his genius into the regions of true simplicity and genuine pathos (as is evinced by the exquisite ballad of Sir Cauline and by many other pieces), yet when he appeared in his own person and character as a poetical writer, he adopted, as in the tale of the Hermit of Warkworth,[42] a diction scarcely in any one of its features distinguishable from the vague, the glossy, and unfeeling language of his day. I mention this remarkable fact[43] with regret, esteeming the genius of Dr. Percy in this kind of writing superior to that of any other man by whom in modern times it has been cultivated. That even Bürger (to whom Klopstock gave, in my hearing, a commendation which he denied to Goethe and Schiller, pronouncing him to be a genuine poet, and one of the few among the Germans whose works would last)[44] had not the fine sensibility of Percy, might be shown from many passages, in which he has deserted his original only to go astray. For example,[45]

> Now daye was gone, and night was come,
> And all were fast asleepe,

All save the Lady Emeline,
Who sate in her bowre to weepe:

And soone she heard her true Love's voice
Low whispering at the walle,
Awake, awake, my dear Ladye,
'Tis I thy true-love call.

Which is thus tricked out and dilated:[46]

Als nun die Nacht Gebirg' und Thal
Vermummt in Rabenschatten,
Und Hochburgs Lampen überall
Schon ausgeflimmert hatten,
Und alles tief entschlafen war;
Doch nur das Fräulein immerdar,
Voll Fieberangst, noch wachte,
Und seinen Ritter dachte:
Da horch! Ein süsser Liebeston
Kam leis' empor geflogen.
'Ho, Trudchen, ho! Da bin ich schon!
Risch auf! Dich angezogen!'

But from humble ballads we must ascend to heroics.

All hail, Macpherson! hail to thee, Sire of Ossian![47] The Phantom was begotten by the snug embrace of an impudent Highlander upon a cloud of tradition—it travelled southward, where it was greeted with acclamation, and the thin Consistence took its course through Europe, upon the breath of popular applause. The Editor of the 'Reliques' had indirectly preferred a claim to the praise of invention, by not concealing that his supplementary labours were considerable![48] how selfish his conduct, contrasted with that of the disinterested Gael, who, like Lear, gives his kingdom away, and is content to become a pensioner upon his own issue for a beggarly pittance!— Open this far-famed Book!—I have done so at random, and the beginning of the 'Epic Poem Temora,' in eight Books, presents itself. 'The blue waves of Ullin roll in light. The green hills are covered with day. Trees shake their dusky heads in the breeze. Grey torrents pour their noisy streams. Two green hills with aged oaks surround a narrow plain. The blue course of a stream is there. On its banks stood Cairbar of Atha. His spear supports the king; the red eyes of his fear are sad. Cormac rises on his soul with all his ghastly wounds.'

Precious memorandums from the pocket-book of the blind Ossian!

If it be unbecoming, as I acknowledge that for the most part it is, to speak disrespectfully of Works that have enjoyed for a length of time a widely-spread reputation, without at the same time producing irrefragable proofs of their unworthiness, let me be forgiven upon this occasion.—Having had the good fortune to be born and reared in a mountainous country, from my very childhood I have felt the falsehood that pervades the volumes imposed upon the world under the name of Ossian. From what I saw with my own eyes, I knew that the imagery was spurious. In nature every thing is distinct, yet nothing defined into absolute independent singleness. In Macpherson's work, it is exactly the reverse; every thing (that is not stolen) is in this manner defined, insulated, dislocated, deadened,—yet nothing distinct. It will always be so when words are substituted for things. To say that the characters never could exist, that the manners are impossible, and that a dream has more substance than the whole state of society, as there depicted, is doing nothing more than pronouncing a censure which Macpherson defied; when, with the steeps of Morven before his eyes, he could talk so familiarly of his Car-borne heroes;—of Morven, which, if one may judge from its appearance at the distance of a few miles, contains scarcely an acre of ground sufficiently accommodating for a sledge to be trailed along its surface.[49]—Mr. Malcolm Laing[50] has ably shown that the diction of this pretended translation is a motley assemblage from all quarters; but he is so fond of making out parallel passages as to call poor Macpherson to account for his '*ands*' and his '*buts!*' and he has weakened his argument by conducting it as if he thought that every striking resemblance was a *conscious* plagiarism. It is enough that the coincidences are too remarkable for its being probable or possible that they could arise in different minds without communication between them. Now as the Translators of the Bible, and Shakspeare, Milton, and Pope, could not be indebted to Macpherson, it follows that he must have owed his fine feathers to them; unless we are prepared gravely to assert, with Madame de Staël, that many of the characteristic beauties of our most celebrated English Poets are derived from the ancient Fingallian;[51] in which case the modern translator would have been but giving back to Ossian his own.—It is consistent that Lucien Buonaparte, who could censure Milton for having surrounded Satan in the infernal regions with courtly and regal splendour, should pronounce the modern Ossian to be the glory of Scotland,[52]—a country that has produced a Dunbar, a

Buchanan,[53] a Thomson, and a Burns! These opinions are of ill omen for the Epic ambition of him who has given them to the world.

Yet, much as those pretended treasures of antiquity have been admired, they have been wholly uninfluential upon the literature of the Country. No succeeding writer appears to have caught from them a ray of inspiration; no author, in the least distinguished, has ventured formally to imitate them—except the boy, Chatterton, on their first appearance. He had perceived, from the successful trials which he himself had made in literary forgery, how few critics were able to distinguish between a real ancient medal and a counterfeit of modern manufacture; and he set himself to the work of filling a magazine with *Saxon Poems*,—counterparts of those of Ossian, as like his as one of his misty stars is to another.[54] This incapability to amalgamate with the literature of the Island, is, in my estimation, a decisive proof that the book is essentially unnatural; nor should I require any other to demonstrate it to be a forgery, audacious as worthless.—Contrast, in this respect, the effect of Macpherson's publication with the Reliques of Percy, so unassuming, so modest in their pretensions!—I have already stated how much Germany is indebted to this latter work; and for our own country, its poetry has been absolutely redeemed by it. I do not think that there is an able writer in verse of the present day who would not be proud to acknowledge his obligations to the Reliques; I know that it is so with my friends; and, for myself, I am happy in this occasion to make a public avowal of my own.

Dr. Johnson, more fortunate in his contempt of the labours of Macpherson than those of his modest friend, was solicited not long after to furnish Prefaces biographical and critical for the works of some of the most eminent English Poets.[55] The booksellers took upon themselves to make the collection; they referred probably to the most popular miscellanies, and, unquestionably, to their books of accounts; and decided upon the claim of authors to be admitted into a body of the most eminent, from the familiarity of their names with the readers of that day, and by the profits, which, from the sale of his works, each had brought and was bringing to the Trade. The Editor was allowed a limited exercise of discretion, and the Authors whom he recommended are scarcely to be mentioned without a smile.[56] We open the volume of Prefatory Lives, and to our astonishment the *first* name we find is that of Cowley!—What is become of the morning-star of English Poetry?[57] Where is the bright Elizabethan constellation? Or, if names be more acceptable than images, where is the ever-to-be-honoured Chaucer? where is Spenser? where Sidney?

and, lastly, where he, whose rights as a poet, contradistinguished from those which he is universally allowed to possess as a dramatist, we have vindicated,—where Shakspeare?—These, and a multitude of others not unworthy to be placed near them, their contemporaries and successors, we have *not*. But in their stead, we have (could better be expected when precedence was to be settled by an abstract or reputation at any given period made, as in this case before us?) Roscommon, and Stepney, and Phillips, and Walsh, and Smith, and Duke, and King, and Spratt—Halifax, Granville, Sheffield, Congreve, Broome, and other reputed Magnates—metrical writers utterly worthless and useless, except for occasions like the present, when their productions are referred to as evidence what a small quantity of brain is necessary to procure a considerable stock of admiration, provided the aspirant will accommodate himself to the likings and fashions of his day.

As I do not mean to bring down this retrospect to our own times, it may with propriety be closed at the era of this distinguished event. From the literature of other ages and countries, proofs equally cogent might have been adduced, that the opinions announced in the former part of this Essay are founded upon truth. It was not an agreeable office, nor a prudent undertaking, to declare them, but their importance seemed to render it a duty. It may still be asked, where lies the particular relation of what has been said to these Volumes?—The question will be easily answered by the discerning Reader who is old enough to remember the taste that prevailed when some of these poems were first published, seventeen years ago,[58] who has also observed to what degree the poetry of this Island has since that period been coloured by them; and who is further aware of the unremitting hostility with which, upon some principle or other, they have each and all been opposed. A sketch of my own notion of the constitution of Fame has been given; and, as far as concerns myself, I have cause to be satisfied. The love, the admiration, the indifference, the slight, the aversion, and even the contempt, with which these Poems have been received, knowing, as I do, the source within my own mind, from which they have proceeded, and the labour and pains, which, when labour and pains appeared needful, have been bestowed upon them, must all, if I think consistently, be received as pledges and tokens, bearing the same general impression, though widely different in value;—they are all proofs that for the present time I have not laboured in vain; and afford assurances, more or less authentic, that the products of my industry will endure.

If there be one conclusion more forcibly pressed upon us than another by the review which has been given of the fortunes and fate of poetical Works, it is this,—that every author, as far as he is great and at the same time *original*, has had the task of *creating* the taste by which he is to be enjoyed: so has it been, so will it continue to be.[59] This remark was long since made to me by the philosophical Friend for the separation of whose poems from my own I have previously expressed my regret. The predecessors of an original Genius of a high order will have smoothed the way for all that he has in common with them;—and much he will have in common; but, for what is peculiarly his own, he will be called upon to clear and often to shape his own road:—he will be in the condition of Hannibal among the Alps.

And where lies the real difficulty of creating that taste by which a truly original poet is to be relished? Is it in breaking the bonds of custom, in overcoming the prejudices of false refinement, and displacing the aversions of inexperience? Or, if he labour for an object which here and elsewhere I have proposed to myself, does it consist in divesting the reader of the pride that induces him to dwell upon those points wherein men differ from each other, to the exclusion of those in which all men are alike, or the same; and in making him ashamed of the vanity that renders him insensible of the appropriate excellence which civil arrangements, less unjust than might appear, and Nature illimitable in her bounty, have conferred on men who may stand below him in the scale of society? Finally, does it lie in establishing that dominion over the spirits of readers by which they are to be humbled and humanised, in order that they may be purified and exalted?

If these ends are to be attained by the mere communication of *knowledge*, it does *not* lie here.—TASTE, I would remind the reader, like IMAGINATION, is a word which has been forced to extend its services far beyond the point to which philosophy would have confined them. It is a metaphor, taken from a *passive* sense of the human body, and transferred to things which are in their essence *not* passive,—to intellectual *acts* and *operations*. The word, Imagination, has been overstrained, from impulses honourable to mankind, to meet the demands of the faculty which is perhaps the noblest of our nature. In the instance of Taste, the process has been reversed; and from the prevalence of dispositions at once injurious and discreditable, being no other than that selfishness which is the child of apathy,—which, as Nations decline in productive and creative power, makes them value themselves upon a presumed refinement of judging. Poverty of language is the primary cause of the use which we make of the word, Imagination; but the word, Taste, has been stretched to the sense which it bears in modern Europe by habits of self-conceit, inducing that inversion in the order of things whereby a passive faculty is made paramount among the faculties conversant with the fine arts. Proportion and congruity, the requisite knowledge being supposed, are subjects upon which taste may be trusted; it is competent to this office;—for in its intercourse with these the mind is *passive*, and is affected painfully or pleasurably as by an instinct. But the profound and the exquisite in feeling, the lofty and universal in thought and imagination; or, in ordinary language, the pathetic and the sublime;—are neither of them, accurately speaking, objects of a faculty which could ever without a sinking in the spirit of Nations have been designated by the metaphor—*Taste*. And why? Because without the exertion of a co-operating *power* in the mind of the Reader, there can be no adequate sympathy with either of these emotions: without this auxiliary impulse, elevated or profound passion cannot exist.

Passion, it must be observed, is derived from a word which signifies *suffering;* but the connection which suffering has with effort, with exertion, and *action*, is immediate and inseparable. How strikingly is this property of human nature exhibited by the fact, that, in popular language, to be in a passion, is to be angry!—But,[60]

> 'Anger in hasty *words* or *blows*
> Itself discharges on its foes.'

To be moved, then, by a passion, is to be excited, often to external, and always to internal, effort; whether for the continuance and strengthening of the passion, or for its suppression, accordingly as the course which it takes may be painful or pleasurable. If the latter, the soul must contribute to its support, or it never becomes vivid,—and soon languishes, and dies. And this brings us to the point. If every great poet with whose writings men are familiar, in the highest exercise of his genius, before he can be thoroughly enjoyed, has to call forth and to communicate *power*, this service, in a still greater degree, falls upon an original writer, at his first appearance in the world.—Of genius the only proof is, the act of doing well what is worthy to be done, and what was never done before: Of genius, in the fine arts, the only infallible sign is the widening the sphere of human sensibility, for the delight, honour, and benefit of human nature. Genius is the introduction of a new element into the intellectual universe: or, if that be not allowed, it is the application of powers to objects on which they had not before been exercised, or the employment of them in such a manner as to produce effects hitherto unknown. What is all this but an advance, or a conquest, made by the soul of the poet? Is it to be supposed that the reader can make progress of this kind, like an Indian prince or general— stretched on his palanquin, and borne by his slaves? No; he is invigorated and inspirited by his leader, in order that he may exert himself; for he cannot proceed in quiescence, he cannot be carried like a dead weight. Therefore to create taste is to call forth and bestow power, of which knowledge is the effect; and *there* lies the true difficulty.

As the pathetic participates of an *animal* sensation, it might seem —that, if the springs of this emotion were genuine, all men, possessed of competent knowledge of the facts and circumstances, would be instantaneously affected. And, doubtless, in the works of every true poet will be found passages of that species of excellence, which is proved by effects immediate and universal. But there are emotions of the pathetic that are simple and direct, and others—that are complex and revolutionary; some—to which the heart yields with gentleness; others—against which it struggles with pride; these varieties are infinite as the combinations of circumstance and the constitutions of character. Remember, also, that the medium through which, in poetry, the heart is to be affected, is language; a thing subject to endless fluctuations and arbitrary associations. The genius of the poet melts these down for his purpose; but they retain their shape and quality to him who is not capable of exerting, within his own mind, a corresponding energy. There is also a meditative, as well as a human, pathos; an enthusiastic, as well as an ordinary, sorrow; a sadness that has its seat in the depths of reason, to which the mind cannot sink gently of itself—but to which it must descend by treading the steps of thought. And for the sublime,—if we consider what are the cares that occupy the passing day, and how remote is the practice and the course of life from the sources of sublimity, in the soul of Man, can it be wondered that there is little existing preparation for a poet charged with a new mission to extend its kingdom, and to augment and spread its enjoyments?[61]

Away, then, with the senseless iteration of the word, *popular*, applied to new works in poetry, as if there were no test of excellence in this first of the fine arts but that all men should run after its productions, as if urged by an appetite, or constrained by a spell!—The qualities of writing best fitted for eager reception are either such as startle the world into attention by their audacity and extravagance; or they are chiefly of a superficial kind, lying upon the surfaces of manners; or arising out of a selection and arrangement of incidents, by which the mind is kept upon the stretch of curiosity, and the fancy amused without the trouble of thought. But in everything which is to send the soul into herself, to be admonished of her weakness, or to be made conscious of her power;—wherever life and nature are described as operated upon by the creative or abstracting virtue of the imagination; wherever the instinctive wisdom of antiquity and her heroic passions uniting, in the heart of the poet, with the meditative wisdom of later ages, have produced that accord of sublimated humanity, which is at once a history of the remote past and a prophetic enunciation of the remotest future, *there*, the poet must reconcile himself for a season to few and scattered hearers. —Grand thoughts (and Shakspeare must often have sighed over this truth), as they are most naturally and most fitly conceived in solitude, so can they not be brought forth in the midst of plaudits, without some violation of their sanctity. Go to a silent exhibition of the productions of the sister Art, and be convinced that the qualities which dazzle at first sight, and kindle the admiration of the multitude, are essentially different from those by which permanent influence is secured. Let us not shrink from following up these principles as far as they will carry us, and conclude with observing—that there never has been a period, and perhaps never will be, in which vicious poetry, of some kind or other, has not excited more zealous admiration, and been far more generally read, than good; but this advantage attends the good, that the *individual*, as well as the species, survives from age to age; whereas, of the depraved, though the species be immortal, the individual quickly *perishes*; the object of present admiration vanishes, being supplanted by some other as easily produced; which, though no better, brings with it at least the irritation of novelty,—with adaptation, more or less skilful, to the changing humours of the majority of those who are most at leisure to regard poetical works when they first solicit their attention.

Is it the result of the whole, that, in the opinion of the Writer, the judgment of the People is not to be respected? The thought is most injurious; and, could the charge be brought against him, he would repel it with indignation. The People have already been justified, and their eulogium pronounced by implication, when it was said, above

—that, of *good* poetry, the *individual*, as well as the species, *survives*. And how does it survive but through the People? What preserves it but their intellect and their wisdom?[62]

> '—Past and future, are the wings
> On whose support, harmoniously conjoined,
> Moves the great Spirit of human knowledge—'
> *MS.*

The voice that issues from this Spirit, is that Vox Populi which the Deity inspires.[63] Foolish must he be who can mistake for this a local acclamation, or a transitory outcry—transitory though it be for years, local though from a Nation. Still more lamentable is his error who can believe that there is any thing of divine infallibility in the clamour of that small though loud portion of the community, ever governed by factitious influence, which, under the name of the PUBLIC, passes itself, upon the unthinking, for the PEOPLE. Towards the Public, the Writer hopes that he feels as much deference as it is entitled to: but to the People, philosophically characterised, and to the embodied spirit of their knowledge, so far as it exists and moves, at the present, faithfully supported by its two wings, the past and the future, his devout respect, his reverence, is due. He offers it willingly and readily; and, this done, takes leave of his Readers, by assuring them—that, if he were not persuaded that the contents of these Volumes, and the Work[64] to which they are subsidiary, evince something of the 'Vision and the Faculty divine;'[65] and that, both in words and things, they will operate in their degree, to extend the domain of sensibility for the delight, the honour, and the benefit of human nature, notwithstanding the many happy hours which he has employed in their composition, and the manifold comforts and enjoyments they have procured to him, he would not, if a wish could do it, save them from immediate destruction;—from becoming at this moment, to the world, as a thing that had never been. 1815.

NOTES

1 The text of 1815 (only) opens with a paragraph protesting against the 'impudent falsehoods and base artifices' of Wordsworth's critics, and asserting his own genius.

2 Matt. 6:24.

3 Cf. the comments on a Unitarian reader of *The Excursion* in No. 13 (p. 220); and *Prose*, iii. 85–6.

4 Unidentified.

5 Unidentified in this form; but 1815 quotes only the two words 'the region', which might have come from *Hamlet*, II. ii. 517, or *Paradise Lost*, vii. 425.

6 Not in classical anecdotes; perhaps from Burton's *Anatomy of Melancholy* or Congreve's *Way of the World*; see *Prose*, iii. 86–7.

7 Wordsworth, discussing 'the poetical literature of this Country', must be thinking mainly of the translations of Du Bartas by Joshua Sylvester (1605–6, and earlier partial editions). For Wordsworth's sources for this survey, see *Prose*, iii. 87–101.

8 *The Faerie Queene*, I. i. 9.

9 The learned Hakewill (a third edition of whose book bears date 1635), writing to refute the error 'touching Nature's perpetual and universal decay,' cites triumphantly the names of Ariosto, Tasso, Bartas, and Spenser, as instances that poetic genius had not degenerated; but he makes no mention of Shakspeare. [Wordsworth's note.] The reference is to George Hakewill, *An Apologie or Declaration of the Power and Providence of God in the Government of the World*, 3rd ed., Oxford, 1635, 290.

10 *Essay of dramatic poesy*, in *Essays*, ed. W. P. Ker, Oxford, 1900, i. 81.

11 Pope's Preface to Shakespeare observes that 'some of the most shining passages are distinguished by commas in the margin'.

12 Voltaire in his *Dictionnaire philosophique*, s.v. 'Art dramatique', says that cultured Continentals take Shakespeare for 'le plus méprisable bouffon qui ait jamais amusé la populace'.

13 Baron Melchior von Grimm (1723–1807) discusses Shakespeare in his correspondence with Diderot (published 1812–14).

14 Probably invented by Wordsworth to typify many such remarks.

15 *Shakespeares Sonnets Never Before Imprinted*, London, 1609. George Steevens reprinted it in his *Twenty of the Plays of Shakespeare*, London, 1766, iv; the criticism which Wordsworth reports is in his *Plays of William Shakespeare*, London, 1793, i. vii–viii. Coleridge's rebuttal (see n. 16—Wordsworth refers to the lectures of 1808) does not appear to survive.

16 This flippant insensibility was publicly reprehended by Mr. Coleridge in a course of Lectures upon Poetry given by him at the Royal Institution. For the various merits of thought and language in Shakspeare's Sonnets, see Numbers, 27, 29, 30, 32, 33, 54, 64, 66, 68, 73, 76, 86, 91, 92, 93, 97, 98, 105, 107, 108, 109, 111, 113, 114, 116, 117, 129, and many others. [Wordsworth's note.]

17 *Paradise Lost*, iv. 829.

18 *A Maske*, 1637; *Lycidas*, 1638; *Poems*, 1645.

19 There are translations of 'L'Allegro' and 'Il Penseroso' in Voss's *Gedichte*, Königsberg, 1795, ii. 269, 280.

20 Boswell's *Life*, ed. G. B. Hill and L. F. Powell, Oxford, 1934–50, iv. 305. There is more in Johnson's *Lives*, i. 169–70.

21 Ibid. 18–19.

22 In 1667.

23 *Paradise Lost*, vii. 31. See No. 10, p. 172, for the reference in the next sentence.

24 *Lives*, i. 143, misquoted. Wordsworth draws on Johnson for the rest of his information.

25 Hughes is express upon this subject: in his dedication of Spenser's Works to Lord Somers, he writes thus. 'It was your Lordship's encouraging a beautiful edition of Paradise Lost that first brought that incomparable Poem to be generally known and esteemed.' [Wordsworth's note.] See Spenser's *Works*, ed. John Hughes, London, 1715, i. v.

26 This opinion seems actually to have been entertained by Adam Smith, the worst critic, David Hume not excepted, that Scotland, a soil to which this sort of weed seems natural, has produced. [Wordsworth's note.] The reference is not certainly identifiable in Smith's works: see *Prose*, iii. 93.

27 Unidentified.

28 'Advice to an Author', in *Characteristicks*, n.p., 1737, i. 217.

29 *The Shepherd's Week in Six Pastorals*, London, 1714. See Johnson, *Lives*, ii. 269, for the anecdote and the quotations following.

30 'Winter', 1726; 'Summer', 1727; 'Spring', 1728; 'Autumn', in a collected edition, 1730.

31 Patrick Murdoch, in Thomson's *Works*, London, 1763, i. vi–vii.

32 Dryden, *Indian Emperor*, III. ii. 1–6; Pope, *The Iliad of Homer*, viii. 687 ff.

33   CORTES *alone in a night-gown.*
        All things are hush'd as Nature's self lay dead;
        The mountains seem to nod their drowsy head.
        The little Birds in dreams their songs repeat,
        And sleeping Flowers beneath the Night-dew sweat:
        Even Lust and Envy sleep; yet Love denies
        Rest to my soul, and slumber to my eyes.
                DRYDEN'S *Indian Emperor.*
                                [Wordsworth's note.]

34 'Spring', 849–1176, especially 963–1112; 'Summer', 1269–370.

35 'Testimonies of Authors' prefixed to *The Dunciad*: 'Mr. Thomson, In his elegant and philosophical poem of the Seasons:' [cites 'Winter', 553–4].

36 Since these observations upon Thomson were written, I have perused

the second edition of his Seasons, and find that even *that* does not contain the most striking passages which Warton points out for admiration; these, with other improvements, throughout the whole work, must have been added at a later period. [Wordsworth's note.] The passages referred to are 'Summer', 936, 977–9, 1048–9.

37 Joseph Warton, *Essay on the Genius and Writings of Pope*, 5th ed., London, 1806, i. 40–9.

38 *Correspondence*, ed. P. Toynbee and L. Whibley, Oxford, 1935, 307: 'there is a poem by Thomson, the Castle of Indolence, with some good Stanzas'.

39 Collins, *Ode Occasion'd by the Death of Mr. Thomson*, London, 1749.

40 This anecdote is given in Langhorne's Memoir in Collins, *Poetical Works*, London, 1765.

41 London, 1765. Percy, in his introductory note to 'Sir Cauline' (see below), says that he added 'several stanzas in the first part, and still more in the second'.

42 London, 1771.

43 Shenstone, in his Schoolmistress, gives a still more remarkable instance of this timidity. On its first appearance, (See D'Israeli's 2d Series of the Curiosities of Literature) the Poem was accompanied with an absurd prose commentary, showing, as indeed some incongruous expressions in the text imply, that the whole was intended for burlesque. In subsequent editions, the commentary was dropped, and the People have since continued to read in seriousness, doing for the Author what he had not courage openly to venture upon for himself. [Wordsworth's note.]

Shenstone's *The Schoolmistress* (1742), a semi-comic poem in Spenserian stanzas, is accompanied by an 'Index' in the first edition. D'Israeli's account draws attention to the Index as a mark of Shenstone's comic intention, which seems clear enough.

44 Klopstock gave this opinion to Wordsworth in 1799; see *Prose*, i. 93.

45 From 'The Child of Elle'.

46 From 'Die Entführung, oder Ritter Karl von Eichenhorst und Fraülein Gertrude von Hochburg': 'As now night masks mountain and valley in raven-shadows, and Hochburg's lights had already flickered out everywhere, all were sound asleep, yet only the maiden, full of feverish anxiety, was still awake and thought of her knight: then hark! A sweet sound of love came softly flying upwards: "Ho, dear Gertrude, ho! I am here already! Make haste! Get dressed!"'

47 James Macpherson (1736–96), virtual author of the 'translation' of the works of the Scottish bard Ossian, widely accepted as authentic, and of considerable influence in England (in spite of Wordsworth's comment below) and on the Continent. First published in sections; first collected edition 1765.

48 See n. 41 above.
49 Wordsworth saw Morven on his Scottish tour of 1803. Although 'car-borne' is a frequent epithet for Macpherson's heroes, I have not found a passage which states that 'cars' were driven on Morven.
50 'Dissertation on the Supposed Authenticity of Ossian's Poems', in *History of Scotland*, 2nd ed., 1804, iv. 409 ff.
51 *Treatise on Ancient and Modern Literature*, London, 1803, i. 273–87. The 'literature of the North' is said to derive from Ossian.
52 *Charlemagne; ou L'Eglise délivrée*, London, 1814. Bonaparte criticizes Milton (and Tasso) for confusing the myths of Pluto and Satan (i. 379); and calls Macpherson, or rather Ossian, 'ce beau génie, l'honneur de l'Ecosse' (i. 376).
53 George Buchanan (1506–82), historian and (Latin) poet.
54 Wordsworth is probably following G. Gregory's 'Life of Chatterton', reprinted in Chatterton's *Works*, London, 1803, i. xxxvii, which refers to 'some pieces called Saxon poems, written in the style of Ossian'.
55 Commonly called *Lives of the Poets*; published (as Prefaces) 1779–81.
56 Watts, Blackmore, Pomfret, and Yalden were included at Johnson's request; and also Thomson, whom Wordsworth discreetly overlooks here.
57 A commonplace for Chaucer, perhaps originated by John Denham, 'On Mr. Abraham Cowley's Death': 'Old *Chaucer*, like the Morning Star,/To us discovers day from far.'
58 In *Lyrical Ballads*, 1798. Wordsworth's claim for their influence seems exaggerated.
59 See No. 7, p. 115. On the removal of Coleridge's poems see No. 11, n. 39.
60 Edmund Waller, 'Of Love', 1–2.
61 This obscure paragraph is based on the ideas of John Dennis; see Introduction, section XIV.
62 *Prel.* (1850), vi. 448–50.
63 Wordsworth is adapting the maxim 'Vox populi, vox Dei' ('the voice of the people is the voice of God').
64 *The Recluse*.
65 *Exc.* i. 79.

13   Letter to Catherine Clarkson
1815

A reply to Mrs Clarkson's report of criticism of *The Excursion* by
Patty Smith, daughter of William Smith, M.P. for Norwich, to
whom Mrs Clarkson had lent her copy of the poem (*MY*, ii. 184).
The letter serves as a gloss on some of the more difficult ideas in the
Essay, Supplementary to the Preface, written at about the same time.
The manuscript of this letter is in Cornell University Library; my
text is from *MY*, ii. 187–92.

[Jan. 1815]

(Transcribed by Mary and Dorothy, on account of the vile penman-
ship) (*Note by W. W.*)

[*Mary begins the copy*]
My dear Friend,[1]
　　I don't know that it is quite *fair* to sit down to answer a letter of
friendship the moment it is received; but allow me to do so in this
case.—Unitarian hymns[2] must by their dispassionate monotony have
deprived your Friend's ear of all compass, which implies of all
discrimination. To you I will whisper, that the Excursion has one
merit if it has no other, a versification to which for *variety* of musical
effect no Poem in the language furnishes a parallel. Tell Patty Smith
this (the name is a secret with me and make her stare); and exhort
her to study with her fingers till she has learned to confess it to herself. Miss S's notion of poetical imagery is probably taken from the
Pleasures of Hope or Gertrude of Wyoming[3] see for instance stanza
first of said poem. There is very little imagery of that kind; but, I
am far from subscribing to your concession that there is little
imagery in the Poem; either collateral in the way of metaphor
coloring the style; illustrative in the way of simile; or directly under
the shape of description or incident: there is a great deal; though not
quite so much as will be found in the other parts of the Poem where

219

the subjects are more lyrically treated and where there is less narration; or description turning upon manners, and those repeated actions which constitute habits, or a course of life.—Poetic Passion (Dennis⁴ has well observed) is of two kinds imaginative and enthusiastic; and merely human and ordinary; of the former it is only to be feared that there is too great a proportion. But all this must inevitably be lost upon Miss P. S.—

The Soul, dear Mrs C. may be re-given when it had been taken away, my own Solitary is an instance of this; but a Soul that has been dwarfed by a course of bad culture cannot after a certain age, be expanded into on[e] of even ordinary proportion.—Mere error of opinion, mere apprehension of ill consequences from supposed mistaken views on my part, could never have rendered your correspondent blind to the innumerable analogies and types of infinity, insensible to the countless awakenings to noble aspiration, which I have transfused into that Poem from the Bible of the Universe as it speaks to the ear of the intelligent, as it lies open to the eyes of the humble-minded. I have alluded to the Ladys errors of opinion—she talks of my being a worshipper of Nature—a passionate expression uttered incautiously in the Poem upon the Wye⁵ has led her into this mistake, she reading in cold-heartedness and substituting the letter for the spirit. Unless I am greatly mistaken, there is nothing of this kind in the Excursion. There is indeed a passage towards the end of the 4th. Book where the Wanderer introduces the simile of the Boy and the Shell, and what follows,⁶ that has something, ordinarily but absurdly called *Spinosistic*. But the intelligent reader will easily see the *dramatic* propriety of the Passage. The Wanderer in the beginning of the book [*Dorothy takes the pen*] had given vent to his own devotional feelings and announced in some degree his own creed; he is here preparing the way for more distinct conceptions of the Deity by reminding the Solitary of such religious feelings as cannot but exist in the minds of those who affect atheism. She condemns me for not distinguishing between nature as the work of God and God himself. But where does she find this doctrine inculcated? Where does she gather that the Author of the Excursion looks upon nature and God as the same? He does not indeed consider the Supreme Being as bearing the same relation to the universe as a watch-maker bears to a watch. In fact, there is nothing in the course of religious education adopted in this country and in the use made by us of the holy scriptures that appears to me so injurious as the perpetually talking about *making* by God—Oh! that your Correspondent had heard a conversation which I had in bed with my sweet little Boy, four and a half years old,[7] upon this subject the other morning. 'How did God make me? Where is God? How does he speak? He never spoke to *me*.' I told him that God was a spirit, that he was not like his flesh which he could touch; but more like his thoughts in his mind which he could *not* touch.—The wind was tossing the fir trees, and the sky and light were dancing about in their dark branches, as seen through the window—Noting these fluctuations he exclaimed eagerly—'There's a bit of him I see it there!' This is not meant entirely for Father's prattle; but, for Heaven's sake, in your religious talk with children say as little as possible about *making*. One of the main objects of the Recluse is, to reduce the calculating understanding to its proper level among the human faculties—Therefore my Book must be disliked by the Unitarians, as their religion rests entirely on that basis; and therefore is, in fact, no religion at all—but—I won't say what. I have done little or nothing towards your request of furnishing you with arguments to cope with my antagonist. Read the Book if it pleases you; the construction of the language is uniformly perspicuous; at least I have taken every possible pains to make it so, therefore you will have no difficulty here. The impediment you may meet with will be of two kinds, such as exist in the ode which concludes my 2d volume of poems.[8] This poem rests entirely upon two recollections of childhood, one that of a splendour in the objects of sense which is passed away, and the other an indisposition to bend to the law of death as applying to our own particular case. A Reader who has not a vivid recollection of these feelings having existed in his mind in childhood cannot understand that poem. So also with regard to some of those elements of the human soul whose importance is insisted upon in the Exn. And some of those images of sense which are dwelt upon as holding that relation to immortality and infinity which I have before alluded to; if a person has not been in the way of receiving these images, it is not likely that he can form such an adequate conception of them as will bring him into lively sympathy with the Poet. For instance one who has never heard the echoes of the flying Raven's voice in a mountainous Country, as described at the close of the 4th Book[9] will not perhaps be able to relish that illustration; yet every one must have been in the way of perceiving similar effects from different causes;—but I have tired myself, and must have tired you—

One word upon ordinary or popular passion. Could your correspondent read the description of Robert, and the fluctuations of

hope and fear in Margaret's mind,[10] and the gradual decay of herself
and her dwelling without a bedimmed eye then I pity her. Could she
read the distress of the Solitary after the loss of his Family and the
picture of his quarrel with his own conscience (though this tends
more to meditative passion) without some agitation then I envy not
her tranquillity. Could the anger of Ellen before she sate down to
weep over her babe, though she were but a poor serving-maid, be
found in a book, and that book be said to be without passion, then,
thank Heaven! that the person so speaking is neither my wife nor
my Sister, nor one whom (unless I could work in her a great altera-
tion) I am forced to daily converse with. What thinks she of those
Relatives about the little Infant, who was unexpectedly given, and
suddenly taken away?[11] But too much of this—Farewell. I wish I
could have written you a more satisfactory letter. Lamb is justifiably
enraged at the spurious Review which his Friends expect to be his.[12]
No Newmarket jockey, no horse-stealer was ever able to play a
hundredth part of the tricks upon the person of an unhappy beast
that the Bavius of the Quarterly Review has done for that sweet composition. So I will not scruple to style it, though I never saw it. And
worst of all, L[amb kept no copy] and the original M S [we] fear,
destroyed.—As [to the Ed Review] I hold the Author[13] [of it in
entire] contempt, and therefore shall not pollute my fingers [with
the touch] of it. There is one sentence in the Ex^n. ending in 'sublime
att[ractions] of the grave'[14] which,—if the poem had contained
nothing else that [I valued,] would have made it almost a matter of
religion with me to [keep out] of the way of the best stuff which so
mean a mind as Mr [Jeffrey's] could produce in connection with it.
His impertinences, to us[e the] mildest te[rm,] if once they had a
place in my memory, would, for a [time] at least, [sti]ck there. You
cannot scower a spot of this kind ou[t of] your mind as you may a
stain out of your clothes. If the m[ind] were under the power of the
will I should read Mr J^y merely to expose his stupidity to his still
more stupid admirers. This not being the case, as I said before, I
shall not pollute my fingers with touching his book. Give my affectionate regards to Henry Robinson, and the sa[me] to Mr Clarkson.
Remember me also kindly to your Father.—I am sure you are
competent to write the Review as well as I could wish to have it
done. I am very sorry for the indisposition under which your last
was written. Headaches are plaguey things, I hope you are better—
   [*Wordsworth ends the remainder in his own hand*]—Sunday
Morning—I have just read over this Letter; it is a sad jumble of

stuff and as ill expressed.—I should not send it but in compliance with the wish of Mary and Dorothy. The reason of the thing being so bad is that your Friends remarks were so monstrous. To talk of the offense of writing the Ex^n and the difficulty of forgiving the Author is carrying audacity and presumption to a height of which I did not think any *Woman* was capable. Had my Poem been much coloured by Books, as many parts of what I have to write must be, I should have been accused as Milton has been of pedantry, and of having a mind which could not support itself but by other mens labours.—Do not you perceive that my conversations almost all take place out of Doors, and all with grand objects of nature surrounding the speakers for the express purpose of their being alluded to in illustration of the subjects treated of. *Much* imagery from books would have been an impertinence and an incumbrance: where it was required it is found. As to passion; it is never to be lost sight of, that the Excursion is *part* of a work; that in its plan it is conversational; and that if I had introduced stories exciting curiosity, and filled with violent conflicts of passion and a rapid interchange of striking incidents, these things could have never harmonized with the rest of the work and all further discourse, comment, or reflections must have been put a stop to.—This I write for you and not for your friend; with whom if you would take my advice, you will neither converse by letter nor *viva voce* upon a subject which she is [in every] respect disqualified to treat. farewell.

[?Your most] affectionate friend   W. W.

You had sent a promise that Mr C would give me an account of the impression my Book made on him.

[*In M.W.'s hand*] Six o'clock Monday morning—Wm and I are going to Bowness to take the Quarterly bath—a fine day—

NOTES

1 Catherine Clarkson, *née* Buck, primarily a friend of Dorothy Words-worth's. Her husband, Thomas Clarkson, was prominent in the anti-slavery movement in Britain; Wordsworth reluctantly came into conflict with him over the Westmorland election of 1818, when Clarkson's views on slavery led him to support Henry Brougham against the Lowther interest.

2 William Smith was a prominent Unitarian as well as Clarkson's ally in opposing slavery.

3 Both poems by Thomas Campbell, published 1799 and 1809.

4 Wordsworth is drawing on the same ideas of Dennis as he uses in No. 12, p. 183. See Introduction, pp. 49–51.

5 'Tintern Abbey', 151–2.

6 *Exc.* iv. 1132–47.

7 William Wordsworth ('Willy'), born 12 May 1810.

8 'Ode: Intimations of Immortality', the last poem in Wordsworth's *Poems, in Two Volumes* (1807).

9 *Exc.* iv. 1175–87.

10 Ibid. i. 566–91, 646 ff.; iii. 680–705, 778–991; vi. 973–82.

11 Ibid. vii. 636–94.

12 Lamb's review of *The Excursion* for the *Quarterly Review*, xii (October 1814), 100–11 (published December 1814), had been tampered with by the editor, William Gifford. Wordsworth wrote to Southey about this time in an attempt to recover Lamb's manuscript (*MY*, ii. 186).

13 Jeffrey reviewed *The Excursion* in the *Edinburgh Review*, xxiv (November 1814), 1–30.

14 *Exc.* iv. 232–8.

Bibliography

Original editions

Lyrical Ballads, with a few other Poems, Bristol *or* London, 1798.
Lyrical Ballads, with other Poems, in two Volumes, by W. Wordsworth, London, 1800.
Lyrical Ballads, with Pastoral and other Poems, in two Volumes, by W. Wordsworth, London, 1802, 1805.
Poems by William Wordsworth: Including Lyrical Ballads . . . With Additional Poems, a New Preface, and a Supplementary Essay, London, 1815.
Poetical Works of William Wordsworth, 6 vols, London, 1849–50.

Modern editions

S. T. COLERIDGE, *Biographia Literaria*, ed. J. Shawcross, 2 vols, Oxford, 1907.
Collected Letters of Samuel Taylor Coleridge, ed. E. L. Griggs, 6 vols, Oxford, 1956–71.
S. T. COLERIDGE, *The Friend*, ed. Barbara E. Rooke, 2 vols, London, 1969.
Critical Works of John Dennis, ed. E. N. Hooker, 2 vols, Baltimore, 1939–43.
Henry Crabb Robinson on Books and their Writers, ed. E. J. Morley, London, 1938.
SAMUEL JOHNSON, *Lives of the English Poets*, ed. G. Birkbeck Hill, 3 vols, Oxford, 1905.
Journals of Dorothy Wordsworth, ed. E. de Selincourt, London, 1941.
Letters of William and Dorothy Wordsworth: The Early Years, ed. E. de Selincourt. Second edition, revised by Chester L. Shaver, Oxford, 1967.
Letters of William and Dorothy Wordsworth: The Middle Years, ed. E. de Selincourt. Second edition, revised by Mary Moorman and A. G. Hill, 2 vols, Oxford, 1969–70.

Literary Criticism of William Wordsworth, ed. P. M. Zall, Lincoln, Neb., 1966.

Lyrical Ballads, 1798: ed. T. Hutchinson, London, 1898; ed. H. Littledale, Oxford, 1911; ed. W. J. B. Owen, London, 1967, 1969.

Lyrical Ballads, 1800–5: ed. G. Sampson, London, 1903; ed. R. L. Brett and A. R. Jones, London, 1963; ed. D. Roper, London, 1968.

Poetical Works of William Wordsworth, eds E. de Selincourt and Helen Darbishire, 5 vols, Oxford, 1940–9.

Preface to Lyrical Ballads; ed. W. J. B. Owen, Copenhagen, 1957.

WILLIAM WORDSWORTH, *The Prelude*, ed. E. de Selincourt. Second edition, revised by Helen Darbishire, Oxford, 1959.

Prose Works of William Wordsworth, eds W. J. B. Owen and Jane Worthington Smyser, 3 vols, Oxford, 1974.

Illustrative and critical material

ABRAMS, M. H., *The Mirror and the Lamp*, New York, 1953.

ABRAMS, M. H., 'Wordsworth and Coleridge on diction and figures', *English Institute Essays 1952*, New York, 1954.

BANERJEE, SRIKUMAR, *Critical Theories and Poetic Practice in the Lyrical Ballads*, London, 1931.

BARSTOW, MARJORIE L., *Wordsworth's Theory of Poetic Diction*, New Haven, 1917.

BEATTY, ARTHUR, *William Wordsworth: His Doctrine and Art in their Historical Relations*, Madison, 1922, 1927.

HEFFERNAN, JAMES A. W., *Wordsworth's Theory of Poetry*, Ithaca and London, 1969.

OWEN, W. J. B., 'The major theme of Wordsworth's 1800 Preface', *Essays in Criticism*, vi (1956).

OWEN, W. J. B., 'Wordsworth and Jeffrey in collaboration', *Review of English Studies*, NS, xv (1964).

OWEN, W. J. B., *Wordsworth as Critic*, Toronto, 1969, 1971; London, 1969.

OWEN, W. J. B., 'Wordsworth, the problem of communication, and John Dennis', in *Wordsworth's Mind and Art*, ed. A. W. Thomson, Edinburgh, 1969.

OWEN, W. J. B., 'The sublime and the beautiful in *The Prelude*', *The Wordsworth Circle*, 4 (1973).

PARRISH, STEPHEN M., '*The Thorn*: Wordsworth's dramatic monologue,' *English Literary History*, xxiv (1957).

PARRISH, STEPHEN M., 'The Wordsworth–Coleridge controversy', *Publications of the Modern Language Association of America*, lxxiii (1958).

PARRISH, STEPHEN M., 'Dramatic technique in the *Lyrical Ballads*', *Publications of the Modern Language Association of America*, lxxiv (1959).

PARRISH, STEPHEN M., 'Wordsworth and Coleridge on meter', *Journal of English and German Philology*, lix (1960).

RAYSOR, THOMAS M., 'Coleridge's criticism of Wordsworth', *Publications of the Modern Language Association of America*, liv (1939).

SCOGGINS, JAMES, *Imagination and Fancy: Complementary Modes in the Poetry of Wordsworth*, Lincoln, Neb., 1966.

SHARROCK, ROGER, 'Wordsworth's revolt against literature', *Essays in Criticism*, iii (1953).

SHARROCK, ROGER, 'The chemist and the poet', *Notes and Records of the Royal Society of London*, xvii (1962).

WELLEK, RENE, 'Wordsworth', in *History of Modern Criticism 1750–1950*, ii, London, 1955.

WHALLEY, GEORGE, *Poetic Process*, London, 1953.

WHALLEY, GEORGE, 'Preface to *Lyrical Ballads*: a portent', *University of Toronto Quarterly*, xxv (1956).

WOODRING, CARL R., *Wordsworth*, Boston, 1965.

Index